RING OF FIRE

The Inside Story of Valentino Rossi
and MotoGP

Rick Broadbent

motorbooks

This edition published in 2010
by Motorbooks, an imprint on MBI Publishing Company,
400 First Avenue North, Suite 300, Minneapolis, MN 55401 USA

Originally published in Great Britain by Bantam Press,
an imprint of Transworld Publishers.

Rick Broadbent has asserted his right under the
Copyright, Designs and Patents Act of 1988 to be identified as the author of this work.

The information in this book is true and complete to the best of our knowledge.
All recommendations are made without any guarantee on the part
of the author or Publisher, who also disclaims any liability incurred in connection
with the use of this data or specific details.

We recognize, further, that some words, model names, and designations mentioned
herein are the property of the trademark holder. We use them for identification
purposes only. This is not an official publication.

Motorbooks titles are also available in at discounts in bulk quantity for industrial or
sales-promotional use. For details write to Special Sales Manager at MBI Publishing
Company, 400 First Avenue North, Suite 300, Minneapolis, MN 55401 USA.

To find out more about our books, visit us online at www.motorbooks.com

The extract from *The Waste Land* by T. S. Eliot is reprinted
with permission of Faber and Faber Ltd.

The author and Publisher have made all reasonable efforts to contact copyright holders
for permission, and apologize for any omissions or errors in the form of credits given.

Corrections may be made to further printings.

Library of Congress Cataloging-in-Publication Data

Broadbent, Rick.
Ring of fire : the inside story of Valentino Rossi and MotoGp / Rick Broadbent.
p. cm.
Includes index.
ISBN 978-0-7603-3954-1 (hb w/ jkt)
1. Grand Prix motorcycle racing. 2. Motorcycle racing. 3. Rossi, Valentino.
4. Motorcyclists. I. Title.
GV1060.B65 2010
796.7'5--dc22
2010020999

ISBN: 978-0-7603-3954-1

Cover photo by Mirco Lazzari.

Printed in the United States of America

Contents

Acknowledgments

Over the years I have been grateful for the knowledge, kindness and enthusiasm of numerous people in motorcycling, including Nick Harris, Iain Mackay, Matthew Roberts, Gavin Emmett, Chris Herring, Ali Forth, Katie Baines, Neil Bramwell, Carl Fogarty, Chaz Davies, James Toseland, Neil Hodgson, Roger Burnett, Dr Martin Raines, Barry and Angela Coleman, Ron, Ann and Leon Haslam, Julian Ryder, Mat Oxley, Matt Birt, Mike Scott, Dave Fern, Toby Moody, Steve Westlake and David Dew.

From another era I am heavily indebted to Pauline Hailwood, Giacomo Agostini, Tommy Robb, Ralph Bryans, Paddy Driver, Bo Granath, Ted Macauley and John Cooper.

Many books and newspapers were referred to, but *Mike the Bike* by Christopher Hilton and Ted Macauley's *Hailwood* and *Mike the Bike – Again* were particularly useful. Thanks to Silvia Nucini, Monty Shadow, Mark Hughes and to *Vanity Fair Italy*, Laureus and Haynes Publishing for their help. Thanks too to Giles Elliott at Transworld and David Luxton at Luxton Harris for getting the idea off the ground.

Finally, I would especially like to thank Valentino Rossi and Max Biaggi, whose rivalry was as good as sporting theatre gets, and Debs, Sam and Erin for letting me live with them.

'Racing is life. Anything that happens before or after is just waiting.'

Steve McQueen

PROLOGUE

THE BIG SLIDE

The racer wakes and climbs into his leathers. He zips himself up and walks, bow-legged, from the hut, helmet in his hand, his thick brown hair like a lion's mane.

This is Japan and this is his home. The mind of the racer is blinkered, all rampaging thoughts crystallizing into the need to go faster, harder, better. The most dominant season in the 250cc class is already fading to sepia in the record books. This is the big time and he cannot think of his son, barely a week old, back with Makiko. He does not think of his wife because from the corner of a large, brown eye he can see Valentino Rossi, the world champion, in neon yellow and orange. This is his year and this is his stage. Faster, harder, better.

He likes Rossi. The previous month they had toured the Honda factories in Japan and been feted as gladiators. They shook hands with the workers, the people with slower, softer, sadder lives, and had their backs slapped by little men with power. They had got drunk together at the Eight Hours. Hopelessly drunk. And he had fallen asleep in his own vomit. Now his gloved hand catches Rossi's. They nod and look over a wall to the people and the yellow metal of a roller coaster writing thrills in the sky.

The engines spark into thunderclaps. They are louder now. The old 500cc bikes have given way to beastly 990cc four-stroke MotoGP machines. Faster, harder, better. Soon these men will top 200mph in races, striving to tame the acceleration like rodeo riders. Loris Capirossi, the Bolognese Bulldog, will even reach 215.86mph in a test at Barcelona. Unimaginable. The senses of the spectators are pummelled, but these men make a routine of the extraordinary. So they ride and lean and scrape their knee-sliders on the tarmac. They go so quickly that the outer world is dulled to a soft monotone and washed canvas. They concentrate and look for the opening.

This is Japan and this is his home. Where he grew up. And where he falls now. Where the colour and noise and danger explode into an incandescent rage. The race goes on. The marshals drag him from the track.

Rossi is oblivious. He is thinking of winning. Only of winning. It is why he is so good. Even at speed his mind is sedate enough to see the yellow flag. Focus. Think. Ride. He could try to go faster but he does not. Know the limit. Seek it, touch it and draw back. Bargain with your bravery and your reason. Be the fastest, the hardest and the best.

Rossi wins. That bastard Biaggi is second. Fuck him. Fuck them all. He has started the new season at the top. He is the man to beat. Capirossi is third. A tough little street-fighter, he will need to scrap and brawl and believe to beat him this year. It is 2003 and Rossi will be king.

So they celebrate and pop the champagne corks. 'Kato fell, the helicopter took him,' the Dorna press officer tells them. It happens. This is racing, a miasma of broken bones, shredded skin and frayed nerves. Only later do they find out Kato hit the wall. Daijiro Kato, the Samurai of Slide, Daijiro Kato, the man Rossi had got drunk with. The wall that they all knew was too close, the wall that means they will never again return to Suzuka. They hear that his heart was revived at trackside. That the marshals pulled him from the circuit without thinking about neck and spinal injuries. And the race went on regardless.

And when two weeks later, with his wife and children red-eyed with pain and what-ifs by his comatose body, he dies, the riders will be so angry that they will form a safety commission. And then they will go to South Africa for another race. They wear No. 74 badges (his official race number) as a memorial and then forget. They think of winning. Only that. Faster, harder, better.

What goes through your mind when you crash? 'Your arse' was what Barry Sheene said and 28 metal screws in his legs gave him some insight. How do you spot a motorcycle racer in a restaurant? 'He's the one gripping his fork with the first two fingers of his left hand' was what Kenny Roberts said. King Kenny who came along and dethroned Barry. That is sport. It is all human drama wrapped up in ephemera. Today's superstar is tomorrow's veteran, the limping figure hanging around in the background with the dodgy table-manners.

But the young do not think about that. They are here for the moment. This bloody brilliant, dangerous moment. When you ride a motorbike you have to live in this moment because it is all that keeps you from disaster.

And Hopper and Shakey are living for the moment as they steal out of the paddock and into a nearby field. They are in the mood for a laugh. It is 2005 and they are rising stars. They are in the big time and they are relishing the moment. 'Come on, Shakey,' Hopper drawls, the California man with East End parents. So they walk into the Tuscan countryside where the fans gathered on Thursday, waiting for the latest instalment of the Rossi and Biaggi feud. Rossi's fans wore yellow, like his old livery. Biaggi's wore red, like his eyes. The battle lines were drawn, fire-crackers exploded and people shouted, 'Fuck Rossi! Fuck Biaggi!'

Hopper and Shakey make their way through unseen. They come to a clearing and Hopper knocks over the drum. Madness but fun. He moves in a circle and pours petrol in his wake. Then he stands in the epicentre and flicks a match. The flame sprints around him. 'Shit!' he cries. 'Jesus!'

The following week Hopper the thrill-seeker arrives on the grid in Barcelona. His face is redder than the shirts at Scarperia or Biaggi's eyes. His nose is badly burnt. He laughs off an enquiry from Suzi Perry, the glamorous BBC presenter. How could he explain? This is motorcycle racing and it is what they do. This is the fast lane and they all dance inside a ring of fire.

CHAPTER ONE

ESTORIL, 2006

It is the unusual that makes sport such an addictive drug. For months and years you watch unspectacular events that soon become forgotten little histories, but you always hope. The sports fan is an archaeologist digging through dust and ruins for naked drama, and the enduring thrill is you never know when you are going to strike it rich.

So as I talk to Iain Mackay in the paddock at Estoril in Portugal, an ugly racetrack prone to showers blowing in off the Atlantic, we cannot know that we are about to witness a sequence of events that people will never forget.

Mack is a die-hard Celtic fan who lives in Amsterdam and works in Honda's press department. A font of all knowledge, he speaks in conspiratorial tones, the words barely making it out from beneath his grey moustache. He thinks Nicky Hayden will win. 'If I didn't I wouldn't be here, would I?' he laughs.

But Hayden and Honda are up against it. Just a few races ago, when he won on home soil in the United States, he held a commanding fifty-one-point lead over Valentino Rossi.

But then his RC211V was hit by the clutch problem that has sabotaged his starts and led to this dramatic denouement. Rossi, the charismatic seven-time world champion, has whittled the lead down to a fragmentary twelve points with only two races to go. He has been making confident noises in the build-up to the Portuguese Grand Prix too, praising his Yamaha team and telling everyone that he feels great.

Hayden is less convincing. In his last four races he has finished ninth, fourth and fifth twice and, despite Mack's softly spoken confidence, the consensus is Hayden is limping towards the line in need of both a tourniquet and a corner turned. 'It's the biggest race of my life,' Hayden says in his Kentucky brogue, the look he gives the pressmen as pointed as his designer sideburns.

Earl Hayden is nervous too. In the old days, back on the farm, when the summers were baking the land and threatening their very existence, he would take his sons Nicky, Tommy and Roger Lee out into the fields and they would raise their hands to the heavens and rub their fingers. 'Pray for rain, boys,' he would say. 'Pray for rain.'

Earlier this season, Earl had done the same thing in Australia when Nicky's clutch problem had seen him drop from first to eighteenth on the very first lap. They needed something to soften the blow and so he went out into the pitlane, raised his hands and rubbed his fingers. The rain came and washed away some of the pain. Nicky recovered to fifth as the conditions worked to his advantage. Now Earl was watching by the wall again, his lucky No. 69 ring on a crossed finger.

Rossi v. Hayden, Honda v. Yamaha, this afternoon v. Earl's pained nerves. It was the crunch, the moment Earl had waited for and the one he had dreaded. This paddock, with its zipping scooters weaving in and out of punters on behind-the-scenes tours, its gargantuan trucks and lackeys washing dismembered parts, its brolly dollies and their PVC hot pants, was free to enjoy the pressure. But not Earl. This was a million miles away from Second Chance Autos and his days spent stripping tobacco. Earl could barely think that, within an hour, his son might be the 2006 MotoGP world champion.

Basi Pedrosa was just as anxious. Her son, Dani, had already had a successful debut year in MotoGP. A world champion at 125cc and 250cc level, Pedrosa had long been billed as the new Rossi. Pedrosa had just turned twenty-one and was Honda's blue-eyed boy, a remorselessly pragmatic Spaniard who punished himself every morning with 800 sit-ups. His time was coming and, although it would take a major turnaround, he still had a mathematical chance of winning the title. That was one reason why Honda said there would be no team orders. Team-mates they might be, but Hayden and Pedrosa had been told to race hard. Satoru Horiike, the managing director of the mighty Honda Racing Corporation, had almost bristled with indignation when the subject of a team plan had been raised. Basi just hoped things would work out for her son. The next hour would suggest she did not hope hard enough.

At 1.50 p.m., with the clouds thickening overhead, Rossi crouched down by his bike. It was a beautiful combination of cutting-edge technology and aesthetic craftsmanship. The YZR-M1 had been revolutionized by Rossi. When he walked out on Honda in 2003 to join Yamaha, they had been a struggling factory, devoid of inspiration and even the inclination to usurp Honda. But by the sheer force of Rossi's will and the motivation of paying him £6 million, they had become the best almost instantly. When Rossi had won his first race for Yamaha in a redneck South African afterthought called Welkom, he dismounted and kissed his bike. He called it 'her' and would often creep out of his motorhome late at night, wander through the deserted paddock and slip into the garage to see her. Sometimes they would even sleep together.

The cameras clicked in his face but Rossi was in his zone. This was all part of a time-honoured routine. Nobody could get to

Rossi when he was on the track. It was his release from the life that meant he called himself a creature of the night. He said everything was more peaceful at night, softer and slower, like a parallel universe. But now it was early afternoon in Estoril and his world title was hanging by a thread. So he thought of winning. Only of winning. Faster, harder, better than Hayden.

Rossi was on pole position after dominating the previous day's qualifying session. Colin Edwards, his team-mate, was next to him in matching yellow. Then Hayden. The Doctor, the Texan Tornado and the Kentucky Kid. The title of a documentary filmed at the United States Grand Prix was now the front row for the climactic scenes of the World Championship. Twelve points. Gossamer. Confidence surged through Rossi. Earl Hayden felt sick.

They circled on the warm-up lap and the crowd roared. Everywhere you looked you saw yellow, signifying deference to the Rossi phenomenon. He had debunked the myths of motor-cycle racing and dragged this sport from the ranks of working-class petrolheads into the mainstream, from the back of the waltzer through the hall of mirrors. The only tattoo Rossi had was a small turtle on his stomach, a joke against himself and his rivals. He was very much the modern sports hero, an unattainable Everyman.

Then at 14.01 the red lights went out and the engines roared. For everyone concerned those first tenths of seconds are torturous as they yearn for the speed to kick in. And when the pack found some shape it was Rossi who led, but Hayden was not far behind. The clutch had not got him this time. It was race on. The title on the line. Earl Hayden on the very edge.

It was febrile fare from the opening corner. Shinya Nakano went down on the lime-green Kawasaki and did not move. The cameras cut away quickly and that exacerbated fears in the press room. Some wondered if the race would be stopped. Rossi, Edwards and Hayden pressed on regardless, thinking only of winning. The TV screens suddenly showed Nakano being carried away on a stretcher. His arm was held up and twitched. Suspended consciences gave way to satisfaction and lust.

On the fourth lap Hayden dived down the inside of Pedrosa at Turn 6. It was a courageous, aggressive move that let Pedrosa know exactly what this meant to the older rider. 'They touched!' someone said. 'They bloody touched!'

And then it happened. As they came to Turn 6 on the next circuit, Rossi led from Edwards, with the Repsol Honda pair of Hayden and Pedrosa in swift pursuit. Too swift in fact. Pedrosa braked late and started to move up the inside of Hayden. The inside of the man who would be king. Inside and out.

It was the season in three seconds. Pedrosa went in too hot, ran up on to the blue and white zebra strips and fell. As he did his mighty RC211V, with its 260-brake horsepower, 990cc engine, extended swing arm and orange wheel trims, preceded him. The glorious machine ploughed into Hayden who was swept away in a torrent of fear, anger and sparks.

It took a nanosecond for Hayden to have the implications sear through his brain. He signalled frantically to marshals to help him, but it was all in vain. Pedrosa was already walking off. He looked behind, as if contemplating going over to apologize, but thought better of it and waved an arm, almost dismissively.

Hayden knelt down. He buried his face in the gravel and beat the ground with a fist. Then he was up and raging. Striding away with tears in his eyes, his face contorted, his mouth screaming, 'That's fucking bullshit!' He knew that was it. The hopes and dreams erased in one moment of rank incompetence from his putative team-mate. 'Fucking bullshit!'

In the press room there was disbelief. It was one of those extraordinary moments. Digging for drama amid the dust and gravel where two Hondas lay like dying carcasses on the Serengeti. I caught Mack's eye as he walked sullenly from the room, his hands in his pockets, no doubt anticipating the furore that Pedrosa had caused.

Rossi's Yamaha team rejoiced in the message hung out on their man's pitboard. 'HAYDEN OUT. EDWARDS 1.0'. Rossi saw the words at 200mph and his heart skipped a beat. As if that was not enough, we then had the race to end all seasons, as Toni Elias, another Spanish fledgling, slithered his way to the front on disintegrating tyres. Never one to settle for second best, Rossi overtook him on the last entry to the chicane. Elias responded. So did Rossi. The lead changed hand four times within a stuttering crescendo before Elias won by inches and two thousandths of a second. It was a photo finish, but Elias knew he had his maiden triumph, while Rossi took defeat well, his disappointment tempered by Honda's internecine implosion.

In most sports those who have made a heinous error or suffered some terrible setback will hide away behind PR men and the safety afforded them by the cult of celebrity. But within an hour Pedrosa was sitting, pale-faced, in the Honda hospitality suite explaining his act. 'I am so sorry,' he said. 'I went to see Nicky to apologize. He was very angry. I was not trying to overtake. I just was going too fast. I have never hit another bike in my life, in practice or anywhere, and it has to be like this. I can't believe it.'

It was impossible not to feel his pain. I had been there early and watched Pedrosa sit at a table with his cheek in a flat palm. Beside him were Basi and Alberto Puig, the former racer who now mentored him. This supremely gifted sportsman looked like a naughty schoolboy. Around him the hospitality men went about their business, replacing great plates of cheese and sausage and peppers. Mack stood in the background, feeling Dani's pain too. Checking his watch.

The timing went awry. Suddenly the melee around Pedrosa disentangled. Everyone swarmed to the other side of the same hospitality suite. A radio man fell in the rush. 'Hayden's here!' someone yelled. So, as Pedrosa completed his heartfelt apology to a disappearing audience, Hayden vented his raw feelings to a hungry pack.

'I know he hates this, he hates this situation, but I don't know if I can forgive him,' he said, mirror shades hiding watery eyes, his voice cracking with disbelief. 'I can't say next week I'll come back and it will all be OK because these chances don't come around every day. I know he's hurting, but so am I.'

A noisy Italian TV man was speaking loudly into a camera as this epistle from the heart was read out. 'Shut up!' Mike Scott, a large, ursine veteran for *Motorcycle News*, demanded. 'Shut up!' He was quite right to do so. Nobody wanted to miss this. It was the ultimate in sporting voyeurism.

The Italian departed and Hayden shied away from the trickier questions, the blunt ones designed for instant headlines. Could he continue to ride in the same team as Pedrosa? 'I don't even want to go there,' he said. 'People have been trying to drive a wedge between us all year. I know he's not dirty, but this hurts like hell. You know, the world title is on the line and we should have had a plan.'

That was a reference to Honda's refusal to issue team orders and perhaps tell Pedrosa to go easy with so much at stake. It was something Rossi was also referring to simultaneously in the podium press conference. 'For sure Colin helped me more than Pedrosa helped Hayden,' he laughed. So did everyone. 'Our team is a magic place,' Rossi gushed. 'Everyone gets on so well and works together. It's a really nice place to be.'

By Honda's cheese and sausages, the hypocrisy of the bystanders was laid bare as they expressed concern for Hayden. 'You know I don't sign his cheques, I can't tell him what to do,' he lamented. And that was it. There was a race left in Valencia but everybody knew 2006 was over. The pressmen gave Hayden a round of applause. Others laughed with Rossi. Pedrosa crept away and was later in tears. It had been the first foot he had put wrong all year, but it was a clown's foot in a minefield.

Wash away all my guilt; from my sins cleanse me. My sacrifice, God, is a broken spirit.

Basi hugged him. It was an unfathomable finish to a season and, as the wounded and the well-fed dispersed, it seemed certain that the rematch in 2007 would be special.

But then they came to Valencia . . . for the final, supposedly straightforward, race . . .

Do not spurn a broken, humbled heart.

I spoke to Mack in the press room on Friday and he looked crestfallen. Ashes to ashen. Rossi was relaxed, exuding the confidence from knowing he could finish second and still win another title. Hayden sat in Honda's hospitality suite once more and tried to grin and bear the lingering pain. 'Did you go home and stew for a few days after Estoril?' I asked him. 'Man, you don't chew yesterday's breakfast,' he said. 'But if I don't win on Sunday I don't know whether I'll ever get over it.' They were not the bullish words of a would-be hero. If Hayden lost the title and did not improve next year, he was facing the scrapheap. You sensed he knew it too.

On Saturday it got worse. Although he had declared that Valencia was not one of his favourite tracks, Rossi broke the lap record to qualify on pole position. Hayden did not even make the front row, struggling back in fifth place. It would take a miracle now.

The tension of two weeks ago had given way to a mutual love-in between Rossi and his people. There were 200,000 of them at

Valencia that Sunday, crammed into the dusty bowl, engulfing the twisty, low-gear track and wondering what post-race stunt Rossi would come up with this time. Last year, he had marked his seventh world crown by posing as Snow White with seven of his friends. So what of the eighth wonder?

And then the red lights faded to black and all the pre-race predictions and confidence were banished. Hayden immediately barged past Rossi, touching him with his knee, leather on leather, spirit on spirit. Rossi seemed shaken or maybe he was just biding his time. Ahead of him Pedrosa ran wide to allow Hayden through. No team orders, just a gentlemen's agreement, Hayden would later say. It went against the grain with Pedrosa, but another calamity could blight his career for ever. Already they had been printing Wanted! posters in the newspapers putting a price on Pedrosa's head.

And then, on the fifth lap, the same lap in which Hayden and Pedrosa had come together in Estoril, *salvation*.

The scenes that followed would never be forgotten. They meant that when darkness descended on Valencia and the riders departed, Hayden for a family meal, Rossi into his night, and some of the others to the all-night paddock party at Spooks nightclub, the stench of newly spawned revenge filtered through the trucks and suites and empty stands. The greatest racer of them all sipped on a beer, shook his head and contemplated the reckoning.

CHAPTER TWO

BEGINNINGS

Five years earlier the self-styled king of motorcycle racing wore a No. 1 pendant and named his Vietnamese pot-bellied pigs after his rivals. He was aggressive, rude and suffused in confidence. But the trouble with Carl Fogarty was that when he crashed at 150mph and joined the ranks of ex-racers, the act lost its relevance. From being a bloody-minded star Fogarty was rendered merely bloody-minded.

It was March 2001, and I sat with him in Ducati's hospitality tent at the first round of the World Superbike Championship in Valencia. He was restless and anxious. Neil Hodgson, a former bricklayer from Burnley, was making his debut in the series and was being billed as the man to take over Fogarty's mantle. 'Neil's one of the favourites,' Fogarty said before adding the poisoned caveat, 'but he's been weak and fragile for five years and can't possibly have the heart. Is he the new Foggy? You're joking. The world's not ready for another Carl Fogarty.'

Valencia is an ugly circuit with square concrete buildings painted a muddy yellow. Few turned up for the superbikes so the vast rows of concrete seats framed the track like a Venetian blind. In Spain it has always been the 500cc World Championship that is the ultimate in two-wheeled racing; only in Britain, where Fogarty's fame added 20,000 to the sales of *Motorcycle News* when he was on the cover, did World Superbikes hold sway.

Fogarty gave me a lift back to our hotel. Neil Bramwell, a freelancer for the *Independent* and friend of Fogarty, was next to me. 'Are you ready for this?' he asked. Bramwell knew Fogarty well, having ghosted the autobiography that confounded literary critics by leaping to the top of the *Sunday Times* bestsellers list. The drive was hair-raising. Fogarty took what seemed incredible risks and circled corners with an apparent disdain for self-preservation. He lost his way and performed an illegal U-turn. I shut my eyes and my head was thrust against the side window. My knuckles were white. Fogarty grinned. If he couldn't shake up the world then he could at least put me through the tumble drier.

'I went to the Ducati team launch in Milan,' he said when we had adjourned to the bar of the Sidi Saler, nestling in the dunes of the Albufera Nature Park. 'I sat in the front row and, when the curtains went back and the riders were on the stage, I felt a lump in my throat. I should have been where they were sitting. It will be the same on Sunday. I was the best in the world at doing something and now I can't do it. That's depressing. I never actually enjoyed racing, just winning. It was twenty years of my life, gone.'

It was hard to imagine the tumult of conflicting thoughts in Fogarty's head. He had been forced to retire at the age of thirty-five and the future was an unknown. Success is transient and heroes come and go. Fogarty wanted to believe that the world could not cope without him, but it was still turning. Hodgson would race for his GSE Ducati team in the first race of the season the following afternoon, while Chris Walker, the other leading Briton, had signed to race for the Shell Advance Honda team in the 500cc World Championship. 'The funny thing is Neil suddenly got better after I'd crashed,' Fogarty mused. 'He wasn't in my shadow any more. But if he's going to take it to another level then he's got to do it soon. When Barry Sheene retired there was no one to take it over and the interest at home dropped off. Now I'm gone, Neil has two years to take it on or bike racing will die in Britain.'

Fogarty was happy to ignore the members of other teams who were loitering in the lobby and bar of the hotel. He was a slight, wiry figure who walked with the semi-arthritic gait of the old racer, the result of too many crashes and broken bones. 'You do think, "Christ, what am I going to do now? What am I good at?"' He could not stop wishing it was different. 'I couldn't have carried on,' he said, almost apologetically. 'The pain in my shoulder is too bad. Doctors have told me it will never be right and you need your arms to throw a superbike around. I'm lucky. Some people end their careers in a box. I can live a normal life and see my kids grow up.'

Would he cope without the attention? 'I don't miss the fame because I never craved it. Someone like Barry Sheene was into self-promotion. He wanted the trappings of success, but I don't want to do aftershave ads. All I ever wanted was to win and go home.'

His manner of peppering his speech with sideswipes at other legends was a default setting. Fogarty did not know why he was like this, but perhaps it stemmed from the perception that he was undervalued. He did not crave fame, but respect was his lifeblood and the irony was he set about achieving that by dis-respecting those he deemed lesser beings. Colin Edwards, the reigning World Superbike champion, had recently posted a question on Fogarty's website. 'Do you actually like anyone other than yourself?' Fogarty had the skin of a rhino but a sensitive core. 'I was never a hell-raiser,' he said. 'People thought I was because of the way I raced, but when I put on the helmet I changed. I hated everyone, but it wasn't really me. I played up to it. People say I'm more mellow now. I think I am. I always had trouble switching off from racing. I took my work home and could be difficult to live with.'

The desire to win and fear of failure were instilled by his father. George Fogarty was a racer and could be a volatile figure himself. John Cooper, the racer known as 'Moon Eyes' because of his distinctive helmet and best known for beating the great Giacomo Agostini at the Race of the Year at Mallory Park in 1971, once told me an informative story. 'We used to stay in a hotel on the Isle of Man for the TT and there was an amusement arcade next door,' he recalled. 'A lad came in and said the arcade boss had just locked the young Carl in the office. George was up and out of there immediately. "Why have you locked up my lad?" he said. The boss said he had been jumping all over the machines and he had warned him. He said it was only for ten minutes. Teach him a lesson. George didn't care. He took a swing and knocked him flying. Then the henchmen jumped in. They had George on the floor and he shouted, "Don't hit me, I'm a TT rider!" I think he got done for GBH. That was George. He fell off at the bottom of Bray Hill and, fucking hell, he was lucky. He was doing 150mph when the forks slipped down and spat him off. He was rolling and rolling and the bike burst into flames. He hardly hurt himself. Les Graham did the same but hit the wall.' Les Graham died.

Crouched over a pool table, pendant dangling, a date to go house-hunting with Michaela, his wife, and Ruben Xaus, the up-and-coming Spanish rider, in the diary for Monday, Fogarty was a man at the crossroads. 'I quit at the top and that's the way to go,' he said, but you could taste the uncertainty. 'There's also a lot of confusion about what's happening in bike racing. Yamaha are developing a four-stroke GP bike and that seems to be the way forward. But you can't have two four-stroke championships. Nobody knows what's going on. All I know is that, without me, Sundays will never be the same.'

The following day Hodgson crashed after barely covering 12 kilometres of his much-vaunted debut. I could envisage Fogarty smiling at the pretender's fate. He chose the aftermath to announce that he was in talks to run a Ducati team in the World Superbike Championship. Paolo Flammini, the World Superbikes boss, said, 'His future should be in superbikes and we are proud and happy for him to stay in the family. He is a very special person.' Flammini also tried to defuse the concern that the series was in trouble because the 500cc championship was to allow four-stroke engines. 'A million people came to our races last season,' he said. 'Two billion watched on television. Our website gets a million hits during a race weekend. That does not sound like a championship in trouble. It will be more of a danger to themselves as they will lack the resources to convert.'

The 2001 season marked a new beginning. The rivalry between the 500cc World Championship and World Superbikes served to confuse the layman, the departure of Fogarty had robbed Britain of its pivotal figure and the sport was crying out for a hero. The 500c title had been won the previous season by Kenny Roberts, a softly spoken American who inspired ambivalence and was not as good as his dad. Would Sundays ever be the same?

I went to Suzuka for the Japanese Grand Prix and to search for a new hero. I met Chris Walker, the man who had the British superbike title in the bag the previous year until his engine blew up at Donington Park. Like Hodgson, he lacked the piratical menace of Fogarty, but when I mentioned that his predecessor did not see the same hunger in Walker's eyes, he deadpanned, 'You look into Foggy's eyes and you think he's on drugs.'

Hodgson had been the same. 'Carl's never one to blow smoke up your arse,' he had said. On that Friday in Japan Walker was upbeat after turning down a move to Suzuki in World Superbikes. 'All over the world GP racing is bigger than superbikes,' he said. 'There is only one reason why superbikes are so big at home and that is Foggy.' He then belied Fogarty's claim that the new generation were too meek and mild to fill his boots, by saying, 'The bottom line is you need the right package. Foggy would not have won his titles if he didn't have a great bike, and there are a lot of riders with a glint in their eye who haven't got a prayer.' Time would show that Walker came into that category as he was battered, bruised, knocked unconscious and then sacked in mid-season. He would suffer from Bell's palsy, leaving his face in a frozen grimace, and would put tampons in his helmet to soak up the sweat. Michaela Fogarty bumped into him during his darkest times and said, 'Oh, I'm sorry, I thought you were Chris Walker.' The transition from next big thing to next best was complete.

But you never know which way sport will turn. On 8 April 2001, motorcycle racing was in a state of flux and turmoil, epitomized by the jarring fortunes of the best British riders. Walker joked that he had the No. 8 bike so that people would be able to identify him when he was upside down, but what the sport really needed was someone to turn it upside down and inside out. Like Fogarty, it needed to be rejuvenated. He had given Hodgson two years to save it from a premature death, but he was looking in the wrong place. If you asked Fogarty who was the greatest racer around then he would ignore the gammy arm and say, 'It's still me.' But it wasn't. Not any more. That day in Suzuka would prove that. After that Sunday, nothing was the same again.

It was already known that Valentino Rossi and Max Biaggi regarded each other with mutual antipathy. They were contrasting figures. Rossi had just turned twenty-two while Biaggi was pushing thirty; Rossi was the fun-loving maverick from Tavullia, a small town of 7,000 close to the Adriatic coast, Biaggi a prickly, urbane figure from Rome; Rossi was the son of Graziano, a former racer with a two-foot ponytail who slept in the back of his beat-up BMW at races, Biaggi the boy who was reportedly abandoned by his mother as a child. 'He's a crazy bastard, but then you would be with his background,' one Italian journalist told me.

They had been chipping away at each other for years. Rossi later pinpointed the genesis of their feud as the Malaysian Grand Prix of 1997 when, as a teenager, he was riding in the 125cc class and Biaggi the 250cc. 'No,' he did not want to be regarded as the Biaggi of 125s, Rossi told the Italian press. 'It's going to be him who dreams of being the Rossi of 250s.' It was a throwaway remark, but Rossi claimed Biaggi reacted badly when the pair met later in the trackside restaurant at Suzuka. 'Wash your mouth out,' Biaggi is alleged to have said. Others have different recollections, one former Yamaha team member saying Rossi and his crowd were being irritatingly rowdy and Biaggi merely shouted to them to keep the noise down. 'Max said that Valentino could never get over the fact he had been spoken to like that in front of his friends,' Ali Forth, the Yamaha press officer at the time, remembered. 'Max said *that* was the reason Valentino hated him so much.'

In 2001 Rossi was already a star-in-the-making. He had won the 125cc and 250cc world titles and finished second to Roberts in the 500cc class in his debut year. Biaggi, a four-time winner of the 250cc class, had been third. That rankled with the Roman. However, Rossi's popularity went beyond speed and success. With him the substance was suffused in style, and teenage Italy had been seduced by his quirky nature and asinine stunts. From popping into a Portaloo on his victory lap in Spain in 1999 to the ever-changing bouffant – the neon blue, the foppish mane, the Max Miller monk – Rossi's rise had bucked the stone-faced stoicism of Biaggi.

He had also resisted no opportunity to slight Biaggi. The love of mockery had caused uproar in the excitable Italian media at the way Rossi had chosen to celebrate a win at Mugello at the Italian Grand Prix in 1997. Newspaper reports had linked Biaggi with Naomi Campbell, then the biggest supermodel in the world, and he himself had pricked Rossi's interest by saying the glamourpuss would be among his guests at Mugello. Rossi had been the owner of a blow-up doll since the previous year, planning to use it for a celebration at some point. Now the chance was too good to waste and his Fan Club, a group of loyal fans and drinking buddies, egged him on. And so Rossi celebrated by giving a pillion ride to a blow-up doll with the moniker 'Claudia Schiffer' scrawled on the back. It was a crude but colourful thumbed nose. Rossi would claim the media misinterpreted the prank and Schiffer was a pun on the word *schifo* meaning 'gross', but the target was clear.

Their colours highlighted the contrast, the neon yellow of Rossi's Honda NSR and the crimson rage of Biaggi's Yamaha. 'Many people can win races, but few can win the title,' Biaggi said. The profundity underscored Rossi's lighthearted behaviour. It made it hard to be in both camps. The fans were divided into red and yellow legions and even hard-bitten journalists took sides. Roberts, Garry McCoy and Loris Capirossi were among those presenting added opposition to the duel, but it was clear from that dramatic day in Japan in April 2001 that this was to be a high-speed arm-wrestle between two sworn enemies.

The start of any season is always flushed with heightened expectation and myths ready to be made and shattered. Capirossi, riding the satellite NSR for Sito Pons' tobacco-backed team, was the first away with Biaggi in febrile pursuit. Rossi was down in the pack, but as the cavalcade snaked its way around Suzuka, he scythed a path towards Biaggi. Capirossi, a teak-tough brawler with a pit-bull physique, drifted backwards with a damaged rear tyre. Walker, meanwhile, had already gone, into the back of the pack and footnote status, his debut a fleeting cameo in one of the most talked about races for years, the cold pain strangling his body later diagnosed as a broken shoulder. Sete Gibernau, another who would come to play a leading role in the Rossi story, also fell. And then came the moment when the bickering and bad-mouthing spilled over into violence. Rossi slipstreamed Biaggi, pulled out and was edging level. Biaggi's will to win and overt hatred for his compatriot clouded his judgement for a nanosecond. The red bike disappeared beneath a red mist and Biaggi appeared to elbow Rossi off the track. Rossi was stunned. Furious. Scared. He tried to control his bike on the grass that lined the straight. He was travelling at 150mph. By the time the crowd had gasped, Rossi had saved himself and was back on the track. No harm done. The race went on.

Rossi was now in the danger zone because the calmness needed to risk life and limb had been replaced by raw anger. 'Fuck Biaggi!' he muttered. Later, in an interview with Monty Shadow for Laureus, he would explain how everything is beautiful at speed. 'Racers take some serious hits. It is a violent way to tell you how fast you are going. It is extremely important to stay calm. As paradoxical as it sounds, the faster you ride, the slower your movements must become, because speed exaggerates everything, automatically doing the rest of the work for you. This is one of the aspects that fascinates me the most; when you are racing and you exceed a certain velocity you start to feel like you're moving faster than everything around you. You feel faster than reality.'

After a brief hiatus, when his emotion seized control of him, Rossi was in this state of heightened reality. He had lost ground so he put his head down, swore and raced. Like never before. 'Speed; too fast, too furious; fast food, fast forward, speed-boat; fast-lane; flat-out; survival of the fastest; I live for speed.'

Biaggi held Rossi at bay for two laps and then the younger man sailed past on a fast right-hander. Everything slowed. Sound, motion, his movements now calm. He lifted his left hand off the handlebars, turned back and raised a finger at Biaggi. Ignorance causes fear, he would say. Moving slowly. Thinking fast.

Rossi increased his lead and now the mayhem was in his wake. Tohru Ukawa crashed and Biaggi was fighting with McCoy and the Japanese duo of Shinya Nakano and Norick Abe. All were on Yamahas and Biaggi was damned if he was going to let them beat him. There were no more elbows, just hard, aggressive racing and the last place on the podium by a mere two-tenths of a second.

The aftermath of that race was strange and showed how divided the press corps had become when it came to the Italians. Many in the media initially sided with Biaggi, suggesting Rossi's overtaking manoeuvre had been dangerous, with plenty more dismissing it as a lot of fuss about nothing. Race control shared that approach and decided there was nothing worth reporting. More startling still, both Honda and Yamaha made no complaints. It was, then, left to Rossi to voice his disbelief by confronting Biaggi and telling him to get a gun next time and shoot him. Biaggi, who generally treated Rossi as an irritating child, ignored him.

Honda preferred to bask in the glow of their five hundredth GP victory. A party was held in one of the function rooms next to the offices and media centre. Rossi was there, along with Mick Doohan who topped the list of winners with fifty-four. Rossi was down in thirty-ninth spot with just three wins and there were some at Suzuka who were somewhat sniffy that a relative novice should have hit the winning runs. Rossi had a beer, chatted with Doohan and then departed into the night. 'There was a bit of fear all right and so I gave him a little wave,' he said of his spat with Biaggi.

Biaggi had already given his version of events at the press conference. 'There was a lot of body contact and I touched Rossi, Haga and Ukawa, but they were legitimate racing manoeuvres,' he said. As the Honda party progressed, and canapés were munched beneath grainy pictures of legends such as Mike Hailwood, people were happier looking to the past rather than the future.

The only man who seemed unimpressed was Francesco Zerbi, the president of the FIM (Fédération Internationale de Motocyclisme), motorcycle racing's governing body, who sent an open letter to Rossi and Biaggi, warning them to avoid a repeat of their behaviour in Japan. He also said that sanctions would be taken if there was any more 'anti-sporting or censurable behaviour'. His letter contained some confusing statements. 'My intervention is a reproach to you both, in order to invite you to more attentively and correctly control your actions and reactions, without taking anything away from your fighting instinct and your desire for victory.' It was a curious message but it scarcely mattered. Chip paper as far as Rossi was concerned.

Never ones to shirk a melodrama, the Italian media whipped up the feud into a frenzy, even calling on Giacomo Agostini, the most successful racer of all, to arbitrate in the dispute. Agostini, now living in a lavish villa in a lush plot on a hill in Bergamo, reasoned that Rossi was at fault for overtaking on the outside. Biaggi loved that and labelled his rival 'bad-mannered'. Rossi, finding it hard to understand how he had been elbowed off the track and cold shouldered into the role of perpetrator, said, 'I told him it would be bad for Italy if we both fell off. He said he didn't care and was only bothered about the chequered flag.'

It meant that by the time I met Rossi at the London Eye that May, he was becoming big news even in a Britain that had steadfastly refused to embrace the prototype 500cc class, favouring its love-fest with Fogarty and the big and bruising superbikes that fans could buy over the counter. Rossi was fulfilling one of his promotional duties to Dorna, the World Championship rights holders, and was dressed in plain jeans and brown jumper. A gaggle of excited tourists, weighed down with cameras and rucksacks walked past. Rossi leant against a wall. To his relief the tourists failed to recognize him, so he lifted his sunglasses, perched them on the top of his head and listened to the sound of the Thames gently lapping against the blackened bricks of the south bank.

'I moved here to get away from the fans at home,' he said. 'I could not go out of my house back home without being mobbed. People would knock on my door at all hours and I got tired of it. It was like being a footballer, so I decided to move to England. It was a very hard decision to make and I miss my family, but here I can have a normal life. Nobody knows who I am, apart from Italians.' He stopped and looked thoughtfully into the muddy waters. 'Unfortunately, London seems to be full of Italians.'

Rossi had just won his third successive grand prix in Jerez, celebrating by getting one of his friends to jump on the back of his NSR in a surgeon's coat. 'In Italy, Rossi is the most common surname,' he explained. 'I wanted something that sounded a bit more special so I have started calling myself Dr Rossi. That's why he was wearing the gown. My celebrations are part of my approach to life. I want to have fun. I am young and this is how I like to party.'

We stepped into one of the capsules of the London Eye and it was easy to think of Rossi living life in a bubble. Already, with only five wins in the elite class of racing, his home in Tavullia had become a shrine for voyeurs and 'Valenteenyboppers'. The locals loved him and the bells of the church rang out when he won, but his love of life was leaving him exposed. Flippantly, I asked him if his move was a tax fiddle. He laughed and widened his blue-green eyes. It was easy to see why the world might fall for his charms.

What he lacked in subtlety Rossi made up for in colour. He was a bubbling maelstrom of energy topped off with a smile that melted the hearts of female fans and PR men alike. Picture Frankie Dettori marinated in coffee and you came close to appreciating his energy levels. Mention of Biaggi's name instantly wiped the smile off Rossi's face. 'It is hard to be friends with other drivers [sic],' he said. 'Biaggi is a great rider but I don't know him personally. I can't say too much about it, but I can tell you I could never be friends with him. We have different ideas about life and how to do things, but I know that my way is the right way.'

Not everyone thought that. Despite the divorce of his parents Graziano and Stefania, Rossi had a normal and carefree childhood, but John Cooper claimed that Rossi had cut all ties with another family who had been supportive of him during his early days. They ran a garage near Tavullia and even had one of Rossi's old mini bikes nailed to the wall. 'They don't know why, but Rossi just refuses to acknowledge them now,' Cooper said when we met in his Derbyshire home in 2008. 'I went to a function where I knew Rossi was going to be so they asked me if I would have a word with him. I went up to Rossi at a quiet moment and showed him a photograph and asked if he recognized anyone. He said no and walked off. They have no idea why he has behaved like that. Even Graziano says he is at a loss to understand.'

He had started his life in the paddock as Graziano eked out a career. The great Agostini, having hung up his leathers to become a team manager, signed Graziano for Yamaha in 1982, but it was a short-lived alliance as Rossi senior suffered a horrendous fall at Imola that year. His best year would remain 1979 when he was third in the 250cc World Championship, the year his wife gave birth to Valentino.

'One of my first heroes was Nigel Mansell,' Rossi said as he looked down over the Houses of Parliament. Maybe he was trying to spot Chinawhite, the Piccadilly nightclub where he was a regular now that he had broken up with his girlfriend, Eliana. 'I sat on my first bike when I was three, but started racing go-karts when I was a small boy. I wanted to be Mansell or Senna, but eventually we realized it was impossible to become a Formula One driver without lots of money. That's why I turned to bikes.'

His early years were marred by erratic performances that

worried his parents and raised a question mark over his ability to tame his raw talent. More often than not, Rossi's races in his debut GP season in 1996 ended in gravel traps, but the following season saw him mature quickly. He became the 125cc world champion and followed it up with the 250cc title two years later. Suddenly, the man with the playful grin was hot property. Everybody wanted a piece of him, but potential sponsors and team owners soon realized Rossi was a strong-willed enigma and his anti-smoking beliefs meant that he refused to join any team sponsored by a tobacco company. Much was made of the stance, not least when it softened and he eventually rode under Camel and Gauloises banners in multi-million-pound deals.

At Honda he teamed up with Doohan, the five-time world champion, who had an advisory role. The partnership appeared to be one made in motorcycle heaven, but Rossi was never a natural apprentice. 'He has tried to advise me, but there is not much he can do,' Rossi said wearily. 'He is old and I am young. Our styles are different. I am very aggressive. People talk about his record of twelve wins in a season, but I don't think that is possible. There are too many good riders now.'

The PR stunt adjourned and we went for a coffee by the aquarium on the South Bank. Rossi could walk freely among the hordes of tourists and only got a quizzical look because of the cameramen in his wake. 'I love it here,' he said. 'I go nightclubbing and love the shops. I am always going to Carnaby Street and Covent Garden. I've a passion for shoes – I've got hundreds of pairs. It can be hard, though. I have a kid brother, Luca, and a kid sister, Clara, back home, and I miss them a lot. Then there is Guido, my English bulldog. It's tough, but feeling free is important.'

We shook hands and I wished him well. He walked off down the Embankment as a virtual unknown. It was one month before he would become front page news in Italy and his feud with Biaggi would reach its explosive nadir.

CHAPTER THREE

BITTER

Somehow the words did not ring true. Straight-faced he may have been, but straight-laced appeared to be beyond Valentino Rossi. Wearing bright pink trousers, the Italian maverick insisted that he was toning down his act after his crash in Italy a fortnight ago. It was a funny way of showing it.

It had been a great stunt. Rossi was told that his widening appeal meant his Fan Club now had a Hawaiian branch. There were only four members but the very idea tickled Rossi and so he consulted the Tribe of the Chihuahua, the band of old school friends with whom he went to the beach in the summer and drank in his downtime. It had been one such alcohol-fuelled session at Mambo's house that led to them realizing they were a tribe; Chihuahua was added because they were a Native American tribe and sounded cool.

The plan was put swiftly in place. The Fan Club got in touch and four men soon found themselves on an all-expenses-paid trip to Mugello for the Italian Grand Prix. Never one to do things by halves, Rossi donned a floral, Hawaiian livery, while his crew swapped their traditional yellow for the same design. As the final touch, Rossi ordered an inflatable trackside swimming pool to be installed, complete with palm trees. 'So they feel at home,' he said. Down the pitlane, Biaggi bristled at the nonsense and resented being drawn into Rossi's pantomime.

It was a great stunt but it went wrong. With the rivals' fans split into huge red and yellow factions, the latter in the clear majority, the stage was set for the latest round of sparring. Rossi arrived with a thirty-four-point lead, healthy but nowhere near insurmountable, with twenty-five points going to each race winner. I caught up with Mack in the media room. 'You know the great thing about Valentino is he says, "We win" and, "I lose".' Mack has been there and seen it all. He was even called into action when Mike Hailwood had gone back to the Isle of Man all those years ago. As such he was not a man easily deceived by the fripperies of success.

A lot of water had gone under the bridge since Hailwood's era and more was doing so now. Mugello was a washout. Torrents of mud ran down the pitlane. The organizers could not cope and made a farce of the programme, ordering a restart of the 125cc race. It was then delayed a second time after another downpour. It meant that when they finally got to the 500cc race the television schedules were in chaos and Channel 5 viewers saw only a handful of laps. By that time Rossi had already crashed once, on the sighting lap. Then he slid out in the race. Biaggi was third behind Alex Barros and Loris Capirossi. The championship was wide open again.

An undercurrent of glee was palpable when it came to Rossi's fate. Many remembered how he had pitched up on the podium at Mugello in 1998 dressed in swimming trunks and carrying a beach towel. It was taken badly, as an insult to the race winner, Marcellino Lucchi, a veteran who lived off crumbs and was having his big moment hijacked. Now Rossi was clowning around again when he should have been focusing on the track. He was behaving like a superstar rather than someone who was still to win the 500cc world title.

'I am always focused when I ride and the other stuff is just fun,' he said in Honda's hospitality suite at the Catalan Grand Prix. The trousers he had turned up in belied the new-found gravitas. 'We are back to our normal colours. The crash has not affected my confidence. Mugello was like the middle of winter and now it's summer, and this is one of my favourite tracks because it is suited to former 125cc and 250cc riders with its long, sweeping curves. There will be no surprises now.' On that point, at least, he would be proved very wrong.

Rossi fell in the first qualifying session but was unhurt. His problems paled into insignificance alongside those of Chris Walker and Leon Haslam, the British duo riding for Shell Advance Honda. Walker was seventeenth in the championship after a baptism of fire and tarmac and had been taking solace in a venerated agony aunt. Having been told he could teach little to Rossi, Mick Doohan had offered a shoulder to cry on. 'He's a big hero of mine and has had a few words,' Walker said. 'It was a big help because he's been there and done it. He talked to me about how I was transferring my weight on the bike. It's around 30 kilos less than the superbikes I'm used to, which means you can't throw it around.' Pep talk delivered, Walker duly fell in qualifying and went to the *clinica mobile* for X-rays. Haslam had already been there, where he was ruled out with the broken wrist he had sustained at Le Mans a month earlier.

It was a bleak time for the British. Over in World Superbikes Neil Hodgson had also failed to live up to the media's billing of the new Fogarty and had been grousing about his treatment. 'There have been a lot of snide comments about me this season and I'm fed up with it,' he told me over the phone. 'I've seen the odd letter in the press and have heard Joe Public say his piece, but the fact is I'm racing as well as ever. They can all piss off.'

Rossi was on pole and I was stuck. The traffic to the circuit in Montmelo was gridlocked. My taxi driver was shrugging and pointing but getting nowhere. I got out and hiked the rest of the journey. I was not the only one struggling. I had seen Garry McCoy at breakfast. McCoy was a wonderfully gifted Australian, one of the few who really knew how to get the 16.5-inch rear tyre sliding into corners, but he was sometimes too wild and had elected not to race after failing to recover from his own broken wrist. As he sat there in the soulless hotel in Granollers he knew his title prospects were over.

For Rossi the next few hours would cement his status as the most flamboyant star the sport had seen since the days when Hailwood and Agostini were double-dating sisters on the Adriatic Riviera. He was on the front row alongside Biaggi and, unlike at the World Superbike races in Valencia, the grandstands in this part of Spain were full. Banners with roughly marked messages dripped from the railings. A helicopter flew overhead. Rossi stood up on his footrests as he left the pits, adjusting his leathers at the crotch, a trademark move that he said was practical not super-stitious. Biaggi knew he needed to win today, but he had taken twenty points off Rossi's lead in Mugello and was confident.

His mood would have improved further had he witnessed the difficulties Rossi encountered on the first lap. A near-miss between Sete Gibernau and Alex Criville, the two Spanish heroes, saw Criville run wide, forcing Rossi on to the limits of the track. He then had to take evasive action to avoid Jay Vincent, yet another struggling Brit, and found himself languishing back in twelfth place by the end of the first circuit. It did not last. Five laps later he was third and Biaggi had been vanquished. When Rossi hauled in Gibernau and then Capirossi the outcome was never in doubt. Biaggi rode hard and fast to get into second place and might have contemplated the unspeakable truth, that this was the natural order, but if he did then he did not show it. 'My dream is to see him on a Yamaha or a Suzuki,' he said. 'Then we will see how good he is.' The line became a mantra for Biaggi.

Hindsight would suggest he should have been more careful in what he wished for.

There were three Italians on the podium that day but there was no sense of camaraderie. Biaggi had grown to despise Rossi, while Capirossi, albeit far more diplomatic, shared a sense of grievance at Rossi's status as Honda's jewel. Nobody in the crowd really knew why the trio looked so downbeat on the podium that day, but the story quickly emerged. Prior to the anthems the trio had been sequestered in an anteroom. It was a chaotic scene with friends, cameramen, Dorna staff and team officials. Rossi celebrated with Gibo Badioli, the former furniture salesman employed as his personal manager. It was too much for Biaggi to see the unbridled joy of this man he overtly hated. He barged his way up the stairs but then found his way blocked by Badioli. He elbowed him out of the way sparking a furious response from the watching Rossi. 'What the fuck are you doing?' he yelled. Biaggi turned, tipping over the edge again, just as he had at Suzuka when that elbow had led to volcanic scenes. 'You want some!' Rossi would claim his enemy raged in his autobiography. 'There's plenty for you too!' It was claimed that Rossi took him at his word and, to the astonishment of various high-ranking officials, stormed up the stairs and landed a punch. Reports of the fight varied but one suggested Biaggi thrust his head back and butted Badioli. Then there were slaps, half-punches and a tightening of the melee before Carlo Fiorani, the bulky Nastro Azzuro team manager, stepped between the two featherweights and shoved his man on to the podium.

Immediately after the anthems the three Italians were shepherded to the press conference room, where confusion reigned. Rumours of a fight between the two leading racers in the world were already throbbing on the grapevine. Some said Capirossi had also been involved, others that Rossi had thrown a headbutt too. However, as the riders sat down, it was clear that

Biaggi, so often the bleeding heart this season, now had a bleeding face. 'Max, can you tell me what happened to your face?' a journalist asked. 'You seem marked.'

'It is a mosquito bite,' he deadpanned and there was a polite ripple of laughter. There were more questions, but both men had taken a quick decision to flatbat the journalists' queries and keep what Rossi termed a 'reciprocal antipathy' deeply personal. They had to give their versions to race stewards, but all decided that the fight was an unseemly episode best covered up. In that year's *Motocourse* annual, the bible of the sport, the incident was dismissed as 'little more than a light diversion', while the stewards' decision to brush the matter under the carpet smacked of myopia. The truth was, in a year when the sport's future was clouded, a rivalry between two men who sickened each other was precisely what was needed.

Ali Forth, Yamaha's press chief, noticed that Federica, Biaggi's faithful assistant, also had blood and scratches on her face. It was weeks before Federica would give her side of the story. A lot of evil words were spoken, she told Forth. She then claimed Rossi and his entourage started the trouble. 'There was a helmet that got smashed against someone,' Forth said. 'It got pretty brutal. There'd been a big football match that day and they were revved up.'

Lin Jarvis, the manager of Biaggi's Marlboro Yamaha team, trotted out a diplomatic line. 'There were a lot of people in a cramped space and a small misunderstanding got out of hand. Both riders have now made a commitment to keeping their well-documented rivalry within acceptable, sporting parameters.' It was a carefully worded statement designed to defuse the story with its bland understatement. It did not work.

The FIM's decision to let both off with a warning was criticized but showed an acute understanding of the duo's importance to the series. A suspension was simply never an option. However, despite final warnings, the enmity showed no sign of abating. 'I will not say I would be ahead if I was on his bike, but if you asked any motorcycle fan then you would get your answer,' Biaggi said to reporters when the dust had settled. Then the mantra. 'My dream is to see him on a Yamaha or a Suzuki. Kenny Roberts told me that if his father, who is forty-nine, had Rossi's bike then he would be on the podium every week too. That made me laugh, but maybe it's true. We're not the same people. Everyone can see that. We don't act the same, don't speak the same. Some of the things he does are, well, I don't want to say too much because it will be turned back on me.'

This was Biaggi's way. He would paint himself as the wounded soldier while saying just enough to damn his rival. He assumed the moral high ground and fooled plenty of people into believing he was an innocent victim of Rossi's rudeness and ruthlessness, but he was just as measured in his dealings with the media. The hurtful part for Biaggi was the slow realization that Rossi could play people better than he could.

It was always easy to find a seam of insecurity when speaking to Biaggi. He could be guarded, cold and dismissive, but he was usually willing to speak to *The Times* and so perhaps I gained a better insight into his nature than some. He did not speak about his background, but it was hard to imagine that his insularity was not a product of his mother walking out. Whatever the cause, his behaviour certainly had consequences. One example came when he sparked a major row when he turned up to a film shoot with the wrong pair of boots. Having spent months liaising with Yamaha, Philip Morris, the sponsors, were unimpressed. There followed a full-scale argument between Biaggi, Yamaha's Japanese chiefs and Philip Morris's sponsorship boss. Biaggi was said to be in tears.

He had dreamt of being a footballer for AS Roma. 'I only got into motorcycling when my friend, Daniela Mariana, took me to the Vallelunga circuit and I was hooked,' he said. 'I raced for the first time the next year and it was incredible to discover I had this talent.' Biaggi won his first 250cc grand prix in 1992, added a quartet of 250cc titles from 1994 to 1997, and became the second-most successful 250cc rider in history. Since graduating to the 500cc class he had finished second, fourth and third. He was the biggest thing Italy had seen for years. Until Rossi. And now Yamaha were spending too long developing the four-stroke YZR-M1 instead of living in the here and now. 'What bothers me is the championship,' he said. 'I want a better package now.' He sounded very much like a spoilt child.

A truce was called at the next race in Assen, a windswept party-town with a festival feel, but the truth lay hidden beneath the forced smiles and cool handshake. Paco Latorre, Dorna's media chief, demanded the duo at least feign an end to hostilities for the cameras, but it was the half-hearted apology of two naughty children with their parents twisting their arms. Nobody took the contrived photo shoot at face value. 'All riders get nervous, especially with so many press people pushing around,' Rossi said. 'However, it's a matter that is closed now and everything is OK between us.' Someone asked how Rossi viewed their relationship. 'We ride together in the same category, but I don't know him very well.' Biaggi was less conciliatory. 'We do ride in the same category, yes, but it's as if Rossi has ridden against me ever since he was in the 125s,' he said in reference to the longevity of their feud. The thinly veiled message was Rossi had started it and turned it into a vendetta. Several months later Rossi's resentment showed when he said: 'Look, "He started it, I started it, he started it, I started it". Who cares? Fack! I mean, look at what happened in the race. I'd won. Why would I start a fight?'

At the pre-race press conference in Assen, Kenny Roberts tried to lighten the mood. 'You're sitting in the wrong place, Max,' he yelled. 'You're a southpaw and you'll never connect from there.' Others were less amused by the public blood-letting. Foremost among them was Capirossi. The man from the wrong side of the tracks in Bologna trailed Biaggi by just nine points and was upset by the public perception that the championship was a two-horse race. He qualified on pole position and sighed, 'It wasn't pretty what they did. I don't think they should have done it. It's not good for any of us.'

Inevitably, the race brought more controversy. Rossi claimed that he had slowed before the red flags were waved for rain and Biaggi passed him. Chastened by the controversy of recent weeks, he declined to make an issue out of it, while Biaggi championed his own riding ability, claiming that in winning he showed that he was at his peak. Capirossi, who felt he had the beating of both and was waiting to make his move, had to make do with third.

Walker was not there. His baptism was now a case of drowning in a font of misery. In Friday's qualifying session he suffered his worst crash yet, touching a white line going into the Meeuwenmeer kink at 150mph. He was tossed down the track, wrote off his bike and was knocked unconscious for half an hour. Helmet technicians reasoned that their protection had saved him and the crushed lining and gaping hole in the back suggested they were right.

Three days later I wandered down Euston Road in London to a hotel where a media day had been called for the British Grand Prix the following Sunday. The first person I spotted was Barry Sheene, the two-time world champion and the man every rider in Britain wanted to replace. Sheene now lived in Australia and, although the face was ruddier and the eyes circled by little crevices, he was still a vibrant figure. Sheene always had the boy-next-door look about him and, although he was now fifty-one and a year away from telling the world that he was fighting a pernicious cancer, he exuded the energy of men half his age. 'People are talking about their fight all the time and it's brilliant for the sport,' he gushed. The incorrigible rogue, who a female colleague once said had spent an entire interview eyeing up her breasts, then sauntered over to Katja Poensgen, a Bavarian blonde tentatively being billed as the Anna Kournikova of motorcycling.

Half an hour later I sat down with the twenty-four-year-old myself. The previous month she had made history by becoming the first woman to score points in a 250cc grand prix. She knew what to expect at Donington. 'I'd like to be treated like a man but it's hard,' she said. 'At Assen last week there were four or five guys with a banner saying, "Katja, we want to have your babies". Then I get emails from fans asking me to marry them. I think they are joking. If I turned up on their doorstep and said, "Right, where's the church?" they'd be scared stiff.'

Poensgen was in a curious position. She wanted to be treated as an equal but, if so, she would not have been called to the media day. She was here because she was an anomaly in a world where hackneyed images of bikers still festered. She was labelled a mix of Bambi and bimbo, too pretty and too fragile, but it was those labels that provided her badge of distinction. 'In races where I've been leading men, they have retired with supposed engine problems,' she claimed. 'Nobody wants to lose to me because I'm a woman.'

Her father was a Suzuki executive, but Poensgen showed few early signs of wanting to race bikes. 'I was a rebel. I hated my parents, didn't want to go to school, dyed my hair green and became a punk. When I was sixteen I had to go with my father to the Calafat track in Spain. I was furious because it was New Year and I was missing a party. On the last day in Spain I rode a 125cc bike out of boredom and that was it. I knew what I wanted.'

Back at Calafat in 1997, her career appeared to be over when a horrific crash left her in a coma. The left side of her body was paralysed for six weeks. Against her father's wishes, she did return, only to break her hand and foot. She blamed those risks for the dearth of women racers rather than any inherent prejudice. 'Women don't like breaking bones,' she said contemptuously. 'It's the fears and doubts of women themselves that prevent them from doing it.'

Inevitably, Biaggi came up during our conversation following claims from Italy that he had made disparaging remarks about Poensgen, insisting she belonged on the catwalk and that her website was dominated by breasts. 'I don't believe he said those things,' she said.

Despite having to deny those reports to the media in London, Biaggi was in good humour. Rossi had not shown up for the press day, sending word that he was delayed in France, but Biaggi and the British media were happy to take that as a snub. With advance ticket sales for the grand prix up by four hundred per cent, nobody was willing to downplay the schism that had dragged the sport into the limelight. 'What happened in Spain is in the past,' Biaggi said as he sipped a mineral water. 'I don't want to waste words and time going over it.' If that was truly the case then Biaggi would have stopped there, but he added a killer postscript. 'But I hope it's opened Dorna's eyes. It should not have happened, but there were too many of Rossi's people there. Why does he need four people around him? When he first arrived people said he was young and playing games. Well, he's not a young boy any more.'

It was not surprising that Biaggi was in such a bright mood. In the past couple of weeks he had trimmed Rossi's lead to twenty-one points, met the Pope and played football against his hero, Gabriel Batistuta, the AS Roma striker. 'I feel good and the win in Assen was very important,' he said. 'I am not thinking about Rossi. No, I don't agree that our rivalry will make the racing more dangerous. We are professionals.'

The dangers were always evident. Beneath pewter skies at Donington the next day, Chris Walker said, 'I feel second-hand, like I've got a bad hangover, but I'm desperate to ride and give my fans something to hold on to.' It was a grim vista and a relic of a circuit, often rendered a quagmire by the rain and with persistent stories of fuel-shedding aeroplanes landing at the neighbouring East Midlands Airport. Walker had now crashed twelve times in seven rounds. What he lacked in cheap insurance, he made up for in courage and, although the last vestiges of his confidence should have departed in the back of the ambulance that transported him from the Assen circuit the previous week, he was ready for more.

Rossi, too, knew all about crashing. Carlo Pernat is still a blatantly Italian presence at every grand prix. He has had myriad jobs in the World Championship, but primarily has been a racing manager and talent scout. With a crook, bulbous nose, wispy long hair and permanent sunglasses, he cuts a middle-aged dash in the paddock and is usually to be found wandering around the garages, exuding intrigue and cigarette smoke. He is also the man who discovered Rossi.

At Donington, as the skies darkened, the shades stayed on. 'I was a friend of his father and he said to me, "Carlo, come with me and watch my boy". So I went to Misano, I was still with Cagiva, and he was unbelievable. He made some overtakes where you either go down or past. I remember he made a big impression on me because he was so similar to Kevin Schwantz. I had tested with Kevin almost ten years earlier in 1987 when his manager said, "Carlo, come with me, you have to see this guy Kevin Schwantz". Nobody knew who he was and he took the most incredible lines on the bike. It was the same watching Valentino. In my mind I thought, "Either he's a champion or he's dead soon" – one of the two. I remember how many crashes he had in 1996 and 1997, but he was crashing when he was second or third. I was sure he would be a champion or dead.'

He crashed at 140mph on Friday afternoon, but was lucky. Walker's mortality was exposed with every hospital trip, but Rossi crashed at almost the same speed and walked away. A champion or dead, Pernat had said. It was a horrible, gruesome equation, and

Rossi's childishness and *joie de vivre* masked the dangers. In a *Vanity Fair Italy* interview with Silvia Nucini in 2006, it was pointed out that his idols included Steve McQueen, John Belushi and Jim Morrison, people who had lived fast and died young. 'Are you fascinated by doomed lives?' he was asked. 'You're born doomed,' he replied. 'And I don't think I have that thing inside of me.'

Biaggi was on pole position. Rossi, his bike destroyed on Friday, was a lowly eleventh. Doomed? Biaggi led from the line and Rossi stuttered in the pack. Roberts, at last dragging some drama from the Suzuki, swooped into the lead by the end of the first lap. Rossi was engineering a path to the front but almost fell when Olivier Jacque mistimed a corner in defending himself against the Italian. Charmed? Rossi was now on a familiar charge, proving he could beat anyone when the tyres started to age and the racing grew ragged. He overhauled Barros and then Biaggi. The scarlet Yamaha stuck with Rossi for a few laps, but it was a matter of time and the gap grew. Biaggi felt the gap widen in his chest, like a drowning man drifting from the surface.

There was no post-race stunt but the joy was uncontained. 'This is my most important win ever,' Rossi said as he walked into the freezing shack passing for a media centre. 'I needed it after the crash in qualifying. I'm in a great position, but the championship is close and I need to stay concentrated.' Biaggi almost handed out a compliment to his rival in the aftermath. 'He's a good rider,' he lamented. 'Sometimes it looks like we are racing two different championships. I played my own game and it would have been impossible to do more. Rossi started from the third row and won so you can see the potential of him and his bike. It's a hard combination to beat.'

It did not look hard in Germany, where Biaggi trounced Rossi. It was bubbling up into a tumultuous last 500cc championship before the advent of the 990cc four-stroke bikes the following season. Rossi was crestfallen at the Sachsenring and refused to speak to the media. That did not go down well, especially with the Italian contingent, who were happy to damn their man as shirking his responsibilities. Rossi hid away in the garage, listening to the journalists lose their temper with the Honda press officers. Rossi would say it was 'absurd', but his reaction was unusual and evidence of just how much the defeat had got to him. Inside the garage Jerry Burgess, the wily Australian crew chief and part-time psychologist, told Rossi to forget about it. He rallied his man with talk of tiredness from testing for the Suzuka Eight Hours and a ten-point lead still being a significant advantage. It was a motivational speech that would have huge implications for both the season and Rossi's future. He lifted himself out of the doldrums and went on holiday.

Walker, meanwhile, was back in England. He had been sacked. To add insult to the manifold injuries he had suffered in a torrid season, his place was taken by Brendan Clarke, a teenage novice who heard the news while in a maths lesson in Melbourne. Walker's team claimed he was sitting out the race because of his head injuries, but Dave Pickworth, his manager, confirmed he had been dismissed. 'The team have not been true to their word,' Walker added. It was the voice of the dumped. 'They have decided to replace me without giving me time to adapt to riding a 500, which was part of the original deal.' Some onlookers were just pleased that the likeable Walker had been sidelined before his bravery took him over the precipice. He was not alone in his suffering. Jay Vincent was on his way to the Czech Republic when he was told his Pulse team had folded. Poensgen, meanwhile, was sacked in a dispute over sponsorship. This was life down among the dead men and women of the World Championship circus.

Brno was mesmerizing. The attractive old town buzzed with anticipation as the riders and teams returned after the mid-season break. It was the race that would effectively settle the outcome of the world title and, like everything in 2001, it would be jaw-dropping. It came down to the two men, two bikes and two minds. Rossi had been emboldened by Burgess' gentle words, while Biaggi tried to stamp out the nagging beacons of doubt. He had moaned so long and so hard about the Yamaha's inferior machinery that he believed it. 'Jesus Christ, it's not like it's a supermarket trolley,' one disillusioned Yamaha insider told me. 'But that's Max.'

In the white heat of a title decider, Rossi toyed with Biaggi. When the older man looked back to see where his rival was, Rossi would risk all by raising his left hand and waving. It was a gesture that was far more telling than the single finger he had shown at Suzuka all those months ago. How that wave must have plagued Biaggi's thinking. Soon after, with the two bikes blurring into one another, it happened. It was innocuous, unbidden. In a season of harsh words and sledgehammer subtlety, ravaged bodies and broken bones, Biaggi merely slipped away. Rossi was now in the lead and could not quite believe what he had seen. 'All my plans disappeared because I had been plotting. Now he was gone.' Down but not out, as it happened, Biaggi remounting and riding desperately to tenth. It was to no avail. Everyone knew now. Biaggi had refuted the suggestion that he could not mix it in a dogfight as the gentle nature of that crash showed just how far over the edge he had been riding. However, it also showed just how adept Rossi was at getting inside the mind of his rival.

'It was like having a bowl of pasta and then having it taken away,' Rossi said, meaning that he wanted to gorge on Biaggi rather than have the win gifted to him. This was Rossi's way. He loved a fight. Biaggi crashed again in Estoril a fortnight later, two days before of the terrorist attack on the Twin Towers, and again remounted, this time finishing fifth. Rossi had suddenly opened up a forty-three-point lead and Biaggi cemented his reputation as a whinger extraordinaire. 'Rossi has the best bike,' he said afterwards. The mantra. 'Everybody knows that. He also has an advantage with his engine over the other Honda riders. This is unfair. At Yamaha everyone has the same equipment and that is the way it should be.'

The march to the 2001 coronation was a staccato affair as Rossi and Biaggi suffered a torrid time in Valencia and another duel between the pair was washed away as the heavens opened just before the race at the Ricardo Tormo circuit. That prompted frenetic scenes and furrowed brows in the pitlane as teams contemplated their tyre choice. Biaggi was the most frustrated victim. Having qualified on pole position for the fourth successive race, his chances were undermined by the wrong tyre choice. He fell slowly back as Rossi set the early pace. Biaggi gained some solace from the drying track that saw Rossi begin to slow in equally dramatic fashion, enabling Gibernau to win his first grand prix on the Suzuki. Biaggi passed Rossi with three laps left, but their respective tenth and eleventh places meant the latter's lead was cut by a single point. Rossi was angry, labelling Paul Butler, the race director, 'an assassin' for sending the riders out in such awful conditions. Gibernau, sensing the global mood, celebrated with a stars and stripes flag. For Biaggi, the pain was more personal, and his mourning song was laced with bitterness by the time they came to Phillip Island.

Although it was still technically possible for Biaggi to overhaul Rossi, he took the extraordinary step of issuing a press release detailing where the season had gone wrong and pointing the finger of blame firmly at his Yamaha employers. 'I felt the weight of responsibility of being the one who always spoke of what was wrong with the factory,' he said to the sound of dropped spanners in the garage. 'It is not what I wanted to do.' There followed criticism of Yamaha for endangering his safety by forcing him to take too many chances. 'The title is gone,' Biaggi moaned. In went the towel and out came the last barbed compliment.

'Congratulations to Rossi, who has been good, smart and clever to use what is in his hands.'

With such a negative preamble pricking Rossi's bubble, the race might have been an anti-climax. Instead, it was one of the best for years. Rossi only needed to finish eighth but that was not his way. Faster, harder, better. Fuck Biaggi. The charmed and the doomed. Rossi had been late to the track for morning practice and was stopped by the police doing 90mph in a 40mph zone. He got a six-month ban, but would have been jailed had he been a mortal Aussie, according to the local newspaper editor. Then he high-sided and could have landed anywhere. A broken wrist or worse might still have changed the outcome of the championship. He landed on his back and walked away.

Back home in Tavullia, Graziano watched and might have wished that his own crash had not been so damaging. That he had never experienced the creasing headaches. That he had left the hospital and gone on to become a world champion too. Graziano had not cut his hair since that accident two decades earlier and now wore it in a snake-like ponytail that reached down to his midriff. He puffed on a cigar. If Valentino won the title this weekend then he would go down to the barber's shop and have it cut off. That is what he had told his son he would do if he completed the hat-trick of 125, 250 and 500cc titles.

The race was a classic. Barros was the first to put his blackened nose in front, but the lead would change hands twenty-five times. Noriyuki Haga had a spell at the front and then Capirossi, fighting to the last. Biaggi, battling in a way his pre-race comments suggested would be beyond him, took over. It was red raw fare, a phalanx of riders strung together by skill and desire. Rossi led on the penultimate lap as Graziano watched on his crackling television set. In the garage Stefania watched her son and prayed he would be safe. She had already felt her heart sink when Rossi and Barros had touched at a breathless 190mph. The contact had expelled a cloud of smoke but the pair stayed upright. For now.

Rossi made a mistake and Biaggi seized on the opportunity. He now had the race. He had long since stopped accepting anything until it was signed, sealed and delivered, but surely this victory was his? In the garage his mechanics watched and wondered. Geoff Crust, the team manager, grimaced. They wanted this badly, if only to show Biaggi that their bike was not the piece of junk he had portrayed it as. Rossi wanted it even more. This was what he had envisaged when he had spoken of having his pasta taken away. This was duelling, just like he had done with his friends in their Apecars and on their scooters when they were kids. Just the two of them. He was glued to the shining exhaust of the red Yamaha. They came to the MG Curve and Biaggi had it. Rossi was climbing all over the rear end of the Yamaha. His elbow even brushed the Yamaha's exhaust. At such speed it was as if everything was moving slowly. It was a gentle touch that might have had violent repercussions. Speed exaggerated everything. Faster than reality. He took the blind corner on Biaggi's outside. They were level. Biaggi began thinking quickly. There was one corner to go. A year came down to these moments and the clarity of thought. He planned to use his fast exit speed to whip past Rossi and take him on the line. It was his only chance. Rossi held his shape and got on the gas just in time. He won by 0.013 seconds, the equivalent of half a tyre. The top nine riders were separated by less than three seconds. It was the closest finish for decades.

It was the start of something special. Of that everyone was sure. The visceral drama of the fight etched indelible memories in the minds of those who saw it. Rossi, who had a habit of recounting races by saying he liked to 'arrive' first, had indeed arrived. Few spared more than fleeting sympathy for Clinton Farr, a twenty-one-year-old wannabe from Melbourne, who had fallen in a support race and been killed, but the accident would never go away for the family. After forty-three years' involvement in the sport, they turned their backs on it, blaming their son's Honda for the fatal fall. Five years later the inquest into his death was reopened. By then the sporting scene had been torn asunder by the Rossi phenomenon, but for the Farrs it would never get beyond 14 October 2001, the day that another fresh-faced Australian raced on the big stage for only the second time as a wild-card. He was called Casey Stoner and he lived in a caravan in Cumbria.

In Tavullia, Graziano put on his braces, a neatly pressed shirt and a tie. He walked into town and sat in a plastic seat, studied himself in the mirror and told the barber to cut it off. His son was busy saying how much it mattered to become part of history, to be the last 500cc champion and the fourth youngest after Freddie Spencer, Mike Hailwood and John Surtees. 'When I was young I used to admire the great legends like Hailwood and Agostini,' he said. 'For me the number one was Hailwood. Mike the Bike.' He genuinely liked being part of a timeline that went back to Hailwood. Later, in his autobiography, he would say how he wished he could take Hailwood for a ride on the Panoramica, a dangerous, cliff-side road winding its way to Pesaro. Rossi could get emotional speaking about Hailwood, who was both charmed and doomed. 'What a life,' Rossi said. 'What a story.'

LAP 1

Mike Hailwood was racked with doubts. He looked out of the aeroplane window and tried to find an oasis of calm above the clouds, but the fears kept on coming back. He had tried to keep the plot hidden from Pauline, but she was well versed in picking through his secrets and half-lies. 'A little bird tells me that you're thinking of riding in the TT again,' she had said. He had smiled at being found out. 'Oh well, you know,' he had spluttered.

And now he was going back. To 'Blood Bath Island' as the *Daily Mirror* once put it. To the Isle of Man TT, the hardest race in the world, the symbolic home of motorcycling. It was 1978 and the island had been shorn of its World Championship status after the likes of Giacomo Agostini had turned their backs on the place because of the pervasive stench of death. You could scarcely blame them. In 1972 Gilberto Parlotti had come to Ago on the Thursday night and asked if he would take him around the TT circuit. He had done so and then wished his friend good luck and good night. The following morning Parlotti was killed riding his 125cc bike. Ago had turned up for the senior TT an hour-and-a-half later and, although nobody told him, he knew. He looked into the eyes of Magni, his mechanic, and his heart sank like a dead weight. Inside he sobbed, but he still rode.

It was dangerous and the bikes were faster now. It was eleven years since Mike had last tamed the Mountain. The previous year he had watched Ago, his old team-mate and rival, struggling horribly on the 500cc Yamaha at the British Grand Prix, caught by the field and the taunt of time. The great Ago, playboy, film star and winner of fifteen world titles. The great Ago now gone, retired the previous December.

Mike was two years older but was going the other way. Out of retirement and into the bearpit. He was thirty-eight and he had this bloody gammy leg. Just like the Old Man. Stan Hailwood had become a legend on the motorcycling circuit, a dapper business-man with a forceful nature and a gleaming white transporter van with 'Ecurie Sportive' emblazoned on the side. He bought, bribed and bullied for Mike, but any initial resentment from the working-class ranks with their dirty transit vans and patched-up bikes evaporated when they got to know the racer.

Stan always had a lopsided gait brought on by falling on a needle when he was a boy and having his leg broken and reset numerous times. At one point they were going to amputate until Mike's grandfather had said he would rather have Stan die with his leg on. The bloody gammy leg ran in the family. It was 1974 and Mike was racing in Formula One when he had the crash at the Nürburgring. He hit the Armco hard at the Pflanzgarten and ripped a path down it before clashing into a post and pirouetting down a hill, debris falling like ash and pockmarking the burnt track.

Mike was conscious and knew it had been bad. Shin, knee and ankle bones dug into him like shards of glass. He wouldn't race a car again. He went home to Durban and his toes began to claw because of the trapped nerves and tendons. He had them filleted. They took out the joints and put in steel rods which stuck out the end so the doctor put corks on each one. When it was time for them to be removed, Mike went to the specialist who popped the corks and got hold of one of the rods. 'You wouldn't,' Mike said. The doctor smiled and yanked the rod clean out. There was no anaesthetic. No way of numbing the pain.

He went back to their home in South Africa and grew depressed. Pauline had only ever seen him cry once before, at Bill Ivy's funeral, but one night over dinner he let the demons get to him. He said his career was over. He asked her whether she could still love him now that he was a cripple. 'How can you think that?' she had told him. 'I love you the person, not the racing star and the rest of it. That's not going to change.' He believed it in the end. But this gimpy, gammy leg.

He remembered talking to Bill, Little Bill, about the dangers. They were both afraid of the Big Slide. It was a recurring dream. The crash that would leave them in a wheelchair or severely crippled for the rest of their lives. The Big Slide that might kill them. That was the gnawing downside to life at the top. Ago had it too. He dreamt of riding into a ravine during a race. *La Diapositiva Grande.* Ago would have to look the other way when his mother told him to go slowly on the island, and Mike had felt the same when he had hugged Pauline at the airport. He didn't want her there.

It was 1978 and he looked out of the aeroplane window and wondered. Was it the right decision? It was almost a year since he had sent a letter to Ted Macauley, a friend and journalist, proposing the idea. In it Mike had admitted he did not think it was a particularly good one himself, since he was out of shape and too old and was letting his selfishness and irresponsibility take over. He was, he confessed, a silly old sod.

But he felt he could still do it. Even with the leg. With the gear change switched to the left side of the bike. He had lost a bit of weight and had kept his hand in with the occasional run-out in low-level races. It was ten years since Honda had summoned him to Japan and told him they were quitting the grand prix series, but he was Mike the Bike. He had won four world 500cc titles and, even if the last had been thirteen years ago, you didn't lose it. At least he hoped not.

The comeback had started as something to occupy his mind and offset the onset of middle age. It would be a challenge and a bit of fun, like the old days, when they would drink and fight and race and party. But now there were ten sponsors on board, led by Martini, and it had become a media circus. The pressure was mounting. He gazed out of the window, remembered the good times and tried to forget about the Big Slide.

CHAPTER FOUR

A TEENAGE DREAM

Chaz Davies could not help but stare at the Japanese rider with the intense eyes and blond flecks in his hair. This was Youchi Ui, the man who had been second in the 125cc championship for the last two seasons and an exotic symbol of the unknown to the Welsh teenager. He was also the rider he most respected. Davies was disturbed from his reverie in the restaurant at Suzuka, the same place where the Rossi and Biaggi feud had fermented, by a nudge in the ribs. He shifted and looked at his new team-mate, Jaroslav Hules, an excitable Czech twelve years his senior who spoke with clipped vowels and a lascivious hunger. 'You see that waitress,' he said. 'I have had every kind of woman – Brazilian, Portuguese, French, Italian Spanish, I have had them all, but I have never had a Japanese woman.' Davies noted that Jarda was actually licking his lips. 'I want it.'

It was an unreal scenario for a fifteen-year-old who had never been outside Europe before, but here he was, on the eve of the first round of the 2002 World Championship, preparing to ride for his new Matteoni team in the 125cc race. He would be the youngest ever rider to compete over a whole grand prix season.

He could scarcely believe it, later acknowledging he was too in awe of everyone, but like every rookie nursing bad school reports and big dreams, he had already been through the emotional wringer. Just like Ui once had, like Jaroslav, or Jarda as he liked to be known, and like his friend Casey who had now moved from the caravan in Cumbria to sign a deal to ride an Aprilia in the 250cc World Championship.

Davies sauntered over to me in the paddock. He was a mature teenager but he had a skittish smile that evinced the excitement of being on the cusp. His friends back at John Beddoes Secondary School on the Welsh border were jealous, but he kept telling them this life was no holiday. 'My dad ran a go-karting circuit and loads of people would come down on a Sunday to have a go,' he recalled. 'I flipped over when I was seven and landed quite hard on my chest. Well, I punctured one lung and tore the best part of the other, so I was breathing on about ten per cent of my normal capacity. Basically, one lung was out and one had a hole in it. I got up at first, I think more from shock than anything, but then I fell back down. I didn't know what was going on. I think most people thought I was OK at first, but then I started coughing up blood.

'They took me on a quad bike back to the house and then they shipped me to hospital in Hereford. They could not figure out what was wrong. Then they took me to Birmingham but the air ambulance was down so they drove me with two police bikes out in front, complete with sirens and flashing blue lights. I was not in a good state and they sent an anaesthetist with me in case I stopped breathing. As soon as I got through the door they were putting pipes into me, draining this and that. One doctor was going mental because he could not get the right pipe. He'd only ever seen anything like it once before. I remember bits vividly. I had a five-hour operation and got a bit stronger. They let me out five weeks later. Did it make me think twice about racing? Nah. I was a kid. You think you're indestructible.'

He was only an adolescent now, but they grow up fast in biking and Davies was a product of a system that fast-tracked talent into brutal reality. He was glad he had Casey to talk to. In 2000 the Australian fledgling had arrived in England with his father, Colin, because he was in a hurry and he would not have been able to start road racing at home until he was sixteen. At that point Stoner was a dirt-track rider, having landed seventy state titles. When he was twelve, he entered a series of classes at a meeting on the New South Wales coast and won thirty-two races in a single weekend. He was talented, but nobody knew whether he would be able to transfer his aggressive dirt-tracking style, which had already resulted in several punch-ups and a dose of back-biting, to the tarmac. The rules were different in Britain, though, and he was damned well going to try.

Both Davies and Stoner entered the British Aprilia RS125 Challenge in 2000. There was a test at the start of the year at Donington Park. 'Me and Craig Jones were the favourites to win the championship,' Davies recalled. 'I did not think anybody else would have a look-in but then I spotted somebody in skanky mustard leathers. I was catching him but not by enough. I thought, "This bloke is doing OK considering I don't know who the hell he is." I knew from that point on that Casey would be pretty tough.'

The teenagers endured a fractious relationship that year as the title neared its climax. 'We were friends at the start of the year and sworn enemies by the end,' Davies recalled. 'There was not a good atmosphere. You know, Casey and his dad had stayed at our house a few times, but by the end our families were not even speaking. There were a few things we weren't happy about. It was such a big deal back then, but we were convinced that he had a couple of bits on his bike that shouldn't have been there. Then there was this time his bike stayed in parc fermé for three hours after the race. There were a lot of worried faces and then, all of a sudden, it was all all right. There was some funny stuff going on. Me and Casey would still acknowledge each other, it was OK enough for that, but it wasn't great.

'It came down to a race at Donington where I had to finish in the top three if Casey won. I was confident of getting the title. Then it rained a couple of hours beforehand. When we started it had just started drying out and there was a real skinny line, the width of a magazine. Casey had gone by and pulled out a couple of seconds. I was trying to keep everyone else at bay and Casey within sight. Then I hit a wet patch going into the hairpin and that was that. I was massively disappointed. I had a pretty sour face afterwards.'

The pair had done enough to be recruited by Alberto Puig, fast garnering a reputation as the sport's pre-eminent talent spotter. Puig had been tasked by Dorna to find up-and-coming talent from beyond Spain and Italy. So Davies and Stoner were entered in the British 125 Championship and the Spanish 125 series. They quickly learnt that Puig, who had once won a 500cc grand prix, was ruthless. 'There were seven of us in the Telefonica Movistar teams,' Davies said. 'Casey was on the best bike, the next level up, because Alberto had pretty much decided *he* was the one. After two races I was upgraded to a bike that was halfway between the bog standard and Casey's. I remember one race where Leon Camier had someone stall in front of him at the start. Leon had to come off the gas to avoid him. Alberto went up to him and said, "What happened with your start?" Leon said that he'd had no choice. Alberto looked at him as if he was a complete idiot and said, "You should have hit him! Hit him!" Leon couldn't believe it. He was saying he should have ridden straight into the other guy, which would have had them both on the floor. Leon had an argument with Alberto a bit later and left. He was hard was Alberto, but right from the start he had decided it was Casey who he wanted to progress.

'It was fine with Casey that year. All the bad feeling of 2000 was swept away because we needed each other. We didn't know anyone, apart from Camier, and that can make you go mental.'

They were two kids on the threshold of the big time. The world was changing. The 500cc class was rebranded MotoGP because the engine capacity had been raised to 990cc, and the grunting four-strokes were battling with the mercurial two-strokes. The one thing that remained the same was walking past Chaz and myself to one of the offices. Valentino Rossi had succumbed to a haircut at the request of his mother and now had wolfish side-burns, but the rest was as last year. Already he had dominated the groundbreaking tests on his new V5 while Biaggi's campaign had been dubbed 'Mission Impossible' by a cynical Italian press after the M1's tardy showing.

Rossi's mind games had started early this year. He had signed a new £10 million, two-year deal with Honda and had spent some of it on producing a T-shirt that listed thirty-five reasons why he was a world champion, simultaneously denting the egos of his rivals and championing his own maverick ways. The eclectic list included 'because I never went to bed before two on the night of a race' and 'because I trained in a cave'. However, for all the quips about wanting to marry the actress Angelina Jolie, and being brought coffee by Biaggi, an increasingly embittered malcontent, it was No. 15 that really hurt the rest. 'Because I learnt to be a phenomenon.'

Rossi was surfing a wave of his rivals' defeatism. When Loris Capirossi suggested the champion could win with one hand, he responded, 'It depends which one.' Kenny Roberts, the 2000 champion, served notice of his intention to walk out on Suzuki if things did not improve. 'People say it will be easy for me, but until the season starts and we race, nobody really knows what will happen,' Rossi responded. 'This is new territory.'

He also had a new rival in Daijiro Kato, who was making his

debut among the elite after the most successful 250cc campaign in history. But Kato was on the Honda two-stroke and the deficit in horsepower seemed certain to count against him. Honda, Yamaha, Suzuki and Aprilia had all produced four-stroke bikes, with Ducati and Kawasaki set to follow. It was a new era with an old hero.

Rossi was only twenty-three and it was not long since he had shared Davies' and Stoner's wonder and ambition. From behind the black pools of his sunglasses, Carlo Pernat breathed smoke and remembered how it had happened. 'It was 1995 and I was still with Cagiva, but I said to Graziano, "Come with me," ' he growled, the uncanny ability to make history sound like folklore accentuated by his broken English. 'We made a three-year contract. It was simple. Just three pages. Valentino was fifteen so I had to go to the father and say, "Sign here," and to the mother the same because they were already divorced. I was stuck in the middle. I had no problem with Stefania, she signed it OK, but Graziano was more difficult. Valentino owes him a lot because for the first three years of his career, he just wanted to protect him, like any father I suppose. I would speak to Stefania three or four times a year, but with Graziano it was three or four times a day!

'I remember in 1998 when Valentino asked me to become his personal manager, but I was at Aprilia, as manager of the factory, so I said no. It wasn't that I didn't want to, but it was impossible for me at the time. It gave me satisfaction that he asked for me, but I had to close that book. We have always stayed friends. If I could go back in time maybe I would have done it differently, but when I look around my life I wouldn't really want to change anything.'

Talk of starting out made Pernat turn nostalgic. There were plenty of people in the paddock who frowned at the pristine transporter trucks and the voluminous hospitality suites. Some thought the soul had been sold. 'I made a contract with Randy

Mamola on a piece of paper in a restaurant,' Pernat said with a chuckle. 'We were in this place in 1987 with two bottles of grappa and his manager, Jumbo Jim Doyle, who later became a problem – it's better not to speak to Randy about this. I remember Jim Doyle drank a lot, we took a piece of paper, I wrote the amount, and we all signed it. Another time in 1985 we made a five-year deal with Lucky Strike. I was in Paris in the Crazy Horse with the man who was responsible for sponsorship. There were dancing girls in front of us. I was drunk and we wrote the amount on a piece of paper that was on the table.

'Twenty years ago you gave your hand to the people and that was the contract. Honestly. The real contract would arrive after two months and it was never withdrawn. Today you need a lawyer, a really nice and good one, to make a forty-page contract. You have to cover everything. It's dangerous if you don't. I have a lawyer in Rome to make the contracts for my riders now. I agree it has to be done in a professional way, but we have lost the spirit of motorcycling. We are not Formula One and we should not try to be.'

Pernat was no old sourpuss griping from the margins. He was still a mover and shaker with his finger on the pulse and his ear to the ground. Rossi and Capirossi were his best-known finds, but there have been scores of others he has helped, nurtured and protected. Even so, he could not help but drift back to what he believed were better days. 'I remember watching races on the television at the Nürburgring, Assen and Hockenheim. Agostini and Hailwood. The grandstands then were like stadiums and they were always full. When a rider made an overtake, the reaction was like a football crowd when the team scored a goal. It was unbelievable, it was the passion.

'One time in the mid-1980s we were in a bar on the night before a race with Kevin Schwantz, Wayne Rainey and Randy Mamola. They all came in drunk, crazy, together. And the next day they went to battle. Another Sunday night in the airport in Vienna after a race in Brno, around 9 p.m., these three came into the bar, drunk, without their clothes, and they climbed on the tables to make chaos. All the people, the old ladies, were screaming and the police came in. But they were just joking. It was a bit of fun. They still did their job, but this was the spirit. They stuck together. Now it is so different. They stay in their truck or their motorhome. The money is too much, the audience is too much and the press write too much.'

For every Pernat looking to the past there was a Davies salivating at the future. His schoolfriends got up in the wee small hours back in Wales to watch his debut. The rain seeping from ash-grey clouds was portentous and Davies slid off with six laps left, one of eighteen riders who failed to finish. Next came the 250cc race and Stoner's bow. It did not last a single lap. The pair were in good company as Rossi, too, had crashed on the two previous days, but as was his way, he dredged the core of his spirit to grab pole position from Capirossi and Shinichi Itoh. He began slowly, but a modicum of caution was sensible in the conditions. All around others lost their heads and balance, Roberts and Biaggi among those sliding out. For a while Rossi was the meat in a Telefonica Movistar sandwich, the blue fairings of Akira Ryo and Sete Gibernau declaring unexpected resilience. It was cut short by Gibernau's slide into a muddy gravel trap, prompting more dissension from Suzuki who blamed Rossi for braking to a virtual stop in front of the Spaniard. 'You can't help wondering what would have happened if Sete hadn't been balked by Rossi,' Garry Taylor, the team manager, said.

Whatever the cause, the exit of the hard-charging Gibernau left Ryo and Rossi clear, with the impressive Carlos Checa, Biaggi's team-mate, content to limit his ambition to fending off Itoh for third. Rossi took the lead at the chicane six laps from home, wobbling and sliding his way to the front, but Ryo refused to concede and almost regained his advantage with two laps remaining. Rossi was relentless, though, and responded to fashion a winning margin of 1.5 seconds. At thirty-four, Ryo consoled himself with having ridden the race of his life, while Checa completed the podium to show that the Yamaha was not the old rust bucket that Biaggi would have his courtiers believe. 'In these conditions nothing is real, but the bike is ready to fight for position,' Checa said after dismounting. With a reputation for crashing, Checa had done well to stay vertical after touching wheels with Itoh. 'I looked at him and he looked at me and we were thinking the same thing – we were lucky to be on our bikes.' Rossi, for once, said little. 'I've destroyed two bikes this weekend so I have decided to stay quiet.'

The writing was nevertheless on the wall. Rossi was all but unbeatable. In the space of a year he had gone from being the precocious pretender, belittling Italy's established star, to a legend-in-the-making. The machinery was key but the talent unquestioned. A wrong tyre choice in South Africa restricted him to second place behind Tohru Ukawa, but he then won seven straight races. Biaggi, by contrast, made the podium only twice in the opening seven races. The landmark season was all but settled in rapid time.

Biaggi was even being beaten by Checa which was the ultimate ignominy, not even the best rider in Yamaha let alone the world. People were pleased for Checa, a pleasant man with a horror story. I heard it when I sat down with him in the anodyne office of his management company by a London railway bridge. It started with a troubled birth, his father rushing to the hospital in Manresa, where Carlos was threatening to arrive, and crashing his motorcycle. It meant that Checa senior ended up being treated for a broken leg in a nearby ward as his son was born. It proved an apposite calamity as Checa developed an invidious reputation for accidents, acquiring the moniker 'Checa the

Wrecker' along the way and crashing thirty times in two bruising years.

Snubbing the riders' traditional playground of Monte Carlo, Checa moved to Great Ayton, a village just south of Middlesbrough and best known for its Captain Cook monument. It was where his team manager hailed from. Later he would find it impractical to be so far north and he would become the only Spanish, Tolkien-loving adrenalin-junkie with a flat next door to Westminster Abbey.

He had won his first 500cc grand prix in Spain in 1996, when King Juan Carlos presented him with the trophy, and he was vying for the title in 1998 until he was nearly killed in a fall at Donington Park. 'We are only playing,' he told me in his nasal Spanish brogue. '*That* was a problem.' Some had likened crashing to taking a spin in a giant tumble drier and, when we met, Checa's fatalism had even made an epiphany from a splenectomy. Being almost done for at Donington had instilled a sense of perspective that explained his love of fell-walking and his decision to air his thoughts on the Iraq war on his personal website.

'I had a stroke and went blind for nineteen hours,' he said of his darkest day. 'I could not move. Then I could not breathe and that was frightening. I remember a nurse hitting my chest very hard. Then nothing. I woke up attached to all sorts of tubes. All I wanted was to be a normal person again. My only rival was myself.'

Incredibly, Checa got back on the bike forty-three days later and finished the season in fourth place. His vision was restored, but only hindsight enabled him to see the folly of his ways. 'It was crazy to come back so soon,' he said. 'The doctors in Spain weren't happy, but I did a test in Barcelona and was only six-tenths slower than Mick Doohan. I was a wreck, eating liquid food because my digestion was not working, but where would I have been if I hadn't done it?

'Everything is positive. I am still here. The worst thing is when you give up because of fears. We ride at 360kph but nothing is safe. Go on the motorway and many people die. Risk is part of life. I do parachuting and my first jump was one of the most emotional experiences I've ever had. It is not natural for a human to leap out of a plane and in that instant you are scared and the emotion is impossible. I loved it.'

I asked Checa why he moved to Great Ayton in the first place. 'I don't have a social life and that suits me,' he said. 'I like the cold and it's close to Scotland which I love. The scenery there is like Middle Earth from *Lord of the Rings*.'

It was hard not to warm to such eccentricity. Checa and Capirossi were the doyens of the grid, much-loved for being elder statesmen who did not sully themselves with psychological wind-ups. Biaggi was less respectful. He and Checa did not speak, and I was told that Biaggi went to great lengths to keep everything that happened on his side of the garage secret.

Checa went on exorcising his demons by exercising an idiosyncratic nature. 'I have got colder, more analytical,' he said when the 2002 championship arrived in Jerez, a pretty old town with vast sherry houses. 'I don't want to make the same mistakes again. I did 7,000 kilometres in testing the new bike and didn't fall once. If you crash many times it can destroy your mind, but if I am riding on the limit and Rossi is still a second quicker then it is hard. Last year we had problems but nobody wanted to fix them. Now the team is working to sort them out.'

Like Britain, Spain needed a new hero. Their last world champion, Alex Criville, was at the track to announce he was retiring because of the fainting fits that had seen him playing Russian roulette with each circuit of the track. Could Checa be the man? Not on that day as it turned out. Rossi blitzed every-body, albeit four of the top six were two-strokes, leading to confused analysis of the V5's omnipotence, while Checa broke down on the last lap. Rossi was hit hard from behind by Roberts' Suzuki but he survived, recovered and won.

Meanwhile, a fresh-faced Mallorcan with a furrowed brow made his debut in the 125cc class. He had been forced to miss the first day of practice because he was just fourteen and, hence, too young. He turned fifteen on Saturday, though, and was free to race and finish twenty-second, two places ahead of Chaz Davies, the boy he had now eclipsed as the youngest teenage dreamer. His name was Jorge Lorenzo.

Things had quickly turned sour for Davies. He had realized that from the moment one of his press team handed him an article from an Italian newspaper that had the headline '*Imposter del Dorna*'. It did not take him long to realize that the team boss, Massimo Matteoni, had blabbed to the media. 'I *was* an impostor from Dorna,' Davies recalled. 'Matteoni had obviously spoken to someone in the media about how they were having to run this English rider instead of an Italian. It was pretty shit.

'I'd been so excited and had been checking out the team and their past results. But then I found out the truth. Dorna had come in and said, "We'll give you this much money to run this guy Davies, you don't have a choice – run him or lose your spot." That left a bitter taste in Matteoni's mouth and from the start he wasn't interested. He's a pretty complicated guy, a weirdo. I had no idea about any of this. It's what I'd been dreaming about but it didn't take long for me to start hating it. Matteoni never paid us any attention. He didn't care. I was eleventh in the wet but only because people were crashing out. It was a bag of shit.'

Prior to the British Grand Prix, Davies went fishing with Stoner on some private land. They caught a few and tried to forget. There were a few newspaper clippings on the wall back at John Beddoes, but reality had sunk its teeth into the friends. Stoner's reputation for reckless abandon reached its apotheosis at an Italian Grand Prix where he merged bravery and pain to worrying effect. Already suffering from a broken scaphoid, a serious injury for any rider, he crashed in the first session and suffered concussion. The following day he was pumped full of painkillers and, even though he was having trouble feeling the throttle, set out. He crashed again. The sensation of falling. Weightlessness. Fear. He broke a finger this time and did not get up. Already they were calling him 'Rolling Stoner' and, awful as it was, you could not help but recall Pernat's early assessment of Rossi. A champion or dead.

Davies' classmates looked at him with a degree of envy when he competed at the school sports day in the build-up to Donington. His project on Seamus Heaney was late and he was behind in his appreciation of Steinbeck's *Of Mice and Men*. He could get away with more, but at least he went to school – Casey had not been since he was twelve – and it was not the privileged life that some of them thought. Davies and Stoner had befriended Matt Roberts, now a BBC presenter but then a member of Dorna's in-house media team, and they shared their burdens. 'I remember Matt with his head in his hands saying Dorna weren't paying him enough,' Davies said. 'We were in the same position. It was all shit. I wasn't getting paid a penny. It was basically me and my dad. There were hire cars and hotels and it was easy to burn £1,500 a weekend. I got a grant from the Welsh Sports Council, but you don't finish the season with any money unless you get lucky on a couple of sponsors. Leather money is hard to get at that level.'

Even as Stoner progressed through the ranks and his reputation spread, he was forced to live a frugal life. 'The Stoners had it hard like you wouldn't believe,' Davies said. 'They rented a motorhome with a double bed at the back and two singles up front. Our parents would stay in that. Me and Casey lived in a little trailer stuck on the back. There was one bunk bed attached to the wall. No air conditioning. It was cramped and smelt like a dog's dinner. We had a crackly TV set with a PlayStation and that was it. Matt wanted to come and do a feature on it, but Casey's mum wouldn't let him; she was too embarrassed.'

They shared the same paddock as Rossi and Biaggi but they inhabited a different world. 'We looked up to Rossi. He was always nice. When we had our chins on the floor he would say things to us to cheer us up. Biaggi was different. The thing that really used to piss us off about him was he would ride his scooter around the paddock flat out, barging people out of the way. He did not have a lot of respect for anyone and so no one had much for him.'

It was a shoestring dream but it was still enjoyable. Davies and Stoner raced their scooters down the straight behind the paddock at the Sachsenring and nursed each other through the black days. 'We didn't talk about the future much – it was more, "Are you going to kick ass today or what?" We had fun. We'd always share cars with Casey and his dad to cut down on the costs. Well, when you went to the flyaways we'd both have two big cases, as well as carrying boots and helmets and shit like that. Casey's dad is super tight and would always get the tiniest car possible. Once we were coming back from a test with loads of tyres. It took ages to fit everything in the car. I've still got a picture of me and Casey, all tangled up with these tyres in the back seat, you can just about see the tops of our heads. My dad gets the car up to 110 and Colin is clenching his teeth and his knuckles are white from gripping the side of his seat. "Jesus," he cried. "You don't have to go this fucking fast! It's getting floaty!"'

The sheer ridiculousness of fifteen-year-old boys racing motorcycles at speeds that sapped common sense was laid bare when they went to Le Mans, a gritty industrial afterthought with an ugly centre but a permanent place in racing lore. The duo had gone to the concession stand at the back of the paddock to buy sweets. Davies filled a bag and put it on the scales. Twenty-six euros. Stoner was still choosing and then dumped a bulging sack in front of the vendor. The scales flicked to forty-two. Stoner began getting his money out. 'Jesus, Casey, have you seen the price?' He took his hand out of his pocket and peered over the bag. 'Yeah, that is a bit expensive isn't it?' They decided to get their parents to bring them some sweets tomorrow, dumped the bags and fled, the curses of the seller ringing in their ears. They were, literally and metaphorically, kids in a sweetshop that year.

Rossi was utterly untouchable and his only problem came from those who had grown inured to his flamboyance. It was a twin-pronged attack. Some said he was killing the sport with his genius, while the more pious felt he was trivializing it with his antics. That had been the case at Mugello where the playfulness did reach slapstick levels. Marco Melandri pitched up with a Spider-Man livery, while Rossi had a neon yellow armchair installed in the garage. Melandri won the 250cc race, but the armchair was tossed out of the garage by a disgruntled Jerry Burgess, Rossi's craggy crew chief. The antics continued. After Rossi's victory, he stopped on the straight where he was approached by two traffic policemen who gave him a speeding ticket. It was a funny stunt and, like all of them, had a loose meaning. With everyone bemoaning Rossi's dominance and apportioning it almost wholly to the pace of the factory Honda, the champion decided to acknowledge his bike's raw power. The policemen were a violin teacher and the father of Alessio Salucci, Rossi's best friend and confidant, whom everyone called Uccio. The uniforms were borrowed from the Tavullia Police Department after forms had been signed to say they would not be improperly used.

It would all have been dismissed as cartoonish fun but for the track invasion that incensed Francesco Zerbi, the FIM President who had first handed out final warnings after the incident with Biaggi the previous year. Another open letter, this time decrying the crowd-pleasing antics of Rossi and Melandri, another open wound.

Rossi could not have cared less. He knew a second title was as good as his and was well aware that Biaggi had exploded during the weekend and rammed the awning of the Yamaha hospitality tent with his scooter. 'Max had decided at the last minute that he wanted to invite about thirty friends into hospitality and have someone cook for them,' Ali Forth, Yamaha's press officer, remembered. 'The head of Marlboro sponsorship said, "No, Max, I know it's your home GP but you can't just snap your fingers." With that he physically attacked the hospitality hoardings and tore them down.' Then he rode his scooter into one of the people working there. The head of Yamaha had to go to apologize to the head of Marlboro.

Forth saw both sides of Biaggi and is more sympathetic than most. 'He had a reputation as a bad boy, but I found him an intriguing character and it was definitely not as black and white as some thought. His biggest problem was he found it very difficult to trust people, but I do know that Max was also prone to incredible moments of sincerity.'

Nothing remained secret in the insular world. Biaggi seemed on the verge of caving in and Rossi, sensing the weakness, would manipulate it for his own ends. 'I would rather there was a challenge from somewhere because that's more fun,' he said in a press conference. 'But this is not my problem. The bike is fantastic and I think it is possible to win all the races.'

That would prove beyond him but he was not far off. The only blip was in the Czech Republic, but Rossi did not see Biaggi's victory there. Having returned to his pit garage with tyre trouble, the world champion turned off his television monitor. Biaggi, who had hitherto been wearing the expression of a man whose leathers were lined with broken glass, was happy to fill in the gaps. 'I give all I can all year, on and off the bike, but it's not fair,' he said. 'When you see Rossi winning all these races it is hard. I have suffered. We all have suffered. Daijiro Kato got the same bike as Rossi for the first time at Brno and came third. Tohru Ukawa is second in the championship on the same bike. You have to read between the lines. I can't compete, but if I was on that bike, well, who knows?'

He got his wish. Soon afterwards Yamaha confirmed that they were getting rid of Biaggi, the constant griping and tantrums creating an uneasy atmosphere. Few in the team lamented his passing. Biaggi would sign for Camel Honda, meaning he was indeed riding for the same manufacturer as Rossi, but with the get-out excuse of being on inferior machinery.

Rossi had won ten out of twelve races by the time he wrapped up the title in Rio. Ever the crowd pleaser, he posed with members of his official Fan Club clad in Brazilian football kit. It was time to celebrate. Honda hosted a party after a season in which they had destroyed the opposition. Rossi's victory margin would be 140 points and might have been more but for the fact he started losing once the title had been decided with four races to spare.

It was a rollicking night. Uccio was there. He liked the fact that his best friend was a magnet for the best-looking women in any room. He would tell Mat Oxley, the journalist, 'We really enjoyed having so many girls around. Maybe some top riders or stars worry, "Is this girl coming to see me because I'm famous or does she really like me?", but Valentino doesn't think like that. He always says, "I don't care why she's coming to see me, I'm just happy that she is coming."' That night was to be one of the great parties. Rossi was already well on the way to drinking himself towards oblivion when he noticed an elfin figure loitering like a wallflower. Dani Pedrosa had just turned seventeen and earlier that day had suffered a torrid time in the 125cc race. He was very much the antithesis of the extroverted bandleader. Rossi rallied his drinking partners and they bowed and began a chant of 'Pedrosa! Pedrosa! Pedrosa!' The teenager blushed. 'I always remember that night in Rio,' he would later tell me. 'It was the first time I ever tried alcohol. Valentino, Marco Melandri and a few others started chanting my name. I couldn't believe it. I was at the bottom and they were at the very top. It was emotional, but at the same time I was grateful.'

Mack was in the bar that night and remembers bumping into Pedrosa at 1 a.m. 'He was drinking Caipirinha, heavy duty stuff, cane spirit over crushed ice with lime. I asked him if he was OK and he said, "Yes, but I have to be in school at 9 a.m. on Monday!" I can't remember seeing him with a drink since.'

The status of Rossi was undisputed. He was now the biggest star the sport had seen since the golden era in the late 1980s, carrying duller, slower men on his burgeoning legend. Where once he had dallied with journalists in the press room on a Sunday night, eager to force his way into the spotlight, now he rationed interviews and restricted his briefings. Roberta, of Great White London, his PR agency, was omnipresent. Endorsements flooded in. Film stars and footballers wanted to meet him. Where would a challenge to all this come from? Biaggi? Kato? Pedrosa? Nobody could guess with any confidence.

It was also at this time that commentators began to gauge where Rossi might stand in the pantheon of two-wheeled legends. It is always a flawed task, trying to bridge generation gaps with different machinery, but the statistics certainly supported Rossi's lobbyists. The likes of Agostini, Hailwood, Rainey and Doohan all had their backers, but for his age, Rossi had surpassed them all. Agostini, who chalked up a peerless 122 wins, had only a single grand prix victory by the time he was twenty-three. Doohan had none. Rossi had forty-five. It truly was the age of youth.

LAP 2

Mike might have spared a thought for the Old Man as the plane neared Douglas. It had been that January 1978, when the news came through from Miami. The Old Man had collapsed on the beach and had been rushed to hospital. He was taken back to Barbados, the place he had gone to feast on the spoils of his success, and was in an irreversible decline. Tanned and indomitable, it was hard to believe that Stan Hailwood was now a fragile figure with an ailing body.

This was the gruff whirlwind that had ushered in his son's legend. Stan had made a fortune from his motorcycle business, King's of Oxford, and lived accordingly, employing a butler at Highmore Hall and sending Mike to boarding school and then Pangbourne Nautical College. It was hardly the normal course for a would-be racer, but Mike himself balked at privilege. He was picked on for his accent and peculiarity, once being summoned to a room where the punishment committee made him drop his trousers and lie face down on a table while a senior boy lashed him with a golf club.

His mother would pick him up from Pangbourne once a month and let him drive her gleaming XK120 Jaguar. He liked it but there was no epiphany on the leafy Oxfordshire lanes. Nor was there when he quit at sixteen and Stan put him to work on the factory floor. Mike came face to face with motorcycle engines, but to him they were just unfathomable metallic puzzles. He would later tell Ted that speed never held a natural attraction for him. He just liked to win.

Stan was hardening him all the time. When he was six he would be forced to swim mammoth distances on holiday in the south of France. There were inevitable rows. Once, when Mike had started to dabble in racing, he fell in a 125cc race and damaged his ankle. The pain was violent and the bruising instant. Stan demanded he get back out there for the 250cc race, but Mike said he was in too much agony. That was when Stan started throwing spanners at him. Later, he threw him out of the house.

Mike sipped a drink and looked out of the plane's window once more. The sun spilt over the clouds like egg yolk. It had been a long, wonderful and sometimes horrible journey, but he had got through. He had survived where so many had not. So why go back? To the hardest race of them all. Why now, in 1978? He had to, he supposed. It was still in him and, anyway, he was good enough. There were plenty of doubters but the fans believed and the ferries were full. And he had read what Tommy Robb had told the press. 'I fancy him to take the Formula One race on the Ducati.' Good old Tommy.

They had first met at Aintree in 1958. 'I had just come over on the boat,' Tommy remembered. 'It was a horrendous journey from Belfast. The gangplank was at about seventy degrees and I had to get the bike up the rungs that stopped people slipping into the water. As soon as the crew saw a racing bike coming they'd get to know you. We used a three-and-a-half-inch jack to get it up this plank. Then we lashed it to the side of the boat with thick rope. When I got to Liverpool the bike was covered in sea salt and the aluminium fairing was beginning to corrode. I had no money so I slept on the floor outside a berth. When I got to Aintree I was walking down the paddock when I saw this good-looking kid. I'd been reading a lot about Mike Hailwood in the papers because he'd been down to South Africa and was winning on an MV. I was getting a bit of coverage at the time too because I was Ireland's new up-and-coming boy. We both put out a finger of recognition. From that moment we became friends.

'I had one NSU which I didn't even own. I looked in the back of Mike's massive transporter and there were 350 and 500 Nortons, a 350 Mondial, a 125 Ducati, spare engines propped up at the side. I thought how the hell can I do battle with this?'

Everyone thought that. The following year, a fresh-faced teenage girl tagged along to Snetterton with some biker friends. They had a 500 Norton but the plugs kept oiling up. 'Dare you to go see Hailwood and ask if we can borrow some,' one of her friends said. Off she marched, but her confidence waned with each step. She walked alongside the huge, white truck and peered in the back. Mike was changing and was down to his underpants. Pauline looked away, but as she did she saw the walls decked out with page 3 pin-ups. She did not know where to put her face, but her brazenness came through and she hurriedly explained the situation. 'You're a cheeky monkey, aren't you?' he said with a melting grin. He studied her and passed her a box. 'Off you go.'

'Thanks very much. I'll bring you the money.'

A wave. 'Don't worry about it.'

She tried to pay him back a few times afterwards, but he always refused. They would nod to each other in the paddock and Pauline would stifle infatuated smiles, but that was the extent of their relationship.

And now he was on his way back to the island, scaling another Mountain, and Pauline was in England with the kids. She was fearful. 'I was terrified, absolutely terrified,' she said. 'I wondered if I'd ever see him again. But I'm a strong believer in fate. You have to be in this world.'

Pauline was safe but the Old Man had gone. He lasted only a month after the heart attack. Stan Hailwood had been there, either in body or in spirit, throughout all of his son's achievements, but he would not be there for *the comeback*. For a moment Mike felt very alone.

CHAPTER FIVE

THE RAVINE

It turned out that Barry Sheene was not bionic after all and, just before the start of the 2003 season, he succumbed to the stomach cancer he had termed 'a bloody pain in the backside'. That was why I was ringing Kenny Roberts for a tribute. When a racer survives his career and is then killed by capriciousness, it always sends a shudder through the paddock. Even Carl Fogarty, son of a backmarker, a man who had rarely found anything good to say about Sheene, was neutered by the news. 'Barry lived his life to the absolute full and did more in his fifty-two years than most people would in a hundred,' he said. 'He was the biggest house-hold name that sport created in Britain and was the first person to make that crossover from racer to celebrity.'

Maybe Fogarty, as he had claimed in the bar at the Sidi Saler, really had mellowed. It could also have been that Fogarty had realized that a modicum of good PR was needed for his new role in charge of Team Foggy Petronas. The Malaysian company had feted Fogarty, flying him to the twin towers in Kuala Lumpur, to discuss the deal that would make him rich beyond even his dreams. Insiders had been quick to scoff at the project, but Fogarty would be laughing the following year when he hurdled the pit wall at Valencia after one of his bikes finished third. 'This has proved a point to certain people,' he would tell me. 'I get knocked because of who I am, but they'll have to find something else to knock me for now.'

By a quirk of fate, the rider of the Petronas that day would be Chris Walker, a man Fogarty had once damned as not being as good as Neil Hodgson, in turn damned for being 'quite vain' and just wanting to 'look pretty, train and eat the right food'. After all his traumas Walker was happy to let bygones be bygones. 'Once, when I was still trying to make a name as a wild card and Carl was in his pomp, he went past me at Donington and stood up and wiggled his bum at me,' he told me at Team Foggy's factory. 'That's Carl.'

Back at the start of 2003 the doctors were at a loss to explain his sunken face. 'It was the weirdest thing and very frightening. They thought I'd had a stroke and ran loads of tests. When they finally diagnosed Bell's palsy it was a relief, but although injuries are bad, illness is shocking. You think, "Why me?"'

Why Walker and why Sheene? It was hard not to think of the latter flicking a V-sign at Kenny Roberts in the old days and not fast-forward to Rossi's gesture to Biaggi at Suzuka. Both were lovable rogues with darker sides, barely needing to lift a finger to forge their way into the public consciousness.

The dawn of the 2003 campaign diverted everyone's attention and the off-season had spawned a winter of discontented riders. Foremost among them was Rossi. His fame meant he was now friends with Vasco Rossi, a fifty-year-old rock singer who was no relation and had been convicted on drug charges. The younger Rossi's life was turning. He had an Ibiza bolt-hole and women throwing themselves at him. Casey Stoner was still living in a tiny trailer in the back of the paddock with Chaz Davies, but Rossi had it all. Yet he had already started to gripe about his treatment by HRC. He talked about how he loved riding the NSR in his

Nastro Azzurro days and, in some ways, he seemed rooted there. The fans still wore bright yellow in homage to his old livery and Rossi, who was irritated that HRC had stalled on a verbal agreement to let him keep his winning NSR from 2001, felt the bike represented a freer time. The move to the official factory team had seen him thrust into a corporate world and he bristled. Even when celebrating his 2002 triumph there were persistent irritations that would ultimately flag up a major debate about whether the rider or the bike was most important. Rossi and his Japanese paymasters had conflicting, unbreakable views on that matter.

It was, hence, very timely of Davide Brivio, Yamaha's team director, to visit Rossi in Ibiza two months before the start of the season. 'We want you,' Brivio had said after pushing the food around his plate over dinner. It was what Rossi's ego needed to hear and the seeds of a divorce were sown.

The immediate opposition was much changed for 2003. Former World Superbike riders Colin Edwards and Troy Bayliss would be there. The pair had just fought out a spellbinding finale to the 2002 season; after seven months, five continents and sixteen hours of racing, it came down to a few tenths of a second as they exchanged the lead five times on the last lap of the season at Imola. Bayliss was phlegmatic in defeat, having signed a deal to ride for Ducati as they made their much-vaunted return to grand prix racing.

Edwards would be riding for Aprilia, although the papers openly wondered why he had not got a seat alongside Rossi at Repsol Honda, instead of another American, Nicky Hayden. The truth was it had been agreed that Edwards' Castrol Honda team would move to MotoGP, with Honda agreeing to supply a four-stroke bike and Castrol putting up the money. A problem then arose because of tyres. Edwards was to ride on Bridgestones, but Michelin regarded the Texan Tornado as one of their best development riders. Somebody made a call to HRC warning that Michelin would not supply any of the MotoGP riders if Edwards was on Bridgestones. The deal fell through.

Edwards was twenty-nine, had a baby daughter and well knew the vagaries of the sport. He had been due to step up to the 500cc series back in 1998, but an ageing French rider named Jean-Philippe Ruggia drafted past him in practice at Monza. 'I remember watching it on the monitor,' Edwards' friend and former Honda employee Chris Herring recalled. 'There was no need for Ruggia to do that at all. It was Saturday morning and they were going down to the Parabolica. God knows why but he tried to outbrake Colin and took him down. He smashed his arm, his knee, you name it. He was proper beaten up. That was Colin's season over.'

He stayed in superbikes and twice won the world title, but MotoGP was the real place to test a dream. So, five years late, Edwards was there on the Aprilia. The paddock was glad to have him. With his wide smile, lackadaisical manner and colourful conversation, Edwards was widely liked. Sometimes his tongue got him into trouble, although he always denied the statement that had caused a furore in Kyalami in 2001. A South African newspaper, the *Saturday Star*, printed an interview in which he was quoted as saying he would like to live in South Africa if they nuked a few townships first. Edwards said he was deeply disappointed with the affair. Others felt Edwards would never have subscribed to such a view, but they knew he had a quick, acerbic tongue. In Bertie Simmonds' book *The Texas Tornado*, his wife, Alyssia, gave an insight into the blunt mindset of Edwards. 'I think the reason we stayed together so long is the fact that Colin is just the same guy he was when we met. I've seen so many people in the race business who, as soon as they become famous, become assholes or treat people bad for no reason. Colin's not like that, he's just a normal guy who thinks about sex all the time.'

There was an American at Honda, though, in the form of Hayden. He was the AMA superbike champion and had coined an equally colourful moniker, the Kentucky Kid. Hayden had also been involved in a turbulent winter after being offered a ride on the factory Yamaha vacated by Biaggi. Under the terms of his existing deal with Honda, they could only keep him if they matched any sum offered by another team. That meant a place at Repsol Honda, but Rossi and Tohru Ukawa had their slots. Versions of events differ, but there is no doubt that American Honda then put pressure on HRC to take Hayden. HRC might have said there was no room for Hayden, but the powerful American arm of the company flexed. I was told, 'It was a case of them saying to HRC, "You don't understand, Nicky *will* ride a Repsol Honda, sort it out."' Ukawa suddenly found himself moved sideways into the satellite Honda team. That was the way people got their rides. It was cloak and dagger in the back stuff.

Hayden was popular too. He had a neat turn of phrase, angular looks and an air of innocence leant credence by him showering in the dark in his hotel at the first pre-season test in Malaysia. The country boy had never been in a hotel where the room key needed to be put in a slot to power the electricity. Hayden also slept in his clothes and two pairs of socks because he could not get the central heating to work. He rang reception but nobody spoke English. He seemed naive and emotional, and was never happier than when surrounded by his racing brothers, Tommy and Roger Lee, and parents, Earl and Rose.

Earl had always told his sons that he was happy as long as they gave it everything. It was a bland instruction that would have deep consequences. The boys raced until dark on the track Earl made by the side of the farmhouse where he bred horses and kept llamas. On Sundays they would attend the Precious Blood Catholic Church in Owensboro, attached to a small elementary school. The trio would ride the mile to school over the fields and park their motorbikes against the fence. The teachers were aghast. Earl pushed them hard. When Roger came off in one race, the medical staff insisted he go for X-rays. 'I don't see any bones sticking out of the skin,' Earl said in his subterranean growl. Nevertheless, the deep affection the family had for each other was refreshing amid the forked tongues and social climbing of MotoGP.

Hayden's good fortune had met with pursed lips in Loris Capirossi's motorhome. He had turned thirty on the Friday before the first race and, although he had taken the beastly Ducati Desmosedici V4 to 204mph in testing, bagging a £30,000 BMW for his trouble, he was still unhappy with Honda. 'They broke a lot of promises and that is the only motivation I have,' he said after being dumped at the end of the previous season. Capirossi was a small, muscle-bound figure but had a natural effervescence that had evaporated the previous year when he was involved in a road accident in which a pensioner was killed. He was blameless but distraught and his treatment by Honda, after two hard years on the two-stroke, embittered him.

Ducati's pre-season form promised much, though. With their radical ninety-degree motor, steel-frame chassis and wronged rider, they meant business. Rossi had watched their progress with interest and wondered what it would be like to ride for an Italian factory, for an independent company instead of a corporate behemoth, for emotional Italians rather than phlegmatic Japanese. 'It was quite spectacular,' he reflected on the test. 'The engine is still only eighty per cent,' Claudio Domenicali, Ducati Corse's managing director, added.

Biaggi's discontent, meanwhile, knew no bounds. On day one of the new campaign he let rip and scraped the scabbing off old wounds. 'Rossi is false,' he said to a gathering of journalists by the track in Japan. 'He is a fake. If people had a chance to watch him when the cameras were not on him then they would get a different impression. He is not always nice and smiling. It's just an image.' Rossi questioned Biaggi's right to brand anyone a fake when, in fact, he was 'a liar'.

It meant there were plenty of questions to be answered by the time the riders lined up on the grid on 6 April 2003 for the first race of the season. Rossi, Biaggi and Capirossi, the Italian triumvirate, against the Texan Tornado and the Kentucky Kid, American newcomers. And then there was Daijiro Kato, the rookie of the season in 2002, who carved out lines that confounded geometry and who was now on the four-stroke Telefonica Movistar Honda. After his learning year in the big league, it was widely felt that Kato could be the man to rival Rossi. He had only qualified in eleventh, but a good start could halve the deficit and give him a chance at a track he knew so well.

This was the moment of reckoning for Kato. Everyone knew he was fast. He could weave a silk thread around every track. Some mechanics felt he was an illusory force, his skill and deft touch making it appear he was actually slower than he was. Kato did not fight the bike like some, he just blended into it. And Rossi was worried. The HRC engineers knew that from the race at Brno the previous season when Rossi's tyre had delaminated; some of them put that down to the pressure from Kato who was on the RC211V for the first time.

Rossi's fear of Kato was partly born of his love of Japanese riders. Long before he was the Doctor, he had taken to calling himself Rossifumi, a mix of his name and Norifumi Abe. Rossi had been obsessed with Abe and especially his debut in the 500cc Japanese Grand Prix in 1994, watching it on video every morning for a month before he went to school. It was the danger and the derring-do, the fact Abe overtook in unusual places. 'He rode like it was his last race not his first,' Rossi would explain. Abe crashed, but Rossi was smitten. Abe and Kato were like brothers and now they were racing together at Suzuka.

He sat on his bike with his helmet off, his thick hair forming a mane around his face. Kato's wife, Makiko, had given birth to their daughter the previous week and he waved to the camera as it passed by. Makiko was at home, while his parents had come to Suzuka with their son, Ikko. They had discussed a name before he left but they had not come to a conclusion. Makiko liked Marin and Daijiro favoured Haruka. They talked about combining the two and calling her Rinka. They would decide for sure afterwards. At Suzuka he showed Gibernau, his team-mate, a photograph.

'What's she called?' Gibernau asked.

'I have a few names in mind,' Kato replied. 'Will you help me decide?'

'Sure,' Gibernau said. 'After the race.'

Takashi Kato was excited. He sensed that his son's time was coming. The speed was there and he had got himself into top physical condition by going to Saipan and sweating himself to fitness. Takashi remembered how he had bought his son a pocket bike when he was three and how he had cried at first because of the noise. Shoji Tachikawa, the Repsol Honda team manager, was less convinced by the strict training regime. He knew how good Kato was but wondered why he had changed his normal routine. Was it pressure? 'He looks so fragile this year,' he said in private.

Ryoichi Mori had been a mechanic for Fausto Gresini for two years and, as he stood by Kato on the grid, felt that this would be the day. Qualifying had not gone well, but Daijiro could waltz through the pack. He could sew another silk line and give the team its greatest moment. Kato put his helmet on and closed the visor. Beneath the tinted plastic, Mori could see Kato smiling. On the grid. Moments before the race. The smile never left his face.

Initially, all that mattered was the lead. Checa had it briefly and then Biaggi before Capirossi gave a vivid exhibition of the Ducati's speed and leapfrogged them all. Kato was picking up places and moving fluently, his fans getting used to the new blue and yellow Movistar colours. By the end of the first lap of the circuit, with its fast sections and top end that, from the air, looked like the head of a guitar, Capirossi led from Biaggi with Rossi third. For the duo's fans, the irony of seeing the older rider on a Honda in bright yellow, the colours worn by Rossi's supporters, was rich. Rossi was not hanging about and was past Biaggi on the second lap. Behind him, Kato had moved up to fifth and was negotiating a path past the stubborn Bayliss on the second Ducati. Mercifully, for Makiko watching on television, the cameras followed the leaders. It was only later when fans started putting shaky clips on the Internet that people saw what had happened. How Kato, trailing Bayliss, had inexplicably veered left and disappeared into a wall at a 120mph right-hander. Bits of the bike shredded and fell down on to the track like confetti. Kato's body was jolted back into the track but he did not move. A boot had come off and was lying further up the track. The bike was wrecked and lay on the infield by the holes it had blasted in the wall.

A flock of racers went past. Some saw him lying on the track. Others concentrated on tiptoeing through the debris. They wondered what had happened but then discarded the thought. There was no time to allow your mind to wander when you were racing at this speed and had to impress your new boss. The six marshals looked at a loss to know what to do. The yellow flag was waved and the stretcher came out. Two men in white hats brushed the remnants of the bike and tyre off the track. Three put Kato on a stretcher as a bike appeared in the distance. Now the crowd was up and pouring towards the fence that the Honda had leapt at like a caged animal. The shock was exacerbated when they realized it was Kato lying there.

Akira Ryo, the Suzuki works rider who had been runner-up to Rossi here the previous year, was watching on a monitor. 'Where is the flag?' he thought. 'Where is the red flag?' The ambulance did not arrive for a few more laps and it was many more before the helicopter took him away. Ryo was angry. 'Where is the flag?'

In the Gresini team suite, Takashi Kato felt sick. He rushed to the medical centre. His wife was playing with Ikko and had not seen the accident, but she could not ignore it for long. Some time afterwards, Daijiro's manager, Shingo-san, came up to her in the Gresini suite and said she was needed.

The track was still tainted by the aftermath of a major accident, but nobody knew for sure. They expected a flag but it did not come and so they raced. Hard and fast and dangerously. Rossi had the lead by the fifth lap and was as masterful as ever. The simmering dissatisfaction with Honda paled as the sheer thrill of racing acted like a Prozac pill. This was what he loved. The rest was just the necessary evil to allow him to live a dream. As he hit the front and pulled away from Biaggi the joy of motorcycle racing flooded through him.

The ecstasy of winning and the thrill of speed were as pure as ever. Rossi popped a champagne cork on the podium and grinned wildly. He looked at Capirossi and realized that Ducati would be a challenger this year. In their first race the discarded Honda man had proved as belligerent as ever by grabbing third. And there was Biaggi, of course. Fuck Biaggi! He was the same as ever, silky smooth on the track and lumpen grace off it. It was going to be a good year.

It was only after the celebrations that they realized. Paco Latorre, Dorna's director of communications, told them Kato had fallen and had been taken away. 'Is it serious?' Rossi asked. Latorre said he did not know. Rossi was not content and went to see Dr Costa at the *clinica mobile* to get a first-hand account. Costa was a verbose figure whose way of commenting on events generally involved poetry and philosophy. Yet even he was tight-lipped this time and refused to tell Rossi.

The mood in the Telefonica Movistar garage was muted. Gibernau had debuted in fourth place and was pleased with his efforts, but he knew from looking at the faces of his team that the news was bad. Fausto Gresini, the team manager, did not stay long before making his way to Yokkaichi City to the Mei Medical Centre. In his absence confusion reigned. Initially, a press statement was put out by Honda suggesting Kato was suffering from 'breathing difficulties', a huge understatement, but the truth gradually filtered out, aided by Costa chatting with journalists in the media centre. Rossi, meanwhile, had finally gleaned the truth himself. Kato was in a coma and the prognosis was bleak. Claudio Macchiagodena, the race medical director, then said, 'Kato suffered serious injuries to the head, chest, neck and back. He remains in intensive care and he is fighting for his life. It's difficult to know what the future is, but we are hoping for some improvement in the next twenty-four to forty-eight hours.'

Immediately, there were twin concerns for the riders, fans and media. They all wanted to know how Kato was and they all wanted to know just why he had twisted off the track and catapulted off a concrete wall shrouded in tyres and ineffectual padding. Theories abounded. The first, put forward by Ukawa, was that he had actually collided with Bayliss, something he was forced to quickly retract. The next was that a fly-by-wire throttle system had jammed. However, the data showed that the throttle had been closed. Maybe it was the brakes or the tyres. Biaggi suggested it was the sheer power of the four-stroke engines that made it harder to control the bikes.

For once the riders refrained from their post-race bickering and presented a united front. 'Somebody needs to get fired over this or somebody needs to get their arse kicked because everybody that's crashed this weekend has hit a wall,' Kenny Roberts junior spat. 'Basically when him and the bike hit the wall they just started continually, like, cartwheeling into the wall. And then his fucking body came back across the track, more than three-quarters of the way back on to the track. And I'm trying to brake as hard as I can and move to the right, which is the inside of the chicane, to avoid his body. The race should've been stopped. They just picked him up and threw him on a stretcher which is typical around here. Today was a total disgrace. The last three days of us testing here is just wasting people. It's just a joke.'

Gibernau, a sensitive Spaniard, had also been stunned by what he had seen. 'I saw him start his braking and change gears. In that place all riders follow the same line – right, left, right – but Kato suddenly went left. I don't know why and even the telemetry doesn't say anything. I could not believe my eyes. I saw him go left and crash into the wall at more than 200kmh.' Gibernau then voiced the unanimous view of the riders. 'It's crazy to crash into a wall in 2003. We can no longer race here at Suzuka. It would be crazy,' Rossi concurred. 'The wall is too close,' he said. 'It is too dangerous.' Rossi, like many riders, loved Suzuka for its excitement, but the lack of run-off areas, which had threatened disaster before, was now unacceptable.

It was a unique show of solidarity by the modern riders. In the distant past, Giacomo Agostini had threatened to lead a strike in Finland because of the torrid conditions. He was used to seeing six of his peers die a year. The death rate provided intimations of mortality but also made him think he was somehow charmed. With every death he would ask why it always happened to other people. It had been like that ever since that day at the Vallelunga track in Rome. A young kid had come up and asked if he could borrow his MV 125cc. 'OK,' Agostini said. The kid had crashed into the rails and Agostini remembered seeing him stand up with no arms. But accidents happened all the time in his day, when the tyres and leathers were thinner and they were trapped within a ring of fire.

In 2003 the last serious accident in the elite class had been a decade before when Wayne Rainey, the three-time champion, had broken his back in a fall at Misano and ended up paralysed. That was also the year of the last fatal accident in grand prix racing when Nobyuki Wakai, a 250cc racer, hit a spectator in the pitlane and died. The last 500cc death had been another ten years before. The sport was safe. Wasn't it?

The most frightening thing about that weekend in Suzuka is that it had been foretold. Rossi had been the one who had questioned the safety of the track, but it was Honda's home circuit and money ruled. That weekend a notable absentee from the race was Marco Melandri, who had been due to make his MotoGP debut for Yamaha as Biaggi's replacement. Instead, he was nursing a broken ankle, nose and femur after crashing in practice on the same part of the track two days beforehand. 'I only had about one hour's sleep last night,' Melandri said before the race. 'The staff at the Japanese hospital have been very good and I have to thank them, but I am happy to be back with the Italian *clinica mobile* staff as they are like a little family. I've had some serious painkillers so things are a little better today.'

Melandri's matter-of-fact update suggested Costa and his rhyming couplets could soothe away all pain, but had things really progressed since the days of Agostini and Hailwood, when riders died as cattle and people shrugged? There was still a macabre voyeurism in seeing young men risk their lives for fleeting glory. The danger provided the fix. Agostini had been ignored and so had Rossi. Riders were better protected and the run-off areas were generally good, but they still made riders race alongside concrete walls. The official version of events from race control at Suzuka was that Kato had fallen as a result of a freak accident.

Costa provided updates. Since 1977 this doctor had been caring for grand prix riders at his increasingly hi-tech mobile clinic. He was proud that, of the hundreds of riders who crashed each year, only six, on average, needed to be treated at a hospital. The new version of the clinic had been opened by Agostini, himself, and had eight beds and an X-ray room. Costa loved motorcycle racers as much as he loved medicine, but was sometimes maligned for making a melodrama out of a crisis. It was thus when, two days after Kato's crash, he recounted what had happened.

'The ambulance doors swing open to reveal Japanese rider Daijiro Kato laid out on a stretcher, being given artificial respiration by a Japanese doctor while his colleagues perform heart massage. My hands move in to alleviate the tired hands of that Japanese doctor, who seems almost relieved at the arrival of this unexpected help.

'There is no pulse, and my hands sink into his chest again and again in an effort to convince that terribly still heart to start beating. More than a massage, it is a caress, soothing the rider's seemingly lifeless body. After an endless few minutes, Kato's young heart starts functioning again, beating out the steady rhythm of life, yet a life marred by terrible suffering.'

Dr Aronne Reverzani, the *clinica mobile*'s resuscitation expert, completed the 'life-saving process' by attaching tubes and catheters and arranging the neck collar. Costa continued, 'Critically injured, the rider made it to hospital alive. And it is here that my words now turn harsh, expressed coldly in that detached manner that plain scientific truth demands: deep coma, serious brain injuries with extensive haemorrhaging that worsens towards the base of the brain stem. Dislocation of the first and second cervical vertebrae with fracturing of the third and, consequently, devastating damage to the spinal cord and upper limb fractures.'

Costa could not restrict himself to the bleached words of science for long and mused on what drove men like Kato to race at such speeds on tracks such as Suzuka. 'The explanation resides in the purely irrational side of human nature,' he said. 'Where intellect and reason encroach on the world of sentiment, the resulting folly gives rise to the magical creature of the soul, that precious inner sense that allows us to see life as beautiful and good, acquitting it of every tragedy and rendering it innocent.

'When riders accelerate on to the race track they play a game of chess with death, doing so because they possess a soul – just like all those other motorcyclists who, whether on the race track or the road, ride their bikes in search of a better world, a world of infinite freedom.'

The riders were not so philosophical. Rossi raged that lives were being put at risk and he had a point. As Kato lay fighting for his life and Costa gave gloomy updates on his condition, warning that he would in all probability be a quadriplegic if he survived, the fact the race had not been stopped looked ever more crass. Rossi talked with some of the other riders and they agreed that they needed their voice to be heard. 'These four-stroke bikes are big weapons,' the oft-injured Garry McCoy said.

The day after the race Nobuatsu Aoki, who had retired on the Proton, bumped into Biaggi in the lobby of their hotel. Biaggi said there was going to be a meeting. That they could not carry on like this. The riders had decided they would seek a summit with Carmelo Ezpelata, the Dorna chief executive, at the next race in South Africa in a fortnight. Top of the list was the fate of Suzuka, which they would demand be removed from the calendar. There would be five delegates. Aoki would be one of them, along with Rossi, Gibernau, Roberts and Alex Barros. They would talk through safety at every track before every race.

There was a stream of well-wishers to the medical centre. Ukawa, who had been the last finisher in the race and had seen Kato fall, was among them. Riders are, by necessity, a fatalistic bunch suspending disbelief and imagining that they will some-how be charmed. Kunimitsu Takahashi felt that way. He had been the first Japanese rider to win a grand prix, in Germany in 1961, and had helped quash a national inferiority complex in the process. He felt Kato's way of riding was perfect and hoped he could recover, just as he had done when he had crashed on the Isle of Man in 1962 and spent ten days in a coma. Noriyuki Haga, twelfth on the Aprilia at Suzuka, knew life was tough because his brother was in a wheelchair from a crash, but he did not blame racing. This was life. It was precarious.

Four days after the crash Costa said Kato was surprising doctors with some improvements, but added he was still dependent on a respirator. It proved a false dawn. Kato died thirteen days after the crash. The cause of death was a brain stem infarction. The cause of the crash remained a mystery. Honda's investigation had been unable to offer a definitive answer. Neither had the police.

Costa posted a message on his website that night which might have churned a few stomachs but was undoubtedly heartfelt. 'Tragedy becomes innocent, in the world of motorcycling as everywhere, if for a minute we picture the great yet minuscule, tender and strong Daijiro rebuilding the bike he had destroyed in the Suzuka inferno.

'Daijiro rebuilds the bike which he had loved like he loved his sweet, young family, to race again on a track, but this time without any walls. The angels look on and marvel at how human beings can live again after the most terrible suffering, helped by hope and love.'

Ukawa was distraught when he saw Kato in his coffin the night before the funeral at the Kaneiji Buddhist Temple in Tokyo on the Tuesday before the South African Grand Prix. Tetsuya Harada, the former 250cc champion who had retired the previous year, could not get a flight home. It was Easter and all seats were taken. Finally, he returned three days later and went to Kato's house to pray beneath the photograph and ashes. He scoffed at suggestions that he would replace Kato for Team Gresini.

Abe, the man Rossi had once idolized and who had befriended Kato, was testing in Europe. He told his team he could not continue and flew home for the funeral. He bowed to Hatsumi and Takashi Kato and wished them well. 'Be careful,' they said. Abe would later say that winning races confirmed a feeling of being alive, while knowing death was nearby. He came through the ring of fire unscathed and rode his last grand prix the following year. And then, in 2007, a lorry driver performed an illegal U-turn in Kawasaki and crashed into Abe, who was following on a motorbike. He died from his injuries. He was thirty-two. Kato was twenty-six.

Gibernau, a thoughtful figure who studied business at university before turning to the family business, was deeply affected. He seemed to have been spending too long with Costa when he gave one of his first considered comments on the crash. 'If you imagine a flock of birds wheeling in the sky, they all turn together, moving together. Suddenly, one bursts off in another direction. But you can't watch it. You have to go with the others.'

The South Africa race was a week after Kato's death. Gibernau told Gresini that he could not go. He went home and endured a sleepless night, but then came to the conclusion that life went on. They flew to the funeral in Tokyo on the Tuesday before the South African Grand Prix. On the Sunday Gibernau won. Nobody liked to say it, but he seemed a better rider after Kato's death.

By the time I sat down with Gibernau in the Gresini hospitality suite at Le Mans a month later, he was causing Rossi to take him seriously. Lots of riders have lost team-mates, but Gibernau seemed to be drawing on the emotional energy of that period. 'I went to Welkom but it was only when I got there that it hit me,' he said. 'It's one thing saying he's gone and another to realize it. When I saw my bikes without his, I had to leave. I think about him now. You go through stages. Now I have a new team-mate and that makes it more real. But Daijiro's family follow the races. His son looks at me and says, "That's Dad's team-mate." '

The first thing most noticed about Gibernau was his sister, a petite blonde with cow-eyes and an engaging smile who worked as his press officer. The second was his biceps. Riders come in varying forms. Rossi was wiry and medium height, Pedrosa was a fey pixie and Biaggi was a small, sinewy man who would soon take to wearing a wig to disguise the onset of veteran status. Gibernau had the arms of a featherweight boxer but attracted much mockery from the media corps. There were those who thought he had had it easy, being the grandson of Paco Bulto, the founder of the Bultaco motorcycle dynasty, and there were others who thought he was a drama queen. One Spanish journalist said to me that he thought Gibernau was loving the attention that had come post-Kato. Such brickbats were cruel. Gibernau, like the rest, raced motorcycles at more than 200mph. Ignoring his bravery was myopic and, anyway, he had shown his potential in pre-season.

'Then everything stopped,' he said, a No. 74, Kato's number, now stitched on to the heart of his leathers. 'What happened to Daijiro is something none of us are programmed for. I don't understand it because we don't really understand what death means. Somehow we need to change the weakness to a strength. I'd got to a peak where everything was right and then it was over. The year we'd expected to be great had turned into our worst nightmare. I thought we were finished. I wondered if we could go on.'

He was handed the factory bike now that Kato was gone, but had crashed it in Spain, blaming over-zealousness in front of his own fans, but he was more confident than I had ever heard him. 'We can aim anywhere now, but what we need is consistency. When Valentino's bike is not great he is on the podium; when it's perfect he wins. Maybe with the new bike we need to take one step backwards and two steps forwards. The trouble is I'm so pumped I don't want to take a backwards step.'

Le Mans was extraordinary. Rossi was cruising to victory when the rain came. The new rules meant they would start again over the remaining distance after coming in to change to a wet set-up. Gibernau led on the last lap, showing a level of bravery and assertiveness that some thought beyond him, but Rossi was not going to give way. Twice he passed Gibernau on the last lap and twice he was passed. At the last corner Rossi, now frantic with desire, ran off the track and Gibernau held the inside to win by a tenth of a second. Gibernau won and pointed a finger at the heavens. The message was clear.

A week later David Jefferies, hoping for a fourth treble, was killed during practice for the TT on the Isle of Man. Jefferies crashed into a telegraph pole in the village of Crosby. Jim Moodie, following, hit the wreckage and was airlifted to hospital in Douglas. It prompted well-worn calls for the TT to be scrapped as a deadly anachronism. And the riders defended their right to risk all. This was the hurting business.

LAP 3

Mike down for dinner with Mick Grant, the new master of the TT, and ran through the rivals. The main one, he knew, was sitting opposite him. Grant was a hirsute Yorkshireman, fast and obdurate, who had suffered a run of crashes in the preamble to the TT but he was fit and ready to go. John Williams, the part-time tanker driver, was also there despite an awful accident at Imola when he had been left in the middle of the track facing a swarm of bikes. Williams had broken ribs and bruised kidneys but the island had restorative powers. It had been this way since Mike had lit up the sporting vista in 1961. Like a frozen bolt of lightning.

This was the game. It was a heady mix of fear and fun. His friend, Tommy Robb, had suffered the Big Slide the year before in 1960. It came as the sun came out and the Ulsterman considered how wonderful the island could be. Down through Ramsey and Parliament Square. And then his goggles had steamed up and he went straight into the wall on Windy Corner. An ambulance driver was parked on the side of the road and watching the bikes flash by. Tommy was the first one to pass him on the left instead of the right. He came to and saw a big light. He heard someone say, 'His neck's broken' and he blacked out again. When he next woke he saw a noose in front of him. 'They're going to hang me,' he thought, but it was for pulling himself up in his hospital bed. Tommy had a neck brace but managed to steer his head sidewards. That was when he saw three other racers next to him. They had all crashed in the fog. When Tommy made it to the toilet they cheered. One of the other victims was Mitsuoh Itoh, who went to the toilet and cut his plaster off with a set of garden shears. He escaped through a window.

Tommy was 10 stone 10 pounds on the morning of the crash and 7 stone 11 pounds three weeks later. They plastered him from his head to his waist. He made sure they cut holes for his ears. He got back on a bike soon after but had to get off at every intersection to look right. He raced again in September but crashed and thought he had paralysed himself for life this time. 'What have you been doing?' the surgeon asked.

'Racing motorcycles.'

'Well, you haven't been doing it very well, have you?'

But Tommy survived his Big Slide and would race for another thirteen years until he finally won at the TT. It was his last race there. He retired at the top and was never tempted back.

Mike had gone to the island in 1961 and become truly famous. Stan helped. He reasoned that his boy needed a Honda and so he would have one. Honda had their seasoned and gifted riders, Jim Redman, Tom Phillis and Luigi Taveri, so they felt no cause to give in to the bullying of this curious man with a natty bow tie. Stan refused to concede, though, and so he ended up with Taveri's spare. The two men then indulged in a close battle, Mike breaking the lap record and Taveri responding and staying in touch, overtaking his rival on the course but still trailing on time. In the end it was enough. Mike had won his first TT race and had done it on a borrowed, 'clapped-out' bike.

Nobody could match Bob McIntyre in the 250cc race that afternoon. He was on course to become the first man to manage the mythical 100mph lap on a 250cc machine, but he spotted oil on his tyre and so did not push to the limit. Even so it was going to be enough to win, but then his engine seized on the last lap and Mike had two wins in half a day.

By Wednesday everybody was talking about the twenty-one-year-old. Mike was an irresistible draw. Women loved him for the noble jaw and rapier eyes, men for his style and skill. Mike was cruising to victory on an AJS in the 350 race when the fates turned against him and he was forced out, suffering the pain of watching from the gutter as Phil Read and Gary Hocking passed. The unpredictability of the TT reared up again in the 500cc race when Hocking suffered mechanical problems and Mike claimed the first ever TT hat-trick. When he wrapped up the 250cc world title later that year Mike was a star.

It was a fearful, fun life. He liked to sleep with a woman the night before a race. It left others spent, but not him. It was scarcely surprising since Stan had been known to turn up to meetings flanked by various young women. With a world title and a TT hat-trick behind him, Mike drank heavily and went to all-night parties. It was the start of the swinging 60s and television sets were sometimes hurled from windows. They raced in Barcelona and were drinking away when Tommy noticed a series of scabbed hands put beer bottles behind their bikes. 'I think we better go, Mike,' he said.

'No, no, Tommy, we're having a great night.'

'Yeah, but I don't think it's going to last very long.'

They got out in time and Tommy fired up the old Thames van. Mike was kneeling behind him between the two seats with his arms around the engine compartment. Tommy breathed a sigh of relief. 'That was close.' Mike then put his hands over his friend's eyes. 'Mike! What the hell are you doing?'

'Let's see how good you really are, Robb,' he said.

'We were on the bloody dual carriageway,' Tommy would

recall. 'I mean he could have written us off. His hands so big and he had these firm wrists. That could have been it. But that was the way it was back then. He never stopped having fun.'

Hockenheim, 1961, was one of the best. Someone dropped a pot plant in the lap of Walter Kaaden, the MZ boss, and that set everyone off. Jim Redman was there and joined in. So did Mike. The room was suddenly drenched in soil and Martini and squashed plants. There was almost a riot when the band said they were stopping at 2 a.m., but they continued until Mike silenced the trombonist by stuffing a plant up his brass bell.

Redman would win at the TT six times, himself, and add six world titles on the smaller bikes. For all the fun there was always the lingering presence of danger, as Jim found out when he crashed through a wooden fence at Spa and was flung like garbage into a muddy ditch. Mike and Ralph Bryans went to see Jim in a curious old building with high ceilings and a staff of nuns. Relieved that Jim had only suffered broken bones, they were making their way out when Mike leant over the reception and asked a nun if he could have a dose of a particular medicine. 'Why do you need that?' she asked.

Mike smiled. 'Well, you see, I've got a dose of the clap.'

They were riotous days but maybe it was best to leave them there, to let them grow brighter at a distance and eventually segue into folklore. Maybe you needed to know when it was time. He was damned sure *the comeback* was not about money, despite what the media said, but what was he trying to prove? It was 1978 and he was thirty-eight years old for Christ's sake. Then he looked over the table at Grant, remembered how good he had been in testing, and felt sure. He would continue to tell people he had no chance, but he was Mike the Bike. Times had changed, but he hadn't.

CHAPTER SIX

THE GAME

It was 10 p.m. in San Piero a Sieve and Valentino Rossi was late. That was not unusual. He was always the last to turn up for the morning session of a grand prix. He was usually the last to bed too. At the end of each day's work he would sleep for a couple of hours in his motorhome and then go out for dinner. Then he would go out *properly*. He had not been joking when he claimed on last year's T-shirt that he never went to bed before 2 a.m. So there we were, waiting for God.

I looked at the pitch and cursed myself for not having proper boots. There was a light sheen of evening dew on the surface. I sat in the changing room with the bunch of Dorna staff as they laughed and joked in Spanish. Matt was there. So was Gavin Emmett. It always amused me that these two could switch instantly from their native Yorkshire brogue to fluent Spanish with their gargled vowels and lisped consonants.

It was the annual football match between Dorna and Rossi's official Fan Club, a motley assortment of grizzled Italians from Tavullia. The Fan Club had been created by a few fans in a bar back in 1995 and had grown bigger every year. Now one member, Flavio Fratesi, had express responsibility for creating Rossi's end-of-season T-shirts. He was also the man who liaised with Rossi over his post-race stunts and, thus, had a position of power within the organization. With Rossi in 2003 there was a hierarchy of worship. A step up from the Fan Club was the Tribe, the group of twenty or so friends from his schooldays, and then there was the Kabbalah, which comprised Rossi and five associates going for a pre-race drink at the same bar. No one else was allowed.

This superstitious nature bordered on nervous disorder and manifested itself in various ways. It was a little-known fact that Rossi insisted on four members of his entourage standing in precisely the same positions during races. He also would only let certain people carry his back protector and they had to carry it in a specific way. It was a neurosis of sorts and, yet, in other ways he was the most carefree of sports stars.

The Dorna team were wearing a horrible polyester blue kit that disappeared against the navy shadows of the trees on the far side of the pitch. San Piero seemed like a ghost town, albeit a picturesque one with its medieval castle and fields of brown vines. The clubhouse was once white but had faded to oyster grey. The ancient toilets did not work and the air was heavy with smoke from a nearby bonfire. The clock ticked round and it got to 11 p.m. I was tired. The lavish buffet lunch in an old villa by the side of the Mugello circuit was taking its toll. I had sat there on the next table to a gnarled face with the skin strained and twisted over jailbreak bones. The hair was long and lank and the eyes scarlet. This was Marco Lucchinelli. He was a middle-aged man who looked like a cross between Keith Richards and Salvador Dali. He had also been an Italian legend, the world champion in 1981. That was before the lifestyle caught up with him and he got five years for cocaine smuggling. He had emerged to almost rapturous acclaim and was now the doyen of rebel racers, the earring, pencil moustache and air of danger making him impossible to ignore as he pushed fifty.

The difference with Rossi was marked. Rossi was a fun-loving extrovert but there was no threat with him. He could cut you dead with his eyes and dismissive chuckle, but boozing with Sete Gibernau in Ibiza and womanizing were modest vices next to Lucchinelli's.

Rossi was appallingly unpunctual, though. The clock ticked on and we had been warming up long enough for me to realize my trainers were going to be no use on the oiled grass. Finally, Paco Latorre decided the game should start. Latorre was a thin, chiselled man with a goatee beard. He ran Dorna's media operation with an iron fist. What he said went. And then, as the Fan Club knocked the ball around at the back, a cloud of dust was thrown up and a car turned into the sports ground. 'He's here,' someone whispered. 'Getting changed. Won't be long.'

Finally, at around 11.30 p.m., he emerged wearing a yellow shirt with a No. 46 on the back. It was less than twelve hours until he would be riding his RC211V in the morning session of the first day of the Italian Grand Prix, the biggest race of the year. You might have realistically expected him to be tucked up at home, but here he was. Nobody was warned off tackling him or told to take it easy. So I didn't. Rossi shielded the ball from me and stuck out his arms. He was 5 foot 10 inches tall and had spidery limbs. Nobody ever saw him working out and he lacked the hard-earned biceps of Gibernau. Rossi laid the ball off, turned and ran upfield. I grabbed at him, but he shrugged me off. My trainers and the surface meant I moved as if I was wearing carpet slippers.

It was a good game. Gav scored a couple and Matt showed plenty of skill in midfield. I did manage to throw out a foot and hit the bar. Then I fell over. One of the Fan Club wingers took to laughing at me because I had the turning circle of a motorhome. I am sorry to say I left my foot in and got my revenge. Well, if Rossi could be late.

'Slow down, Vale,' I said as he went past me again. No response.

He had already got one goal when he lined up a free kick from David Beckham distance. He stood over the ball and probably imagined that he was in the San Siro. Rossi was a big Inter Milan fan and the fact Biaggi had his AS Roma allegiance was another subplot in their little war. It had been a contributory factor to their fight back in 2001. Biaggi, too, was a regular footballer, playing alongside Didier Deschamps, the former France captain, in a league in Monaco every Monday night. It would have been good to see them play together, a bit like Leeds versus Chelsea and the do-it-yourself skin grafts of the 1970s. Rossi walked casually up to the ball and stroked a right-footed shot into the top of the net. It had not gone quite into the corner and I wondered briefly whether the goalkeeper had let the ball in. We were basically courtiers playing games with the king. The Fan Club won 4-2. Rossi was feted. He laughed with Uccio and wandered to the side of the pitch. I shook his hand and imagined this was as close to normal as he got.

The following day Mugello was a riot of noise and colour. Rossi was clearly refreshed when we sat down, but there was a sense that all was not right in his world. We were in the transporter this time, away from the Italian journalists lingering in hospitality with their espressos after his daily briefing. He still spoke with the same boyish energy, 'fack' and 'for sure' peppering his speech, but he did not seem like a man having the sort of fun he did the night before. 'Tough game?' I said and he put down the bike magazine that he was half looking at and fixed me with his big clear eyes. 'I suppose that was your last freedom of the weekend?'

He sighed. 'When I'm not racing I try to forget that I am Valentino Rossi,' he said. 'I am just normal, like other guys of my age. I like to go out to nightclubs and drink and have some fun. It is important because of the pressure. There is always a lot of pressure. Everybody wants to talk to me or have a picture.'

'How long do you think you can keep up this life?'

The eyes stretched to saucers. 'I want to stay with motorbikes for three years and then maybe try driving a car,' he said. He had already started, an ill-fated assault on the previous year's Rally of Great Britain having failed to douse his ambition. 'If that is no good, then I hope to have a lot of money for a long holiday.' He laughed but it was hollow. He was only twenty-four and he was telling me he would be retired by the time he was twenty-seven. Like George Best. Gone at the top. Before he was old and in decline. While he was still charmed.

I didn't know at that point just how depressed Rossi was with his winning streak at Honda. Earlier that week Davide Brivio had made the next move in his attempt to wrestle Rossi away from Honda. He met with Masao Furusawa, the head of technological development at Yamaha, and told him Rossi was the key to reviving the ailing factory's fortunes. Furusawa was not convinced. It was natural for the Japanese to think their machinery was all-important and that the rider was icing on the cake. That was the same at Yamaha as it was at Honda. Brivio played a careful game, putting his side across forcibly but politely. The drama went on with Honda exacerbating the situation through their ignorance about the plot. Rossi, knowing his own worth, was playing a game but it was one which inevitably caused him to feel unsettled.

For the moment he welcomed the rise of Gibernau. 'He has a good style for MotoGP because he has good control of the bike,' he said. The door slid open like something from a James Bond film and Mack came in. He grabbed a folder and left. The door slid shut. 'Where were we, ah, yes, Gibernau.' Rossi had a habit of pushing people away when they became threats. The speed of his mind matched his tongue and he could throw out barbed compliments at will. It was a defence mechanism and he did it then when I asked if he had been surprised by how fast Gibernau was. 'Has he surprised me? I am surprised by his head because he made some stupid mistakes last year. But the problem for the show is when one man dominates. This year will be harder but more fun. For sure the points ranking will be closer.'

I went to see Biaggi next. He was with Federica, his faithful friend who always drove his customized Smart car, with the distinctive Biaggi logo and No. 3 on the side. We sat in his office in the Yamaha transporter and he was relaxed. I had always found Biaggi to be affable and courteous, belying the jaundiced image you got from those ensconced in the Rossi camp. Some said he was a difficult man with a chip on his shoulder. Others, including Mick Doohan, criticized his precise riding style, great for 250s but not brutish 990s. Most portrayed him as a joyless figure who spent his days sticking pins into his voodoo doll emblazoned with the No. 46.

The irony was that where Rossi was deemed the man of the people, he was actually the one forced to squirrel himself away in his motorhome, while Biaggi could take his annual ride to the top of the hill at Mugello. 'If I wasn't riding then I'd be a fan and my dream would be to see my favourite rider,' he said. 'It costs me an hour-and-a-half and makes them happy for ever.' He had plenty of fans too. Not as many as Rossi, who had become a phenomenon, but enough. Even Rossi, though he did not like to admit it, once had a Biaggi poster on his bedroom wall.

His voice was duller and less excitable than Rossi's, but he was in good spirits as we watched the men's semi-final from the French Open tennis playing on a television set raised in a corner. Juan Carlos Ferrero clinched the second set on tie-break to take it to a decider. Biaggi was pleased. It was an all-Spanish affair, but Biaggi liked all sport. He had his flaws, but who didn't?

He said he had built a gymnasium on the balcony of his lavish Monaco flat overlooking the sea. He trained every day and, when results went wrong, did not wallow in self-pity. 'If you have a champion's mind, you take a negative result and make it positive,' he said. 'One hour after a bad race I've taken all my anger and am reversing it. This is why I so often bounce back with a good result. It is my character.'

His father, Pietro, was a football coach, sparking his early ambitions, but I was told that being abandoned by his mother hit like a steam hammer. He found a refuge in bikes in his late teens and won the Italian 125cc Sports Production Championship with Aprilia. Five years after he rode his first bike he was the 250cc world champion. 'I look around now and think it was good that I came to motorcycles so late,' he remarked. I wondered if this was an anti-Rossi dig. 'Starting later you are so much more mature.' Yes it was. 'That's especially important when you are working with 200 horsepower. If you don't know what you are doing it's going to get dangerous very quickly. If you are young and all you know is motorcycling then you can become tired. You must be a hundred per cent in the body and the mind. Ninety per cent is no good.'

Biaggi was a complicated character. A crazy bastard, I'd been told, but that seemed an overly harsh and biased view. He claimed he was turning his negatives into positives an hour after the end of a race, but five minutes later told me the disappointment festered longer. 'Mondays are a bad day for me,' he said. 'I wake up early because I still have that adrenalin rush. I analyse everything. I am searching for something even when there is nothing to search for.'

Like Rossi, Biaggi was forced to live in exile, but had chosen Monaco. 'I miss Rome because all my old friends are there.' Rossi brought his friends with him, the Fan Club with their football boots, and the Tribe. He even imported fans from Hawaii. Biaggi, by contrast, always looked one of the loneliest figures in the paddock. 'I miss having a cappuccino and saying hello to the guy selling newspapers. I get back for ten days a year, which is nothing. It's good to go home because the pressure is huge. It never goes. At the track I know I can't make a single mistake.' It was obvious that he was deeply jealous of Rossi, not his ability but his bike. The mantra was always close to hand. 'There are many little differences with the factory Honda and, by the end of a long race, they add up to one thing, but my bike is good. If I can't win this year then maybe next season.'

We chatted about Monaco and how hard Mugello was for the Italian riders. 'Thanks,' he said as I got up to leave and Ferrero wrapped up his victory. 'That's the nicest interview I've done this weekend. It's good to speak about other things than motorcycles.' It was days like these which made it hard to picture Biaggi as the man who locked himself in his motorhome for hours when things did not go his way. 'Sometimes he has to be dealt with like a child,' one team member told me.

I saw Chaz Davies walking down the pitlane with the riders' hunched, splayed-leg gait. I let him be. I'd spoken to him before we came out because the poor sod had his GCSEs this weekend. He had taken maths, English and history and was due back in the makeshift classroom high in the Tuscan hills on Monday for science.

The results on the track did not bode well. He had suffered from food poisoning at the first round of 2003 in Suzuka and came into the pits on his 250cc German Aprilia feeling drained and dizzy. 'I was running on empty. I'd only had an orange juice but could not keep it down and let it all out. It formed a little orange stream in the pitlane. My concentration level was zero.' Stoner had gone the other way and was now in the 125cc class, alongside another young Briton, Leon Camier, who was sixteen and had been learning the Mugello circuit on his PlayStation. This was real pressure. Davies' mother, Sam, had thrown in her job to find more sponsorship and Camier's parents had remortgaged their house. Camier said they had spent £130,000 on him this year and that he would need another £200,000 to be anywhere near the front next season. 'Do you just keep a happy, smiley face and hope something will happen or do you call it a day?' he said. At sixteen.

Meanwhile, word emerged that Rossi was seeking close to £6 million a year from Honda. It was a calculated ultimatum. Now the price was out they could either pay it or lose him. He also upset the powers-that-be by snubbing a gala dinner with the Italian president. Agostini and others were there, but Rossi was too busy. Not too busy to please himself on the football pitch, but too busy for the glitterati. It was another side to Rossi that went unreported. It also reminded me of another time Rossi had missed a gathering of top riders. Chris Herring explained, 'Of all the living Italian riders who had ever won a GP only two were missing. One was on his deathbed and sent his son to read out his story. The other was Rossi.' The story went that Rossi was in Ibiza with a woman. 'I always felt that Honda never got to put their side in the row with Rossi,' Herring continued. 'He was going round saying he had had enough of this guy at Honda or that guy. But there was a culture clash. They say Italians admit to six lies every day while the Japanese culture is not to give a tit-for-tat response.'

The racing always got him out of any holes and in Mugello it was spectacular. It was baking hot. The temperature rose into the nineties, the trackside temperature way over a hundred degrees. Having qualified on pole, Rossi found himself sixth by the end of the first corner. Capirossi, desperate for a good performance in Ducati's first home race for thirty-one years, tore into the lead and held it until he ran wide five laps later, allowing Biaggi to pass. Rossi did not panic, however, and exchanged second place with Capirossi before edging the Repsol Honda into the lead at just over half distance.

The vast 72,000 crowd, crammed into the natural bowl, urged Biaggi and Capirossi to hang on. They responded but their personal duel proved costly. The pair touched on several occasions, a frightening scenario given that Capirossi was recorded doing 206mph, and swapped positions on five occasions before the opera-loving terrier from Bologna began to edge away.

Capirossi's bike now wobbled and slid around the track as it was forced to the boundaries of its capabilities. He managed to bite into Rossi's lead, but the championship leader withstood his efforts and won by 1.4 seconds. Nevertheless, Capirossi's second place was cherished as a win by Ducati, who had shaken up the status quo in MotoGP after only five races.

It was a great race but almost immediately attention returned to the politics and in-fighting. Nobody was talking about Kato any more, even though Rossi voiced concerns about the speeds they were now reaching. 'With four-stroke it is possible to have 300 horsepower tomorrow,' he told me. 'The problem is who will ride the bike? In the last five years of 500s the bikes basically remained the same but they improved the tyres. With the four-strokes we are already one second faster than last year. That is very good but it is also a risk. We need to have some rules so that we don't make the bikes too fast because we are on the limit.' Nobody else seemed too concerned. Kato, tragic as he was, was another grisly statistic. Another inscription on a memorial.

People wanted to know about Rossi. He was news. Where would he be riding next season? Rossi's team fed information to the media, prompting *La Gazzetta dello Sport*, the influential Italian daily paper, to predict that he would become the country's highest-paid sportsman when he signed a new deal. His closest rivals were football stars Alessandro Del Piero and Christian Vieri, who earned €9.5 million and €9.3 million a year respectively. Rossi's new contract would top that. Carlo Fiorani, HRC's team manager, said he wanted the matter resolved as quickly as possible. He did not know the half of it. In the support races Davies was thirteenth in the 250cc grand prix, while in the

125cc race Camier was thirtieth and Stoner eighteenth. They were a world away from Rossi and the money was drying up.

It was then that the wheels fell off for Rossi. Capirossi won the Catalan Grand Prix for Ducati, their first since Mike Hailwood in 1959, after Rossi had made a basic error and run off the track with nine laps left. He had recovered brilliantly and cut a swathe through the field, picking off rider after rider until only Capirossi remained. He had clawed back six seconds but was still half a straight adrift.

At Assen, Neil Hodgson, now cruising to the title in World Superbikes, visited, but the differing stature of the championships was shown when a fan asked if he would take a picture of him and Randy Mamola. The fan had no idea who Hodgson was but was excited by the presence of a former great like Mamola. I would come back to Assen and see Hodgson clinch the world title. That was the weekend Fogarty, Neil Bramwell and I went for a ride down Groningen's major red light street. Fogarty, who loved Assen for its racing and lived in its bubble, was wide-eyed at the sight of the curtained windows and fans and team officials nipping in and out of doors with their neon trims. 'Fuck me,' he said as we read a sign that explained how the lady in the window would electrify your testicles for a little extra. 'The dirty bastards. All these years I thought they were coming here to see me race.'

Rossi had a meeting with Suguru Kanazawa, the HRC president, during MotoGP's weekend in Assen, but no deal was done. HRC were not the sort of company to bow to threats and they were incredulous at the figures Rossi's team were demanding. In the race Rossi lost again, beaten fairly and squarely by Gibernau.

It got worse. At Donington Park, close to midnight, a figure crept into the Yamaha garage. The door was slammed shut after him. This was Rossi's first meeting with the Yamaha M1. He sat on it and thought it ugly and weak. It felt uncomfortable. Brivio looked nervously at Lin Jarvis, the team boss. It might have ended there, but the M1's chief designer, suitably named Yoda, made a joke and Rossi laughed. So did Gibo. It was a throwaway comment that Rossi would later claim convinced him Yamaha would be more fun.

That week Rossi commandeered a boat to cruise up and down the Thames as a PR stunt. I was there and marvelled at the ingenuity of Nick Harris, the Dorna press officer who each year came up with something for Rossi to do to publicize the British Grand Prix. I helped myself to the buffet and asked Rossi whether he would like to ride for Ducati. 'It would be a dream for an Italian to ride for an Italian team,' he said candidly. He was the captain of the ship, co-ordinating the headlines and sending blunt messages to Honda. To his critics, he was behaving like the office flirt at the Christmas party. He spoke of leaving, of Honda's bureaucracy, of Ducati, even of packing it all in to go and race in Formula One. And he lost again. This time he crossed the line first but was given a ten-second penalty for overtaking under a yellow flag on the second lap. The men at race control had not seen anything wrong and the decision was not made until long after the prize-giving after a tip-off from others in the paddock. 'I race on the track not in the office,' Rossi said. Biaggi was elevated to first place, but Rossi made sure he kept the trophy.

Before the German Grand Prix, Rossi and Gibo Badioli drove to Bologna to meet Livio Suppi, the Ducati team director. They got a tour of the factory. The small, emotional team appeared a perfect fit, while the Desmosedici was already far more competitive than the ailing Yamaha. Alex Barros' third place in France would prove the only podium finish for Yamaha in 2003, but Rossi now craved a team that would give him a challenge and acknowledge that he was the most important facet of the equation, not Honda's V5 engine or Ducati's pneumatic valve system. It was clear that the winner in the fight for Rossi's signature would not be the team with the fastest bike or even most money, but the one which bowed to his will.

Rossi lost again at the Sachsenring. This time he showed a new level of doubt, squandering a huge lead and prompting the knives to come out in the Italian media. It came down to a last-lap duel with Gibernau. Rossi led with two corners remaining, ran wide, allowed Gibernau to draw level and could not fend him off as the race went to the line. The winning margin was only six-hundredths of a second but it was enough. The headlines were scathing. Rossi, they declared, was washed up. He still led Gibernau by nineteen points, but back in Italy the gap had been forty-three points. The pressure was on like never before.

It was during the mid-season break in Ibiza that Rossi made up his mind to go to Yamaha. At the next race at Brno he arranged a last clandestine meeting with Brivio and Jarvis. Uccio and Badioli accompanied Rossi. They decided to meet at the *clinica mobile* which was at the far end of the paddock, away from the gossip and late-night workers. They disguised themselves and broke into the awning attached to the clinic. They heard a scooter and all dived under a table. It was slapstick fare but the deal was done with a handshake.

And then, almost as if a burden had been lifted, Rossi started winning again. The first, at Brno, was great. This time the gap to Gibernau was four-hundredths of a second. Afterwards he wore a ball and chain on the podium to signify the pressure he had been under from the Italian media. He was back on the chain gang, back to playing games.

At Motegi Honda presented him with a final contract. Even then they felt they had the negotiating power. Rossi went back to the hotel on the hill that he likened to the one in *The Shining* and left it there. He had bigger problems to worry about. In Rio he had called his team together and told them he was thinking of leaving and needed to know if they would come with him. There was a touch of arrogance about him demanding a quick answer, given Honda's equally stern approach had so irked him. That day in Motegi Jerry Burgess told him the team was not coming. Rossi would have to go it alone.

Publicly there was no decision by the time we arrived at Sepang in Malaysia for the title decider. Rossi was fifty-eight points clear with three races left. First or second place would do it. Malaysia is a strange race as it is possible to forget you are abroad. Most race personnel stay in the Pan Pacific Hotel, which is attached by a walkway to Kuala Lumpur Airport. This means that from the time you enter Heathrow Airport to going to bed you need not step outside. Mike Scott, one of the best writers in the paddock, was holding a drinks party to celebrate his anniversary. Then we went to the bar, a sprawling semi-circle with dancing girls in Burberry bikinis dancing on top of it. This was one of the curiosities of the East – the higher class the hotel the sleazier they often were; when the series moved to China there would be a procession of people in official team uniform hopping up and down the stairs to the silhouetted windows of the 'private rooms' above the dancefloor of our five-star hotel.

Gibernau did his best to delay the inevitable. From a dismal seventh on the grid he surged past Rossi and gave it absolutely everything. He held the lead until the eighth lap, but once Rossi was past there was no catching him, a second equating to a land-slide in the Italian's world. Gibernau had done enough to undermine the mocking moniker bestowed on him by Rossi – 'Hollywood' – and next year he might be a real threat. Rossi staged another stunt on his victory lap, stopping to sever the chains of his friends who were clad in prison uniform, a symbolic gesture marking the end of his partnership with Honda. The official announcement would not come until Valencia, where Gibernau could barely contain his excitement. Rossi to Yamaha? He could see the title on the horizon.

Why did he go? There is no doubt Rossi hated the clinical world of Honda where everything was voted on by committee. He was also disgruntled by the fact Ducati wanted him to do sixty promotional days a year. Yamaha were in chaos, but Rossi knew they could up their game and that he was better than Checa. So the stance against tobacco sponsorship faded in the face of becoming Italy's richest revolutionary.

Unseen to many, Biaggi actually softened a little in the Malaysian aftermath. He found Rossi and shook his hand. 'He deserves it,' he later said. Rossi was happy but still downbeat about the loss of his crew. He saw no irony in questioning their loyalty while planning his exit from Honda, the factory that had made him a multi-million-pound megastar. Rossi went to a glass-fronted high rise and got drunk with his Honda team that night. He slept in and was late for the meeting to sign his Yamaha contract.

In the bar at the Pan Pacific that night I had a drink with a few journalists. Some riders, such as John Hopkins and Marco Melandri, were sitting at a table to the rear, surrounded by friends. The alcohol was flowing and the Burberry dancing girls were surrounded by a phalanx of lusting Europeans, high on success and testosterone.

By the entry to the bar was a blue pool table. A small boy with jet-black hair and olive skin was playing alone. I offered to give him a game. We didn't speak, but when he smiled I could see the braces on his teeth. He looked embarrassed by the Burberry girls. And that was how Dani Pedrosa celebrated winning the 125cc world title.

LAP 4

Ted Macauley had arranged for the team to be based beneath the Castle Mona Hotel. It was literally an underground movement and Mike was already grateful. Not only did the huge cellars beneath the mansion give Nobby Clark, his rubber-faced mechanic, the secrecy he craved to work away on the Yamaha bikes, but Mike was already realizing just how big *the comeback* had become. Everywhere he went people waved and shook his hand and asked for autographs. One man had even followed him into the toilet to get his signature.

It was impossible in that summer of 1978 not to look out over Douglas Bay and be transported back in time on the roll of the waves crashing into the promenade. It was 1962 and Pauline was walking through the pits. Elvis Presley's 'Good Luck Charm' was number one and poured out of a transistor radio. Mike was sitting on a tool box, alongside Bill Ivy and Phil Read. There were other people around whom Pauline did not recognize. She caught Mike's eye and nodded almost imperceptibly. He bounced up and ran after her. 'Hello, you old ratbag, what you doing tonight?' She knew she should have been insulted. She knew that she should say she was busy and she knew how her mother would react if she could see her now. 'Nothing,' she said. He did not know her name, but they arranged to meet outside the Villa Marina, the former governor's residence with its white marble floors and sweeping spiral staircase.

'Oh God, what am I going to wear?' Pauline thought as soon as they had separated. She had only decided to come to practice week with about half an hour to spare, and had hastily thrown some jeans and T-shirts into a bag. She was staying in a tiny guesthouse in Douglas with her friends. They were almost out of money and were due to leave the following morning. 'I can't go out with Mike Hailwood in any old thing,' she told herself and so she rushed into Douglas and found a knee-high skirt and a top for 19s 11d. 'It was clean and it was new, which was all I cared about.' At 7 p.m. she stood outside the grand entrance to the Villa Marina and waited nervously. The clock ticked around to 7.15 and she started to reprimand herself. 'You stupid girl,' she hissed. 'You should have told him to clear off.' Still the minutes passed with no sign. 'What were you thinking?' She looked towards the Douglas Bay Hotel, a grand establishment up on the point, where she knew he was staying. And then, at 7.25, she saw a white Jaguar coming down the hill. Her heart leapt. In her haste and excitement she realized that she had got the time wrong and they had arranged to meet at half past. She would find that Mike was always on time, even if it meant arriving early and sitting up the road in his car for ten minutes.

They went to see *A Kind of Loving*, a gritty tale of a man struggling to come to terms with his girlfriend's pregnancy, and then went for a drink. They met up again the next day.

'I've got to go home,' she told him.

'No you don't.'

'I do. All my friends are leaving this afternoon and I've got no money.'

'Don't worry about that. Let's go to the Douglas Bay and see if they've got a room up there. You've got to stay for race week.' So she did. Pauline asked her friends to pop in on her mother and break the news. 'Tell her I'll be back next week,' she said to her own disbelief.

Mike's star was in the ascendant. He had been headhunted by Count Domenico Agusta to ride for MV in 1962. The Italian had a touch of the Mafiosi boss about him with his slicked-back hair, suave suits and desk raised on a platform so that he could look down on his subjects. His main business was producing helicopters, but he liked motorcycle racing and was creating a sporting dynasty that served as a useful publicity machine. Riders, though, were dispensable. John Surtees knew that. After an interminable wait, Surtees had once been shown into the Count's office. He recalled that the Count said little and then a tiny lady with a vinegary mien, partly hidden by a black veil, came in. She circled the man who would win four world titles for MV, and uttered a few sour words in Italian. She looked at Surtees, walked around him again and then left. 'The Countess has agreed that you can become one of the family,' the interpreter said.

His wife was just as enigmatic. Ago was in the Hotel Quisisana in Capri one day, waiting for the Count. Suddenly, he heard a commotion and saw the Count heading towards him. At first he did not see the tiny woman in his wake, but he could certainly hear her. 'Bastard of a fucking Count!' she raged to a shocked lobby. Later Ago would recall how he was given an appointment to meet the Count at 4 p.m. He got there half an hour early but did not get to see him until 10 p.m. Tired and hungry he walked into the office where the Count barked, 'Who are you and what do you want?'

Inevitably, Mike also suffered his whims. He was made to wait two days to see the Count and, his patience finally exhausted, he stormed out of the factory and tore up his contract. He was halfway to the airport before one of the Count's lackeys convinced him to go back.

But the bikes were good and they gave Mike another TT win on the island in 1962 as Pauline looked on. It proved an irrelevance and any hopes for romance were damned by the danger. The junior TT win was a fantastic race with Mike getting the better of his MV partner, Gary Hocking, but behind them Tom Phillis crashed and died at Laurel Bank. The tragedy cloaked the racers in a sobering gloom. Phillis, once mocked as 'Autumn Leaves' because of his habit of falling in his early days, was a huge talent and a close friend of Mike. They all took it hard. Hocking decided enough was enough and retired. 'My retirement will not stop anyone being killed – except myself,' he said. Jim Redman also thought about quitting but was talked out of it by Bob McIntyre. 'You can't bring him back, Jim,' he said.

Redman reasoned that a rider had three crashes a year and that six riders were killed each year. So he ticked off his crashes and hoped. Two months later McIntyre, the first man to achieve the fabled 100mph lap at the Isle of Man, crashed at Oulton Park and ploughed into the trackside trees. His wife, Joyce, who had just had their first child, spent nine days at his hospital bedside before he died. Redman was distraught. Two Honda team-mates gone in a summer. Mike cruised to the first of his 500cc world titles on the MV, but the death toll had shaken him like the rest. While Redman struggled with his emotions, Mike decided that a racer lived with a narrow margin between life and death and so there was no room for additional worry. But then Gary Hocking, the man who had quit to save himself after Tom's death, was killed racing a car in South Africa. Socks, who read a chapter of the Bible each night, gone too.

At the TT that summer Pauline went to pay for her room at the Douglas Bay but was told it had been taken care of. She asked Mike how much it was, but he told her not to worry. He went back to Oxford and she went home to Essex. He liked her a lot, but there was no way he was ever going to get married while he was in this life. There was little room for sentiment when you were ticking off the crashes and going to funerals.

CHAPTER SEVEN

THE KING

The factories were no longer run as dictatorships but it was still reckless to upset the great dames of the sport. Not that Valentino Rossi was bothered. During his ascent through the junior ranks, the fresh-faced boy with the girlish fringe had taken to wearing the letters WLF on his leathers. Rossi had always taken an active role in the fripperies of racing, placing the stickers on his bike and coming up with comic-book logos, but now it was felt he had gone too far. Asked what WLF stood for, Rossi gave the honest answer. It stood for *Viva La Figa*, which roughly translated to 'long live pussy'. The wife of Ivano Beggio, the chief executive of Aprilia, was unamused and demanded Rossi remove the letters. 'I will take nothing from my leathers,' he replied. The letters stayed.

It was easy to imagine Rossi being happier clashing with pint-sized powderkegs at the old Italian factories than the corporate behemoths from Japan. At least the Count was a personality and thrived on power plays and mind games. The previous season Rossi had felt like just another employee, a cog in a wheel designed to promote the great god Honda. It was anathema to an emotional man from the hills nestling into the Adriatic. He would rather have someone ranting about the bastard of a fucking

Count than a bland teleconference delivered in passionless prose.

So he had gone. Honda was history and he was in South Africa for the first round of the 2004 season. It was a move that had rocked the MotoGP world off its axis. In *The Times*, Alastair Campbell, the former press aide to Tony Blair, was writing a series on the greatest sportsman of all time. He deemed that Rossi would be considered a candidate if he could win the title with a factory that had been in the doldrums for a decade. Meanwhile, *Rolling Stone* had launched an Italian edition that winter. Michele Lupi, a journalist for GQ who had written a book, *Racers*, about motorcycling, was given the task of editing it. There was a paltry budget and Lupi needed something big to make an impact. He pulled off a masterstroke in the second edition when he convinced Rossi to dress up as Elvis Presley for the front cover. 'Rossi is one of the biggest stars in Italy, our answer to David Beckham,' he reflected. 'He understood that we were trying to do something different and he was very helpful. There were loads of calls from people who wanted that photo so, from then on, we realized it would be a good idea not to concentrate only on musicians.'

Rossi gave good interviews but did not enjoy the job. His profile was rising sky high and the questions would waver between the hackneyed and the surreal. Who would he give a Grade F to? 'There are plenty of people in MotoGP I'd give this mark to,' he told Silvia Nucini in an interview for *Vanity Fair Italy*. 'They are especially the people who only think about the money at each race and don't give a shit about the riders. Passion doesn't exist for them. *Zero in Condotta* also for the journalists who have no idea about what they are writing and do not even recognize the riders. They are not all this way, but there are enough of them. Out of the paddock I give a *Zero in Condotta* to the people that give up their opinion as soon as they are faced with important people.'

The media now followed him everywhere he went. While still

enjoying a degree of normality in London, Rossi was hunted at home. He had made the headlines for crashing his Porsche on the way to a party. An image was being created. In actual fact, it had been Graziano who had crashed the car while Rossi had taken a call on his mobile in the back seat. It was becoming increasingly hard to separate truth and myth.

The shutters went up so the media sought others to get their fix. Uccio, as his most loyal friend, confidant and driver of his motorhome, was also in demand and, for a while, was happy to oblige with tales from Tavullia. 'Once Valentino and I were trying to reach a tray with sweets that was on a shelf,' he told a journalist. 'Since we couldn't reach it, I asked Valentino to put another chair on top of the one we were already using. You can probably imagine what happened, the chair moved, Valentino lost his balance, I couldn't hold him and he ended up with a broken arm.'

Gibo Badioli, his manager, was another. 'The secret of this guy is that on the one hand he is even more uncomplicated than he seems and on the other hand he is much more complex than you may think. Everyone that describes him maybe knows one part of him. He then quoted from a song by Francesco de Gregori, likening him to Buffalo Bill and Jesus Christ.

Things were getting out of hand. Rossi had taken a quantum leap by leaving Honda, but the references to Elvis and Jesus showed how the reality had been clouded by hype. Rossi had not helped to that end by breaking his own lap record at Sepang in January, forcing him to downplay his prospects. Yamaha had failed to win a single race the previous season and had not won the title since Wayne Rainey had pipped Mick Doohan by four points in 1992, but the test had raised expectations and there were problems at Honda that fed the optimism. Few doubted that Sete Gibernau and Max Biaggi were Rossi's main threats, but the factory Honda bikes were going to Nicky Hayden and Alex Barros, who had finished a distant fifth and ninth in the championship in 2003. Honda vowed to build a bike to 'crush' Rossi, but Yamaha pulled out all the stops. The entire philosophy had changed with Rossi insisting the power delivery was all wrong. Having jumped ship, Rossi would now sink or swim. It was an almighty gamble.

Welkom was a strange setting for a new era. The place was a throwback, set amid the gold fields of Free State and with the words 'Speed Kills' inscribed on the back of the 'Welcome to Welkom' sign. The endemic racism that had torn the country asunder during apartheid still rumbled on. In the bar at the press centre a couple of locals had bluffed their way in and, powered by several beers, began to turn nasty. They then questioned the masculinity of myself and Mark Graham, another journalist, for our views. We left just in time.

On the Thursday night I went for dinner with Nick Harris, the Dorna press officer, and Randy Mamola, now working as a commentator for Eurosport. We bumped into Chaz Davies, who was there with his dad and Casey Stoner. It was still tough for Chaz and he would not make the top ten in the 250cc class until they got to Brno in August. Casey, though, was gathering a reputation for speed in tandem with crashing. He had won the final 125cc race of the 2003 season at Valencia, keeping his nerve as Hector Barbera ran wide at the death, and felt he could now threaten for the title with the KTM team. It was hard not to feel a tinge of sadness at how these friends' paths were diverging.

Rossi wondered whether Yamaha were capable of pushing for a podium. Jerry Burgess had told him that they were. Rossi respected Burgess more than anyone, which is why he had celebrated when the methodical Australian said he and his team would be following him to Yamaha after all. Rossi remembered the first time he had met Burgess at a track on his debut for Honda and had been stunned by the horrible woolly jumper and the ancient toolbox in the back of a rented van. But Burgess had remained the best purveyor of reality checks and he had delivered another when he said the Yamaha could make rapid strides and win from day one. 'Are you sure?' Rossi had asked incredulously. Burgess gave into a knowing, thin smile. 'I've never gone into a season not thinking I could win the world title,' he said. 'I'm not playing at it.'

Publicly, Rossi tried to relieve the pressure at every available opportunity. 'I have only ridden this bike from January and we have not done enough kilometres in testing,' he said at his daily briefing. 'It will be a good year if we finish in the top three and improve the bike.' It was impossible not to go over old ground, though. 'My work was done with Honda and I don't know if I had enough power to stay for another two years,' Rossi explained again. 'If I had I might have won another two championships, but this is a new adventure. The atmosphere at Yamaha is more gentle because they have not won for so long. If I won last year people said it was because of the bike. If I was second it was a disaster. This was not true and now I have more enthusiasm. Beating Honda would be a great satisfaction.'

The first race was stunning. Rossi led but was overhauled by the stalking Biaggi after three laps. That dive down the inside lit Rossi's fuse and the lead exchanged hands four more times. The last came with two laps to go and was a hard, aggressive move that smacked of desperation and forced both men to run wide. Biaggi hung on and rallied himself for one last move. In the garage Rossi's crew watched and wondered. Uccio, always a nervous wreck, clasped his hands together. Badioli might have counted the dollars. Even by Rossi's vertiginous standards, this was something else. The press centre hummed. Biaggi was smooth and precise, as he always was at his best, while Rossi's bike tossed him around. The effort was intense and the gap negligible, but it stayed constant and Rossi won by two-tenths of a second.

The press room broke out into a spontaneous round of

applause. The Yamaha garage went wild. On the screen they watched as Rossi came to halt by a tyre wall, dismounted and sat down on the grass. He bowed his head and, though he would later deny it, appeared to be crying. Then he kissed *her*.

We were in Welkom because Suzuka had been dropped from the calendar. The traditional curtain-raiser had paid the price for Kato's accident. Prior to the start of the season the official report into his death was published. Professor Ichiro Kageyama of Nihon University's College of Industrial Technology chaired the report which effectively absolved Honda of any blame. 'According to the on-board data, we conclude that the engagement of the front brake abruptly changed the load on the rear wheel, which lifted almost entirely off the ground, causing a lateral skid,' the report read.

The detailed analysis made it clear that any blame lay with the circuit organizers and a gap in the barrier on the wall. 'As the foam barrier was unable to completely absorb the motor-cycle's substantial kinetic energy at that point, the bike flipped forward into the air, springing up higher than the top of the foam barrier, and landing in the grassy area to the left side of the course 48 metres forward from where it initially struck the tyre barrier.

'After impacting the foam barrier, Kato was separated from his bike. He plunged head first into the foam barrier, and was then thrown into the air. Rotating horizontally through the air in the manner of a discus, he landed face up in the centre of the course 33 metres forward and to the right of the point where he first struck the tyre barrier.'

It was an elaborate way of saying what everyone knew – that the wall was too close. Safety meetings were now held prior to every grand prix, but sometimes a representative was too busy with promotional duties or the business of racing. Only Rossi always fulfilled all his commitments.

After South Africa Rossi realized dream-catching was a trying task. In the rain of Jerez he was off the rostrum for the first time since his rear tyre had delaminated under pressure from Kato in the Czech Republic in 2002. The next race saw him embarrassed as he stalled at the start of the warm-up lap. He then infringed rules by having four mechanics and Mike Trimby, the IRTA general secretary, help him get going. Most people felt Rossi should have started from the pitlane rather than the front row and the knives re-emerged, the media accusing Dorna of bending the rules in his favour. By the time the series got to Mugello for an emotion-charged Italian Grand Prix, Rossi was fifteen points behind Gibernau in the championship and five adrift of Biaggi.

It did not look good for him. Mugello is a track suited to power and there was no doubt Honda held sway in that department. Rossi had a bespoke helmet for the race with a wooden medal design, a self-deprecating joke against himself after his failure to get onto the podium, and was heard whingeing in the preamble. He was not alone. Neil Hodgson was now the latest Briton trying to rub shoulders and ruffle feathers with the elite. He had made bold pre-season predictions about only coming when the deal was right and the bike competitive. He was the World Superbike champion but Carl Fogarty had damned it as a hollow triumph in a weakened field and, while Hodgson would never agree with his fellow Lancastrian, he needed a challenge. He was, in effect, Rossi-lite.

And then he arrived at D'Antin Ducati and, like Davies and others before him, tasted the bitter truth. Mechanical failure on his debut in Welkom was followed by further misery in the wet of Spain and a horrendous accident at Le Mans in which he brought down John Hopkins. The American was spitting blood afterwards, but his two broken thumbs were as nothing compared with Hodgson's problems – two broken ribs, torn shoulder muscles and two fractured vertebrae. At the very least his insistence on riding ended any lingering doubts about the quality of his backbone.

Prior to Mugello I flew to the Isle of Man where Hodgson was now living in a wet and windy tax haven. He said he had given himself three years to win the MotoGP world crown, which sounded hopelessly ambitious, not least given his sombre mood. 'People said the atmosphere in GPs was more cut-throat and not as friendly,' he moaned. 'They are right but it's not the riders. I flew back from a test in first class with Rossi and a more down-to-earth unassuming bloke you could not wish to meet. But the mechanics and the hangers-on! Jesus! You've never seen so many egos. I'm walking down the paddock and someone will give me a dirty look. I'm biting my lip and thinking, "Don't you bloody look down your nose at me." My view is that wheel-cleaner, tyre-fitter, rider – we all do the same job. We all go racing.'

He was not a happy figure. I remembered the fun of World Superbikes and pitching up at a hotel near the Monza circuit one night where Hodgson's mechanics were in the throes of a drunken night. In the hotel restaurant they had cleared the tables and were taking it in turns to jump over a growing number of bodies on a mountain bike. Needless to say, it all ended in tears and a big bill. MotoGP was more serious and there was a sense of self-regard about some of the employees. It was populated by job-sworths and hangers-on whose *raison d'être* was preventing people from going into their hospitality suites.

'The Isle of Man is a fantastic place to live,' Hodgson said as he looked out of his hotel window in Douglas. 'There's no crime and I never lock the car because there's nowhere for anyone to take it. I never get asked for autographs because a lot of films get made here for tax reasons and they're used to well-known faces.' He looked over to his wife, Kathryn, and asked, 'Johnny Depp's here at the moment isn't he?' Kathryn shook her head. 'I'd know if he was.' They were a happy couple, a world away from the sleazy side of the street where one MotoGP team member confessed his rider had demanded he watch him have sex with his girlfriend as it was the only way he could get aroused.

For all the domestic bliss and family harmony, Hodgson had the racer's need to prove himself, which is why he had become embroiled in a media-inflated rift with Fogarty. 'All I said was Mick Doohan was a better rider than Carl,' Hodgson muttered. 'Everyone knows that. Even Carl knows that. I'm not putting Carl down because what he achieved was fantastic.' Hodgson paused. 'But he never went to GPs.'

It was the line that was always thrown at Fogarty and so here was Hodgson, trying not to make the same mistakes but struggling among the also-rans. 'I met a bloke from Michelin at a winter test and asked why we didn't have any tyres. He said because my team hadn't paid for any.' He raised his eyebrows. 'The bottom line is the team wasn't ready for the start of the season. Then you've got Honda who are going a second faster than last year and Yamaha who have upped their game and are going 1.5 seconds quicker.'

Did he regret it now that he was licking his wounds in a hyperbaric oxygen chamber? 'I feel like I've been hit by a sledgehammer,' he said. 'If I've had seventy crashes in my career then that was in the top ten. If I was a footballer I'd be out for the season, but this is motorcycling. I stop myself because I find myself crying on the shoulders of mates who have really crap jobs. I'm moaning like hell and then I realize this guy earns £170 a week working in a factory. Yeah, I could have stayed in superbikes. Sure. But when I go to bed at night I know it wouldn't be enough.'

All around the paddock people needed a big result in Tuscany. Foremost among the desperate was Hayden, who had finished eleventh in Le Mans, was almost forty points adrift of Gibernau and was being outgunned by his team-mate, the veteran Barros. Ever since he was a twelve-year-old driving his father's car across mid-America at 100mph, police sirens sounding in his wake, Hayden had been on the fast track to the big time. Barros, with

196 MotoGP races behind him, had been recruited as a reliable figure capable of stopping the bleeding, but more had been expected of the twenty-two-year-old. It was not happening, though, and the naysayers were questioning Honda's choice. In a tent at the back of the hospitality suite, he drank a Coke and talked over Earl's guttural growl in the background. 'It wasn't easy being Rossi's team-mate last year,' he said. 'We didn't really work together, he was winning and I was struggling. I'd been doing great in America and everything was going smoothly, but then I came to GPs and I had to check my ego. It was like starting from the bottom.'

Earl would glance over now and again. Like Stan Hailwood before him, he had brought his kids up to fend for themselves but he also knew they needed him. Hayden had been homesick the previous year and now he had decided to fly back to the States whenever he could between races. It was tiring and expensive, but Hayden had spoken to Freddie Spencer, another gifted rider sometimes deemed emotionally fragile, and had decided it was the best option. The most alarming thing for Hayden, and indeed Honda, was his strengths had been leavened by the advance of technology. It was felt that when the series had embraced the giant four-strokes, the way ahead was to recruit former superbike riders like Hayden, Colin Edwards, Troy Bayliss and Hodgson. But the improvements in traction control and better tyres meant the physicality of the superbike riders was being negated. Hayden was backing himself to pull through and had Earl there to cheerlead. 'Look, my background hardened me,' he said. 'Travelling around with my brothers in the back of a van. I was riding when I could walk and had my first race when I was five. My dad rode, my mother rode, my sister rode – it's in the blood.'

Hayden admitted one popular story was untrue – that he once installed a trackside rocking chair for his grandfather – but the farm boy image and family ties were unquestionable. Earl liked telling the tale of how he let the young Nicky drive him to a race in Washington State while he slept in the back. Only the peal of the police cars woke Earl, who scrambled into the front before pulling over. 'I felt I was under a lot more pressure last season,' Hayden said. 'Honda just didn't want me crashing because these bikes are no toy. But Honda have a lot of old guys and maybe they won't be here for long. I want to be part of the future.'

It looked bleak for Hayden as the year wore on. He broke his collarbone and tore knee ligaments after falling off a Supermoto bike, resulting in a metal plate and seven screws being inserted into the damage. At the final race of the year in Valencia, Tommy and Roger Lee would join their brother in a show of support, only for their car to be broken into, forcing all three to drive to Madrid to get replacement passports. It seemed like Hayden was going nowhere fast. There were five Hondas ahead of him in the standings and he had failed to win a single race in two seasons. For many he had become a totem of Honda's folly.

The atmosphere at Mugello was manic. The heat was intimidating and the fans almost rabid with expectation. Down at the Poggio Secco corner stood three Scotsmen in kilts wearing T-shirts with an Italian slogan. The loose translation was 'Valentino Rossi for President of Scotland'. 'He's brought the masses back to bike racing,' one said. 'He's just pure entertainment.'

Nearby were David and Jean Lace, a Cumbrian couple who had recently gone to Tavullia to see where their idol came from. They had passed the church where Father Don Cesare was known to postpone Mass to watch Rossi race and where the bells rang out after each victory. Unbeknown to the Laces, they then stumbled into the headquarters of the Tribe of the Chihuahua where they were promptly adopted. Now they were at Mugello as special guests. 'They brought us, fed us, watered us,' Jean said. 'They even picked us up from the airport in their motorhome. We were stunned.'

Uccio's father, Rino, was there that day. He ran the Fan Club now and sometimes wondered how it had grown from a band of nine co-drinkers to an organization that required four secretarial staff. 'Valentino has a special character, free and open, free with words, he loves to play and is the same when he comes home as when he went away.' It was easy to find people with similar views as the staccato growl of engine tuning punctuated the summer haze. 'He is sincere and has something special inside,' Piero Meratti said. 'He has the same spirit as someone like Ayrton Senna.' Meratti had painted his Mercedes van in the blue and yellow of Rossi's Yamaha, which you would put down to teenage infatuation were it not for the fact he was well into his sixties.

A few yards from Meratti was a woman named Leticia who showed off a photograph attached to a neck chain. 'My son was killed in a motorcycle accident and we formed a group in his memory,' she said. 'He was such a big motorcycle fan, only twenty-two years old. Valentino has been so kind to me that it has given me the strength to carry on.' Davide, a nine-year-old, said, 'We talk about Valentino in school like other kids talk about pop stars.' They were all there, the men in kilts, the women in love, the boys in thrall and the pensioners in blue and yellow vans, all waiting for a miracle.

Gibernau qualified fastest followed by Hayden, finally showing some resilience, and Rossi. The drama was intense and even harrowing as Shinya Nakano suffered a traumatic crash at close to 200mph. Nakano was catapulted along the fastest straight on the calendar and came to a stop with his head resting against a concrete wall. The marshals leapt into action to clear the track of shredded rubber and green shrapnel from the demolished Kawasaki. Nakano raised his arms to show he was uninjured, except for what was later diagnosed as a broken thumb. The riders who had seen the green blur from the corner of an eye caught their breath and ploughed on, all except Alex Hofmann, the other Kawasaki rider, who saw the debris and slowed. The crash inevitably evoked awful memories of Kato and served as a reminder of how courageous the battle at the front truly was.

A lap after the crash Gibernau sampled the lead for the first time, but there was little daylight between a gaggle of riders including Rossi, Biaggi and Makoto Tamada, his Camel Honda team-mate. There was no quarter given and the lead changed hands twenty-eight times during some of the most dramatic racing Mugello had ever witnessed.

Tamada was the surprise member of the group but he felt a vibration from the rear of the bike. Having witnessed Nakano's rear tyre disaster, he slowed to a disappointing finale. Hayden was out too, paying the price for his ambition as he tried to make up ground on the leaders. Rossi had snaffled the lead from Gibernau and was dazzling the crowd at Poggio Secco and beyond, but the Spaniard had a nice rhythm and felt he could take Rossi at will. It was a question of whether to hold off and surprise him or take the first available opportunity and then defend aggressively. The decision was taken out of their hands as the rain came, meaning the Italian Grand Prix would be settled by a six-lap sprint with grid positions taken from the situation when the heavens opened.

That meant Rossi, Gibernau and Biaggi formed the front row, but the rain had made a mockery of the previous seventeen laps and it was anyone's race now. Norick Abe, one of Rossi's boyhood heroes, led the charge and Barros also hit the front. More surprising still, Ruben Xaus, Neil Hodgson's beleaguered team-mate, took over briefly, as did Troy Bayliss on the factory Ducati. It looked as if Mugello might witness a crazily contrived result, but Rossi held his nerve and overhauled the interlopers. He went on to win by three-tenths of a second from Gibernau, who griped that the rain had aided Rossi. 'I don't know if his fans were doing a rain dance or something, because I felt I had a good chance of winning if we'd continued,' he said. Rossi was rendered almost speechless and did not bother countering. He had won the race twice in his mind and, with a hill of fans chanting his name, said it was the most emotional experience of his life. That slight from Gibernau did not go unnoticed, though, and would be returned with interest as the season exploded into anger and alliances were severed.

There had been a time when Rossi and Gibernau would meet up in Ibiza to discuss nightclubs and property prices. Not any more. Gibernau's remark after that coruscating Italian Grand Prix was a black mark against him, as far as Rossi was concerned. The dispute over whether Gibernau had overtaken under a yellow flag waved as Nakano lay prostrate by a wall was another. Ominously for Gibernau, the stunts were back too, Rossi wearing a stethoscope and placing it against his Yamaha after winning on the Spaniard's home turf in Barcelona. 'I was just checking everything is OK and the girl is fine,' Rossi quipped.

The relationship came to an end at Assen when the pair clashed on the last lap. Gibernau clearly felt Rossi had been dangerously aggressive and had a snapped mudguard to prove it, but the Italian said he had nearly fallen and that any block had been an innocent accident.

I met Gibernau in a small office below the main stand at the Sachsenring ahead of the German Grand Prix and the memory of Assen was still burning inside him. He was in a foul mood. 'Is this going to take long?' he snapped. Riders were like this. I had suffered it with Bayliss the previous year. For some reason he had taken exception to a piece I had written about him, which I had thought was honest and, if anything, complimentary. He collared me in Ducati's hospitality suite and said, 'You ever write anything else like that and you won't speak to me again.' Bayliss had a reputation for being one of the nicest riders in the paddock, but he was a straight-talking Aussie and hard as nails. I remembered one of the photographers telling me how they had seen him challenge a mechanic to a competition in which they beat plastic containers into a pulp with their bare hands. 'His knuckles were a mess and there was blood everywhere,' he recalled.

I could understand Gibernau being tetchy in Germany. He and Rossi were tied on the same number of points, had synchronized crashes in Rio two weeks earlier, and he probably sensed it was this year or never. Rossi's move in Assen had also shown just how hard it was going to be to win from here on. 'I don't compare myself with anyone,' he said sniffily. 'I've always had the talent but now I have the tools. What happened in Assen is history. Valentino needed something desperate like that because, without it, he knew he couldn't beat me. He took it to the complete limit, but I have nothing against him.' He then suggested Rossi get a bit of perspective. 'Why do you have to hate anyone? We don't have the right to get upset about racing.'

Chaz Davies was thinking the same. He was struggling along and knew a podium was a distant dream, but it was only a few days since the funeral of Jaroslav Hules, his former team-mate when he first arrived on the grand prix circuit. Hules had ridden his last race the previous season and had grown increasingly depressed. So much so that he had tried to hang himself in his home town of Pisek on his thirtieth birthday and had died in hospital six days later. 'He was a great bloke but totally crazy,' Davies told me years later. 'He could be completely mad and good fun, but then there were also times when he was really down.' Midway through their season together Jarda had quit the team and ditched his manager, claiming he was pushing him too hard and the pressure was too much to bear.

The pressure got to Gibernau in Germany and he crashed again. Suddenly, it was Biaggi who was back in the role of chief antagonist. He trailed Rossi by a single point after fending off Barros' factory Honda, and was relishing seeing his nemesis show signs of vulnerability on the Yamaha. The mantra had come true and Biaggi was intent on fulfilling his prophecy and ramming years of insults down his detractor's throat. However, with the title race so close it was inevitable that Rossi would start to play games and, as ever, he twisted his words to twist his opponents.

Against this backdrop the British Grand Prix now assumed huge importance. Rossi sat in the grotty hangar with its makeshift desks on the Thursday and sprinkled seeds of discontent. 'It is the Honda Racing Corporation versus Valentino Rossi,' he said dramatically. 'I had a good relationship with my engineers at Honda, but not with the leaders. I had to leave. Now it is me against six Hondas. In the last race in Germany I needed a lion-tamer for the bike. For sure, I am more on edge than the Honda guys and, when you are on the limit, it is possible to make a mistake and for your tyres to wear out.'

Now that Biaggi was twelve points closer to him in the standings, Rossi delivered a carefully planned punchline. 'For me, Sete is faster than Biaggi.' The use of Christian names had a clear role in Rossi's power play. 'When I fight with Sete I feel the difference between the engines is not so much, but when I race Biaggi I feel he rides a bit slower but his engine is better. Us? We are a little bit in the shit.'

It did not show. Rossi qualified on pole and rode superbly to win at a track he loves. Gibernau was only third and Biaggi, having been belittled and badmouthed, was a distant twelfth through no fault of his own. He limped away from the garage with a bloody foot after his gear-shifter failed. There were plenty of races left but the momentum had gone. Rossi laughed with journalists and said when he heard the rain on Sunday morning he was in the toilet with a noose around his neck, an inappropriate comment in light of Hules' death, but nobody said anything. The king was back.

The finale to that season was riotously entertaining and summed up the psychological strength of Rossi. Chris Herring, once of Honda, believes the force of Rossi's will played a major role in his success. 'To be honest, Biaggi was not a very clever person. He tried to play mind games with people but they could read him like a book. It's clear people like Melandri and Gibernau had mental issues. You saw a peak and trough pattern to their results. That's inherent in a lot of riders. Hats off to Rossi, the guy's been there week in, week out for years. And if the guy can beat you on the track, he can absolutely destroy you off it.'

Gibernau was destroyed over the course of one week in October. The evening before the first Qatari Grand Prix, Rossi would claim he saw Biaggi's mechanics cleaning his grid spot, an illegal practice but, given the amount of sand being blown on to the circuit, a good way of ensuring more grip. Yamaha's response to this was hardly subtle and a number of mechanics performed burnouts on team scooters in an attempt to leave some rubber on Rossi's starting position. Unsurprisingly, given the paddock thrives on gossip and intrigue, their actions were known to all by race day. Numerous teams wanted to protest against Yamaha, but as the result would be the same, race direction only took one. As it happened this was from Repsol Honda. The upshot was Rossi was given a six-second penalty which meant he started from the back of the grid. He fumed. His clarity of thought was hampered by a sense of injustice, but he channelled the bitterness to fly from the back of the grid to eighth place by the end of a devilish first lap. He was thinking too fast, though. Driven to avenge himself he roared his way into contention before crashing out. On the last lap Gibernau finally noticed Rossi's bike on the side of the track and his heart skipped a beat. The championship lead had been trimmed from thirty-nine points to an assailable fourteen.

Rossi used the next week to foster a sense of grievance and he pointed the finger at Gibernau, even though several teams had complained about Yamaha's actions. However, Repsol's riders, Hayden and Barros, were irrelevant to the title race, so Rossi managed to convince the Italian media that he had been the victim of a conspiracy led by Gibernau. Biaggi was far more culpable given that his team had been guilty of the same tactics and, indeed, he had also been sent to the back of the grid, but Rossi placed Gibernau at the centre of the row and sought to dismantle him before the next, pivotal race in Malaysia.

He stormed into a live interview on Italian television and called the protest *bastardata*, 'a bastard act'. Gibernau, meanwhile, was labelled a 'spy' and a 'baby' while his race engineer, Juan Martinez, having once worked with Rossi, was painted as a traitor. This would have been knockabout stuff but for Rossi's thespian powers. At the pre-race press conference he sat stone-faced and let everyone know he had been sinned against. Gibernau, a decent man who would rather have been Rossi's friend, was lured into defending himself. 'It was HRC who protested,' he said. The pair sat side by side at the frostiest of press conferences and Gibernau's unease was palpable. 'Racing is cruel and we have all been there,' he mused. 'In the heat of the moment we all say things, but as far as I'm concerned, it is over.' Rossi was not about to let the matter lie, though, and assumed the moral high ground again. 'Sete started all this. He behaved like a baby and played the role of spy. I feel exactly the same way I did last Saturday.'

Jerry Burgess said that he marked the track in exactly the same way during his time with both Mick Doohan and Wayne Rainey. Rossi then finished the debate after Gibernau had unsuccessfully tried to defend himself for something he had not done. 'I've been looking for an excuse to stop talking to him and now I have it,' Rossi bleated. 'It's a knife in the back.'

Rossi won the race in imperious fashion, never looking in danger once he had slipped past Barros in the early exchanges. Biaggi, no longer worth venting a spleen over, was a long way adrift in second while Gibernau suffered from chatter and was only seventh. Rossi was not finished with him, though, and indulged in a post-race stunt that was pure panto. Still clad in his retro Gauloises leathers and yellow crescent helmet, he dismounted and was handed a broom whereupon he started pawing at the track. Soon afterwards the T-shirts were handed out. Rossi and Burgess both pulled them on. The slogan was La Rapida cleaning services and the cartoon image was of the king and his chief in Mrs Mop mode. To add further insult to injury, Rossi then let it be known Gibernau would not win again. He later claimed he meant in 2004, but this became known as the Rossi curse and, with each passing failure, the pressure and embarrassment on Gibernau grew.

The 'gift to the world' was wrapped up and delivered at Phillip Island in Australia, the penultimate race of the year. Biaggi was disgruntled. His mantra had been exposed as flawed thinking, but he wondered why he could not have got Yamaha to reorganize in the way Rossi had. Furusawa provided a radically revised crankshaft and a longer chassis, while Rossi worked tirelessly on set-up, especially on the bumpy tracks that rendered him a 'lion-tamer'.

He was happy to rub salt into Honda's seeping wounds. 'Honda did not treat me well,' he said, a comment that provoked real anger in a factory that had given him the best bikes in the business and a leg up to the Forbes rich list. 'They treat you like a state employee. You can win thirty GPs and all they try to do is belittle the achievements you had. Their attitude pissed me off.'

Amid all the trash-talking, the fact was Rossi had done something nobody expected. I bumped into Wayne Gardner, the former world champion, in Australia and he gave his appraisal. 'I never thought he could do it.' The pack was demoralized. 'I just want this season over,' said Neil Hodgson, who would end up seventeenth a year on from being a world champion. Shakey Byrne, another Brit, was twentieth and battered after the highside in which he landed on his head in the Czech Republic. Bayliss, meanwhile, was reflecting on being sacked by the factory Ducati team. 'It's the final kick in the teeth,' he said. Garry McCoy, another oft-bruised Aussie, was the most demoralized of all. 'It's really tough with Honda and Yamaha dominating,' he said. 'Your confidence level drops so much you just don't feel like racing any more.'

Rossi, as is his wont, won the title on the last lap. It was a thriller. 'The last lap was incredible, unbelievable,' he said and he was not exaggerating. Rossi and Gibernau, the two best riders of the year, swapped the lead three times. The last came when Rossi ran around the outside at Lukey Heights. In the garage his brother Luca cheered. Stefania hugged him. It was a breathtaking move and cut the core of Rossi. He liked the excitement and the drama whereas others would win via the percentages if they could.

The only question, voiced in the aftermath, was whether anyone could stop him. He had won four successive crowns, a feat only matched by Hailwood, Agostini and Doohan. He had already beaten Agostini's mark of twenty-two successive podiums and was now only the second man, after Eddie Lawson, to win back-to-back titles on different makes of motorcycle. It seemed that only his own ambition might derail the record-breaking. The rumours about Ferrari were mounting and there were precedents. Hailwood, still regarded by many as the greatest, raced in Formula One, while Surtees had followed up four 500cc crowns by driving a Ferrari to the 1964 title.

Everyone agreed there was more of Hailwood about Rossi. The Bentley-chauffeured Briton had a voracious appetite for life, won a George Medal and celebrated a TT triumph with blood pouring from his chin. If there was a ring of apocrypha about Hailwood it was because, like Rossi, he seemed too good to be true.

LAP 5

The conversation with Mick Grant had buoyed Mike. All this time away and he had come to the same conclusions about the opposition as one of the modern guys. They had spent that evening going through the entry list for the 1978 TT and assessing each racer's strengths and weaknesses. Mike had nothing to fear but himself. *The comeback* was on.

Like no end of racers Mike was at his most comfortable on the bike. He was a natural. There was something metaphysical about the way he sunk into it like a centaur, but he was buggered if he knew how he did it. Mike had little clue about the mechanics of his success. The great Ago could tell if his bike was half a centimetre shorter than another and would put tape on his brakes so that water would not seep in if the rain came. 'Mike was a very, very good rider but he didn't care about the bike,' Ago said when we met at his Bergamo villa in the winter of 2008. 'They were all the same to him.' Ago, by contrast, was a perfectionist and would seek out every tiny advantage. Mike just assumed he would win.

He was a raging conundrum of confidence and insecurity, which is why Ted was so pleased to see flickers of excitement in the face opposite him. Mike was telling him how he had almost hit a sheep while riding around the island to get used to it again. He had slammed on the brakes and his old pal, Jim Scaysbrook, busy watching a man digging in the neighbouring field, had careered into the back of him. It had been a miracle that neither man had fallen. Ted could imagine the fury on the faces of the Martini chiefs if they knew how close their man had been to disaster. They were not even into practice week and *the comeback* was throwing up little dramas.

Ted had a drink that night but Mike abstained. That might have surprised the party in the bar at the Castle Mona, with their biker jackets, flared jeans and wayward bouffants, but the image of Mike as a heavy-drinking playboy was only partly true. Sure he could be wild. In the company of close friends he was the epi-centre of the party, downing his vodka and lemonades with a devil-may-care profligacy, but he was also a professional. 'Mike was not stupid,' Ago would say. 'He drank when he had the opportunity, but it was not as if he was drunk every night. He drank like you and me, well maybe a little bit more, but I went looking for him on the Isle of Man one year and he was in his bed-room at 9 p.m., drinking mineral water. People say, "Oh yeah, Mike was a drinker", but it was not like that.'

The vodka and the beer flowed like rainwater one night in Rimini. The group, including Mike and Ralph Bryans, ran up a mammoth bill. They returned the following night, but suspecting they had been taken for a ride by the bar manager, decided to pay as they went this time. 'We still got a massive bill at the end of the night,' Ralph recalled. 'We tried to explain, but they weren't listening. There was a heated argument and when we left the local hoods were waiting for us. One guy got smacked in the eye and was in a bad way for a month. Then Mike hit someone so hard that he broke two fingers and could not race the following week. It was Phil Read who had the last word, though. Just when it had all calmed down he picked up a brick and heaved it through the nightclub's window.'

This was part of the racing culture of the swinging 60s and the bikers were guilty as often as innocent. Ginger Molloy, a New Zealander, became renowned for escaping restaurants without reimbursing proprietors and was a key figure in the Opatija nightclub riot in Yugoslavia; another row over a bill resulted in a floored chief of police, a full-scale brawl, several split skulls and a number of riders being locked up.

It was an era of raw characters such as Edy Lenz, an Austrian racer and rumoured owner of a Viennese whorehouse, and Bo Granath, a Swedish privateer and suspected booze runner. 'Please tell me honestly,' Bo's wife once asked Mack. 'Is Bo smuggling narcotics?' She was at a loss to understand where the money was coming from.

There was also Paddy Driver, one of Mike's closest friends whom he had befriended during his early days racing in South Africa. Paddy had a clipped black beard, rugged good looks and a love of guns. The first time Jim Redman had gone to his house he had stayed in the car while Paddy had danced around the drive with a .45 revolver in one hand and .38 in the other, whooping and hollering and firing bullets into the air. Jim later noticed bullet holes in the walls and ceiling of Paddy's house. When Mike started staying with Paddy he was a shy boy who wanted to be left alone, so he shut his bedroom door and played his banjo. Paddy soon enticed him out and the two shot tin cans down the bottom of the garden. 'We partied a lot and the police often came,' Paddy said fondly of those times. 'Once we were at Clermont-Ferrand with a couple of car drivers. We went outside and let the air out of the police car tyres. They didn't like that and let off a few shots. The bullets were ricocheting off telegraph poles and buildings.'

Despite his background at Highmore Hall and Pangbourne Nautical College, Mike fitted in with this motley crew of gifted reprobates. One night at Spa Tommy Robb was woken by a strange, mechanical noise. He stumbled out of his bed and went to the window of his caravan, where he saw Mike. Tommy rapped on the window. 'What are you doing?' Mike looked up and, even through the muddied window, Tommy could tell he was paralytic. 'Go to shleep,' Mike slurred. The caravan lurched and Tommy jerked backwards. He went to the rear of the caravan and noticed Ralph at the back with a jack. He later found out that their grand plan had been to hitch him to their van and tow him to middle of the Masta straight about five miles away.

Having been sent packing, Mike and Ralph staggered towards the next caravan, belonging to Gyula Marsovsky. The unsuspecting Swiss racer was soon jolted into consciousness after Mike attached electrodes from a Honda generator to his fingers. That was the time. It was one for living in the bloody, brilliant moment and trying to banish thoughts about your three yearly lives.

The results kept coming for Mike in 1963. He had expected Gilera to mount a threat but it never happened. He won six straight races on his MV and attracted the occasional whinge about his superior machinery. The snipers had a point as he was competing against singles, but they all knew Mike could ride. At the Sachsenring that year he won three grands prix in a day – the 250cc, 350cc and 500cc races – and he added another senior TT title that summer. He was both irresistible force and immovable object.

But the demons still lingered. He was the happy drunk but he was also given to periods of introspection. Tommy sampled that side of Mike much later when they drove into Spa one night. Adjourning to a bar, Mike fixed Tommy with a wistful look. 'Tommy, you travel with the paddock lads week in, week out. I'm not thrown into the same contact like you, I just wondered, Tommy, what do they think of me?' His old friend was staggered by the question. Mike was a living legend, on the track and off it, and Tommy could not fathom that, despite all the trappings of success, deep down he was still plagued by the same insecurities as the common man. 'Mike,' he said, 'they think you're the greatest. What on earth makes you ask the question?' Mike took a sip of vodka. 'I was just never sure.'

Eight years on and he still wasn't sure. Some people thought he was a gimmick with a gammy leg while others thought *the comeback* was his pension. But Mike also knew there was a tidal wave of goodwill rolling in across Douglas Bay. He just hoped the present could live up to expectations imposed by the past.

CHAPTER EIGHT

RING OF FIRE

It was late. The flickers from the last campfires lit hillsides strewn with rubbish. A lone biker chugged his path along the ridge. The thick, black lines on the Mugello track and the churned earth where the fans had danced were the only betrayals of that after-noon's drama. This was the calm after the storm, the post-coital slump of satisfaction that follows any grand prix.

John Hopkins and Shakey Byrne were there. So were Colin Edwards and Kurtis Roberts, the grizzled son of King Kenny. 'Come on,' Hopper shouted. 'It'll be around here somewhere.' It was not hard to find. Biaggi's Smart car was emblazoned with his yellow and blue colour scheme, the Roman Emperor logo and a giant No. 3. The quartet laughed as they found it. Shakey had reason to be pleased after finishing tenth. He did not know it but, four races into his MotoGP career, he had peaked. The following year would be his last in MotoGP. That was the frustrating future, though, and for now Shakey was living in the bloody, brilliant moment of being a top-flight racer. 'There it is!' he shouted.

The little car stood out in the paddock. Everyone else drove bland hire cars. For the trio of blunt Americans and Shakey, who was so down to earth that he had once laid sleepers on the

London Underground, it smacked of vanity. It screamed 'Look at me!' They all felt Biaggi was precious and needed teaching a lesson and so here they were. Under the cloak of darkness they giggled and set about their clandestine mission.

Kurtis started it. He pushed the Smart car with his hands and got it to rock. The others joined in. The momentum grew until it reached the tipping point and crashed on to its side with a groan. The windows shattered. 'Fucking hell!' someone laughed. Shakey doubled up. The four friends had not finished and Kurtis picked up some rubbish lying on the floor and shoved it inside the car. The others followed. Before long Biaggi's mini-masterpiece was battered, broken and stuffed with the leftovers of race day.

That was when the door to the nearest motorhome swung open. A figure came out. It lumbered towards them through the half shadows. The guilty were now trying to fix Biaggi's car, but the wheels had come off, literally and otherwise. The new figure surveyed the scene and burst out laughing. 'No, no,' he said with one of his infectious grins. 'It's better on its roof.' The others looked at Valentino Rossi, the winner of the race that afternoon, and quickly agreed. And so Kurtis led them in barging the vehicle on to its roof so that it was upside down. Rossi was now crippled with laughter, himself, and the noise grew and other doors opened, while the racers spun the car like a top.

By the time the policeman arrived on his motorcycle, Kurtis was flushed with adrenalin. He was a hard-nosed kid from California, whose brother and dad had both been world champions. That must have been hard. Once, as a young boy, he had almost strangled Kenny junior over a game of Monopoly. He was a chip off the old blockhead too; Kenny senior did not suffer fools gladly or even miserably. As the policeman investigated the bizarre sight of an overturned car surrounded by an assortment of the world's finest motorcyclists, Kurtis fired up the police bike and tore around the Mugello circuit with the sirens blaring. Any pretence at secrecy was removed and Biaggi quickly learnt the truth. It must have hurt.

One week later they were in Barcelona for the Catalan Grand Prix. Talk of the midnight escapade the week before had filtered through to the powers-that-be and the guilty men were called before IRTA. Edwards was the first to confess. 'Yeah, man . . .' They were given a routine dressing-down and warned about their behaviour. They barely managed to stifle their sniggers but agreed to pay for repairs.

The tale of Biaggi's Smart car was indicative of his standing in the eyes of his peers. He had an unparalleled ability to get up people's noses. That was borne out at the test session at Jerez at the beginning of 2005 when Biaggi, as was his habit, rode perilously close to other riders. He shrugged off any criticism, implying the only problem was a weakness in the dissenter, but it was a little cameo of posturing and Nicky Hayden snapped. Enough was enough.

The pair had been teamed together at Repsol Honda, but it was always a rocky partnership. Biaggi, despite having the factory Honda ride that he had spent a large portion of his career craving, was far from flushed with bonhomie. Hayden, meanwhile, was suffering. He scoured newspapers for reports on the AMA series where his brothers were competing, but that world, which had been so vivid and vital for them all, was an afterthought in Europe. It meant Hayden would sometimes get up in the middle of the night to track his brothers' progress by watching the changing lap times on the AMA website. The brothers corresponded by emails and telephone, but it wasn't the same.

The Haydens had trained together at a self-styled boot camp in California before the start of the 2005 season. It had been going well and they were pushing each other on as they went cycling in the searing heat. Nobody had seen the metal pipe fall off the truck, but Nicky and Tommy noticed it lying there just in time to take evasive action. Roger Lee crashed straight over it, though, and bounced along the road. It was only when he got up that he noticed his Lycra was ripped and that a tendon was hanging out of his knee. To the brothers' amusement, Nicky had not bothered to stop. Roger Lee said that was fine. Nicky needed the training. It was going to be a hard year.

And now Biaggi was cutting him up in a test. Shit, they were on the same team. This time he had just had it. He stormed into the garage, shoved Biaggi against the wall and shouted, 'You ever do that again and I'll kill you!' Biaggi looked around at the crew, but the wronged-man expression was already wearing thin. Fuck Biaggi! Honda reprimanded him for his behaviour on the track and that fuelled his sense of injustice. He threw a hissy fit and locked himself in his motorhome. Fuck them!

This was meant to be *his* year. He was on the Repsol Honda, a legendary machine that had become synonymous with success under Mick Doohan and then Rossi. Now Biaggi had finally got what he wanted, but he was anxious. He knew what was at stake but he had suffered a serious setback when he had broken his ankle the previous November. As a result he had only had limited time on the RC211V. 'This is my most important year,' he said when we gathered in Jerez soon afterwards for the first race of the season. 'The injury put my career at risk so my motivation is really high. Everybody wants to ride a factory Honda. Nobody wants to ride a Proton. I'm sorry, but that's the reality.'

Rossi, with four successive titles behind him, for two manufacturers, was content to pour water on his own chances for 2005. He was the champion on a bike that had been developed almost beyond recognition – Yamaha arrived with a brand new chassis, gear-driven camshafts and a smaller, more sensitive engine – but he managed to place the burden of expectation squarely on Biaggi's shoulders. 'Last year we were a big surprise, but now we do not have this effect,' Rossi said when we sat down for our annual pre-season meeting in Jerez. 'All the Hondas have been fast in tests. In past years we have made big leaps, but now we need to make small changes to the bike. It is going to be hard.'

He was a master of manipulation. Rossi was the smiling assassin whose words were often subtle sideswipes designed to undermine his rivals. He was the best on the track and the best off it. 'I want to stay in MotoGP with Yamaha next year,' he said. 'We have to talk about a contract. And then, maybe rallying, maybe Formula One. Sincerely, I have not decided, but I like a challenge.' This was a coded message to Yamaha to get their finger out. It also let Biaggi and Gibernau know that he was so good he was almost bored by his success. 'I'm a little tired,' he added. 'It's difficult to have the same motivation as last year. That was special, but if I'm not motivated it's better to stay at home. Last year Honda did not take us seriously, but now they are going a hundred per cent to beat us.' He said he had more fun, a favourite word, at Yamaha. 'If I didn't win at Honda it was a disaster, if I did then they were a little bit happy.' He was also happy to bring up the misery of Qatar and Gibernau and Honda's treachery. The spy and the bastards. 'That was bad for me, but bad for him too,' Rossi said pointedly. The curse was still in place. 'He made a mess. When the battle is very close, the mental war is more difficult and he lost some motivation after that.'

Rossi was on pole with Gibernau second and Marco Melandri, his new team-mate and another prodigiously gifted Italian, completing the front row. Hayden was fourth but Biaggi was a disastrous sixteenth. It was the first race of the year, but already the pressure, exacerbated by the rift with Hayden, was on.

There were 127,000 fans in Jerez and they demanded a Gibernau victory. For once, Rossi was the enemy, an obstacle in the way of a Spanish fiesta. He slid off in morning practice and the vast banks erupted in glee. It was clear from the start that these two men were going to dominate. Hayden managed to keep pace but was wringing every vestige of boot camp brio from his body. Eventually, the pace was too much for him and he flirted with the limit just too recklessly. He crashed with seven laps left and the race was on. Rossi versus Gibernau. The new rivalry. Gibernau was fast and smooth on his Honda. Comfortable. But he knew Rossi was there. He could hear him and see him in his peripheral vision. Blue and yellow blurring. Thinking fast. Moving slowly. We do not have the right to hate, he had said, but he hated Rossi at times. He was in front but he was a fly on Rossi's windscreen.

Three laps from the end Rossi made his move and you wondered how much he had in reserve. It looked like he was toying with his favourite plaything, a fly to a wanton boy. Now he would kill him off. But Gibernau's occasional melodrama belied an igneous core. He held on and plotted. Every corner limited his options and reduced the percentages. The crowd were on their feet, pounding the bleachers and waving flags. The engines roared back and strained under the effort.

Rossi was not flawless and felt the pressure too. He wanted his rivals to think he was a carefree genius who could move mountains, but his bike was wilting beneath him. He craved an extra five metres, a quick exit, a late brake. Daylight. And then he tried too hard and messed up his braking at the end of the back straight. Gibernau's heart was squeezed up his gullet. This was the race. Right here. There was a gentle touch. For the briefest of moments they were conjoined riders. Melandri, in third place, was half a lap away. But before Gibernau had time to contemplate hanging on to the lead, it was gone. Rossi was alongside him. His nose in front. This was the thrill for him. After all the easy wins and the fight with his concentration, this was the brutal, physical contact of racing. He was now only inches behind with one corner left. Ducados. Turn 13. Unlucky for some.

What happened next would be the source of great conjecture.

What is clear is there are different ways of approaching Ducados and Gibernau left the semblance of a gap. Rossi, being a belligerent bully on a bike, was never going to sit on Gibernau's wheel and rely on his exit speed. So he pushed his bike into the gap. His left leg dangled off the footpeg as it usually does when straddling success and disaster. Gibernau tried to slam the door shut but found Rossi's handlebar wedged in the space. It bashed into Gibernau's left shoulder. Both men ran off line but Rossi had the track and turned out of Ducados to victory, while Gibernau rode into the huge sand trap to the right. He still had time to get back on and finish ten seconds ahead of Melandri but he was fuming.

Rossi celebrated in his usual style, fisting the air and waving to the massed banks of Spaniards. At first he did not realize that they were not cheering but booing. Then came an almighty chant. 'HIJO DE PUTA! HIJO DE PUTA! HIJO DE PUTA!' 'Son of a whore!' The Spanish were unamused. Rossi was already laughing and hugging in parc fermé by the time Gibernau arrived. He was not good at confrontations but knew he needed to do something. He walked past Rossi to the far corner of the small square where the first three bikes were parked. He looked at his rival and glared. Rossi ignored him and grinned widely. Uccio exchanged words with Gibernau's equivalent lackey. Gibernau held his palms out and shrugged.

Gav Emmett was there and collared Rossi for the BBC. A couple of platitudes and then he cut to the question about the last corner. Rossi was animated and buoyant. 'It was a hard overtake,' he said. 'For sure Sete is angry. But this is the races.' He also got his defence in quickly. Gibernau had touched him at the hairpin and braked in the middle of the track. The Spanish were enraged but most people passed it off as an example of audacious, off-the-bone overtaking. 'I don't think anyone will make anything of that,' Steve Parrish told Suzi Perry at trackside. He was wrong.

Tempers were simmering in the anteroom by the podium and it brought back memories of Rossi's brawl with Biaggi four years earlier. Gibernau was the first up another narrow stairway but he stopped halfway up and clutched his shoulder. Rossi looked up and raised his eyebrows into a camera. He clearly felt 'Hollywood' was acting. On the podium there was a cold pause and finally Gibernau offered the briefest of handshakes. There was no brawl this time. Gibernau was not Biaggi and suffered in relative silence. At least publicly. Behind the scenes, he called Rossi a son of a whore too, but at the press conference he merely said he had been injured in the collision with Rossi. 'Ask me about anything else but not the last lap.'

Rossi was more expansive. 'I made a big mistake on the last lap and from that moment it was a hard battle. We touched two or three times, but I had half a metre to overtake and we are here to make motorbike races.' The implication was this was a sport for grown-ups. 'This isn't ballroom dancing,' Jerry Burgess would add.

The incident provoked another letter from Frencesco Zerbi, the FIM president. In turn that sparked Fausto Gresini, Gibernau's team manager, into a bitter riposte. 'Why is he warning both riders when my man did nothing wrong?' he protested. Rossi later acknowledged that his handlebar had indeed speared Gibernau's shoulder, but he was not about to apologize. To do so would be a concession of sorts. Gibernau felt he was dignified in his response to Rossi, but many wished he would vent his spleen and front up to him. Silence just gave Rossi more room to manoeuvre.

Gibernau fell away after that. He did not get on the podium again until the fourth round at Le Mans, by which time he trailed Rossi by forty-two points. Biaggi was faring no better. Hayden was nowhere. Alex Barros won in Estoril on the Camel Honda, but nobody truly expected him to challenge Rossi. When Barros had lied about his age to enter his first grand prix, Rossi was a six-year-old sprite on a scooter, annoying his neighbours on a dusty Italian mountainside. Since then Rossi had blazed a trail out of Tavullia while the career of the journeyman from São Paulo had been a slow-burning affair. He had suffered 150 crashes and gambled his entire $2 million fortune on funding a ride in the 1990s. Burgess had scoffed at Barros' attempts to develop the RC211V the previous year, while others said seven wins from 243 grands prix was evidence of mediocrity rather than resilience. 'Last season I was not physically fit, but this time it's possible,' he said over a coffee in one of the stylish huts shrouded by decking at the back of the Shanghai paddock. 'It's about emotion this sport. You can't win anything with a cold heart.'

Rossi did not care much for Shanghai. He flew in late on Thursday, ignoring the time difference, and departed on the first available plane. In the interim he won the first MotoGP race in China on a rain-sodden track that had been lit by lightning the previous day. The state-of-the-art facilities jarred against the lack of interest, an official crowd figure of 25,000 looking optimistic to the naked eye.

For Rossi it was just another day, for Olivier Jacque it was a rebirth of sorts. He had not ridden a bike for seven months until he got the call to replace the injured Alex Hofmann on the Kawasaki. The Frenchman had been the 250cc world champion in 2000, but was dropped by Yamaha at the end of the 2003 season after a string of crashes. Since then he had been dabbling in rally driving. It meant that when he began catching Rossi in the Chinese rain, the Yamaha pit crew did not even have his name to tell their rider who was in pursuit. 'They just had an "O" on my pitboard,' Rossi said before heading straight for the airport. 'I thought, "Who is that?" I don't know an O. Is he a Chinese rider?"'
Jacque's vision was impaired by spray and steam, so he was equally unsure who he was chasing during the finale. 'I thought it looked like a blue bike and thought, "I don't remember passing

Rossi, it could be him." My visor fogged up so I had to turn my head and peek out with one eye. It is a magical result.'

Others were dumbfounded by how cavalier Rossi seemed to be taking things. He often quipped about his bad timekeeping, but this time it had almost seen him miss his plane to China. Burgess stood in the interview room, the blackening sky blurring the grandstands, and growled, 'He's always here on Sunday isn't he? That's what matters.'

He was not there on Saturday though. Yamaha China had organized a major conference and invited 600 dealers from all around the country to Shanghai. The highlight of the function was to be an appearance by Rossi. The date had been inked in for months and the top brass at Yamaha were assured Rossi would be there. He was even staying in a hotel close to where the conference was taking place. However, the day beforehand Gibo Badioli informed Yamaha China that Rossi would not be attending after all. He was tired and he did not want to be out late on the eve of a race. Unsurprisingly, Yamaha China were up in arms. Colin Edwards and the other Yamaha riders, Toni Elias and Ruben Xaus, went along, but it was not the same.

Afterwards, Edwards, Ali Forth, Lin Jarvis and Masao Furusawa went for a meal to pick over the bones. They sat in a semi-circle and were having a nice meal when Rossi walked in with Uccio, Badioli and assorted friends. They were preparing for their Saturday night out and had been caught red-handed. Rossi's face dropped for a moment, but Furusawa began to laugh at his man's audacity. Rossi then put his head on the counter and, while his entourage talked excitedly to each other and drank beer, fell sound asleep. He woke as his group were finishing their meal. Then they went out clubbing into the wee small hours. The next day he got up and won. He was, indeed, always there on Sunday.

The race in China summed up the chasm between the champion and the rest. The Jacques of the world were feeding off crumbs and seeking fleeting magic. Chaz Davies was still plugging away, but it was hard. He was not on one of the factory 250cc Hondas or the factory-assisted Aprilias and so had little cause to expect to finish in the top twelve. He managed it a few times, but tenth place did not impress the talent-spotters. The covetous eyes were looking at Dani Pedrosa, the young Spanish kid with the permafrown, and Casey Stoner, a spiky Aussie who might just be the real deal if only he could stop crashing.

'You have to put yourself in the kid's shoes,' said Randy Mamola, often regarded as the greatest rider never to win the title, when we spoke about Davies. 'At Le Mans everybody was going out in qualifying and falling off on the first straight because the rain was so torrential. Some teams were sending their riders out because they said they had to learn, but it was crazy. There was no use doing that and that's what I told Chaz. I'm trying to keep his mind healthy, sharing my experience with his inexperience.'

Mamola was a bald bundle of energy with a big heart. He felt for Davies, so he pushed him towards the Familie management company, part of the amorphous Wasserman Media Group, which had interests in Arsenal, Wembley and Formula One. Hopkins, aka Hopper, was their only other MotoGP client. 'It's hard for kids like Chaz,' Mamola said. 'He has got a lot of natural talent. Why do I think that? Because when it rains he goes out and pushes it when others don't. That shows he has confidence in his own ability.'

Davies was still enjoying himself. The arrival of Shakey Byrne had helped. Byrne was a jack-the-lad Londoner who liked a laugh and helped relieve the tedium. Thursdays were boring for racers. There was the press conference for a few top riders, but it was the dullest of days as they waited for the circus to lumber into life. Davies was kicking around the paddock in France and counting down when he saw Byrne walking towards him carrying a large tray in front of him.

'What's that?'

'Eggs,' said Byrne.

'Eggs?'

'Yeah. Come on. Let's go for a drive.'

They found Hopper and went down into Le Mans and pulled up opposite a bus stop. A few people were looking hopefully down the grey road. Hopper put the windows down and then the trio started throwing the eggs at the side of the shelter. That was how MotoGP racers passed the time on a Thursday.

Byrne was good company. Other British riders had come and gone, but Davies gelled with the older man and they managed to put their on-track problems behind them as they took advantage of MotoGP's afterlife. It had been a riot when they went into a bar in Brazil after the race there. Everyone loved Brazil and the women seduced by the scent of MotoGP. In that Rio bar Byrne caught the eye of a transvestite and nudged Davies. 'Bloody hell, Chadwick, look at that!' The bleached blonde hair, red lipstick and oversized hands meant she cut an incongruous figure. That was when Hopper went over and started chatting to her. The next thing they knew Hopper had his arm around her. Byrne could not contain himself. He laughed violently as he and Davies watched their friend in action. When Hopper finally came over, Byrne cried, 'Fucking hell, John, have you not seen the Adam's apple on that?' Hopper took a swig of his beer. 'He didn't give a shit,' Davies recalled.

Hopper was out again in Mugello. It was a year after they had wrecked Biaggi's car. The race had been mesmerizing as Biaggi found his old form and battled wheel for wheel with Rossi. It was like old times. Rossi fought hard and won. Biaggi was three tenths of a second behind but had wrung every iota of power from the Repsol Honda. It was a race that made you wonder just why he could not do it every week. Loris Capirossi was third for an ecstatic Ducati and the paddock raised a collective smile. His wife, Ingrid, had shown her devotion by getting Capirossi's signature tattooed on one of her ankles, which was now moving swiftly down the paddock in a high heel. Marco Melandri had made his own mark by finishing in a carefully crafted fourth. 'You watch Marco,' Mack would routinely tell me when we passed in the paddock. 'He's going to be the one.'

The Motor Sports Manufacturers Association announced that the engines would be smaller from 2007. Something had to be done to stop these beasts from wrecking lap records with a death wish. So they would come down from 990cc to 800cc. The vote was unanimous but there was a murmur of discord from the fans who craved speed. Faster, harder, better.

It was late again. The flickers from the last campfires lit hillsides strewn with more rubbish. The lines on the track were black and earth was churned. Toby Moody, the Eurosport commentator, no doubt felt relieved that the one road out was no longer a river of fans; in a previous attempt to escape Mugello early Moody had taken his hire car through the neighbouring quarry and turned it over. Now he was still finishing his work in the commentary booth and would take the road this time. There was an air of calm. That post-coital slump of satisfaction.

Hopper crept out with Byrne. It had been another mixed weekend. Hopper had qualified in an impressive fifth, but had to settle for eleventh in the race on his Suzuki. Byrne, riding for Team Roberts, had qualified in eighteenth place, finished sixteenth and was moderately pleased that the bike had not broken down. They wandered into the night and the grassy environs of Mugello. Behind the paddock is a two-tiered grassy bank and they made their way up it. Byrne had his camcorder with him. They found the two 25-litre petrol drums. They started dousing things in petrol and throwing fireballs. The edgy camcorder caught the scenes. Then Hopper poured the petrol along the grass ledge. He said he wanted to torch 'the whole goddamn valley'. He said,

'Shit! Fuck!' The tentacles of flame flicked up and burnt him. 'Fuck, man! It's in my face!'

Byrne had it all on his camcorder. He played it back to Davies a week later in Barcelona. There was pitch black and then a shaft of arcing light. Then the screen was white with the torching of Mugello and the burning of Hopper, the soundtrack blue with the off-camera swearing. Davies bumped into Hopper, himself, the following day in Barcelona. He looked odd and it took a while for the Briton to realize that his friend had no eyelashes. They had been burnt off in the blaze of Mugello. His hair, a long wavy 1970s mop, was singed at the front too. Hopper's face was also red, his nose a crimson reminder of the previous week's misbehaviour.

He had just turned twenty-two when he set fire to his face but Hopper had already been in MotoGP for four years. Some said he was lucky to have been plucked from obscurity and given a Yamaha at the age of eighteen, but he had been through the mill. Hopper had English parents, but they emigrated to America before he was born. His father died from lung cancer when Hopper was only twelve. Before he passed away he told Hopper's mother to keep on with the racing. She did and Hopper learnt to ride near the Mexican border. He had thick round earrings and a goatee beard. There was a tattoo of a woman waving a chequered flag on his back, a blue flame and the lettering 'HOPPER' on his right shoulder.

He had a wild streak but he kept it hidden from the press. These were tough times for American riders and it was good sense to keep your head down. The great days of Roberts, Rainey, Schwantz and Lawson were long gone. Hopper was battling. So was Kenny junior, who was now a pale imitation of his former self, let alone his father. He was the milder Roberts. Kenny junior would tell stories of his father's legendary birthday parties held on New Year's Eve and you could not help thinking he sounded out of place amid the guns, the hard alcohol and the topless girls.

Hayden, too, was finding life hard. He had hoped that when Rossi moved on his life would get easier. 'Team-mates? It just means you have the same colour bikes.' Halfway through his year with Biaggi he was struggling again. His team-mate was an aloof figure, alienating both his team and the likes of Davies and Stoner as he cut them up on his paddock scooter, but he was beating Hayden. The American rode hard and fast, he was aggressive yet emotional, but another bleak year and he might be facing the end. Once you were considered to have blown a big chance in MotoGP, there were few people who would ever give you another.

The last of the Americans was Edwards. He had two World Superbike titles, a wife and a family, and there were those who wondered whether he had the killer instinct. Even his friend, Chris Herring, had raised the subject when the golfing buddies went out for a meal one night early in 2005. 'You've turned thirty, you've got a kid, you've been earning a million dollars for the last ten years, what's motivating you?' Edwards replied that he wanted to win, but being picked as Rossi's team-mate was a double-edged sword. 'Rossi was always extremely careful in selecting his team-mates,' Herring would tell me. 'He knew if there was one guy who he could beat but who would be fast and would give him huge technical support then it was Colin.'

Rossi even broached the matter when the pair sat down in a Yamaha office together in 2005. 'A lot of people say that when you have a child you go slower by half a second,' Rossi mused. 'In Italian we have a special phrase for it. What do you think?'

Edwards had heard it said before. 'I know what you mean. They also say that when you get married you lose half a second. You're always losing time, time, time. But when I got married in 1999 I won the championship the next year.'

'So it's not a problem?' Rossi said.

'In 2002, when I found out Alyssia was pregnant and we were going to have a kid, I won all nine races after that in superbikes.'

'Ah.'

'I understand that some people will say, "Now he's got a family he'll roll off the gas and protect himself", but for me now I have everything. So now is the time to go *with* the gas.'

'Yes, yes. Is that.'

'I've everything I want.'

Edwards could, indeed, be aggressive. Aaron Slight knew that. The most experienced World Superbike rider in history with 229 starts was taking his first steps on the comeback trail by driving in the British Touring Car Championship when we spoke in 2001. With a clean bill of health and a metal plate in his skull, he harboured hopes of a return to the two-wheeled arena at thirty-five, but he was philosophical as he reflected on a past comprising brain surgeons, back-stabbing and a Vietnamese pot-bellied pig.

Slight recalled how Edwards had rammed him off the track at Donington Park in 1999. Slight, a New Zealander who had a bitter rivalry with Carl Fogarty, fell and stuck a finger up at Edwards as he looked backwards. He restarted and, after a trip to the pits, found himself in front of Edwards. He raised his finger in front of the Texan again. Then he crashed again. This time there was blood on the handlebars and the finger was hanging off. When Edwards came to visit Slight in his motorhome, he tried to dismiss it as a racing incident. Slight said there was no concern about his finger. His father-in-law took Edwards outside before the scene turned ugly.

Slight's story showed how fate could derail the best-laid plans. It hinted at why riders are among the most insecure of million-aires. I interviewed him when his life was already unravelling and he was seeking a way back. He told me that in the darkest of many funereal hours, he had entertained fleeting thoughts of suicide. Depression stalked every waking moment. He stood at the edge of the abyss, his skills neutered by unexplained blurred vision and dizzy spells.

'I honestly felt like topping myself at the end of 1999,' he said bluntly. 'The depression was bad. I knew something was wrong but I'd had every test known to man and nothing was showing up. I thought, "Am I going crazy?" The doctors said I had glandular fever but I knew it was more than that. I ended up losing two years of my life.'

Matters came to a head at a pre-season test at Eastern Creek in Australia in February 2000. 'I was six seconds off the pace and came back to the pits almost in tears,' he said. 'I couldn't see properly because of blurred vision. I told my team, "Something's wrong. I can't go on like this." So I went back to the doctors in Sydney for one last time. They gave me an MRI scan and found a two-and-a-half-centimetre blood-clot. I thought, "Great". It was a huge relief that I wasn't imagining it all.'

Slight had a rare congenital condition called arteriovenous mal-formation, which meant that blood was leaking into his brain from a ruptured vein. He underwent a five-hour operation, which saved his life but left him a brittle shell of the man who had earned eighty-seven podium finishes, a record bettered only by Fogarty, the rival who named his pet pig Aaron. 'I went on a five-minute walk to the shops and was knackered,' Slight said. 'The operation knocked it out of me. I remember sitting under a tree one day for seven hours and not moving. I said to myself, "This isn't me." The doctors told me I'd feel crap for two years but they put a plate in my head instead of gluing it because they knew I wanted to ride again.'

You knew that there was nowhere for Slight to go and his denial was awful to behold. 'I look at the championship now and know that, if I was there, I'd be out in front,' he said. 'Nobody is taking it by the balls and they're going so slow. I could still be world champion. No question. The trouble is getting a chance. Some people see me as damaged goods.'

When Slight first vowed to return after his brain surgery, most people felt the New Zealander's talk betrayed a hopeless romanticism. Few believed he could turn back the clock. Yet, incredibly, he missed just three rounds of the 2000 season, only to be replaced by Tady Okada for 2001. 'I feel bad about it,' he said. 'I gave them options and said, "Look, I'll be right in 2001. I've been ill for two years." The next thing I know they're ditching me for a guy who can't even find the track. I'd been with Honda for seven years and they ended it just like that. What's happened has made me view things differently. I'm grateful for what I've got but I still need a challenge.'

This was motorcycling. You could have a stroke and risk death by riding with blinding headaches and a bleeding brain, but there was no sentiment. Slight would not race bikes again. Damaged goods. Doomed not charmed. You did not get time in bikes. He knew it. Edwards knew it. Hopper and Hayden knew it too. For different reasons the pressure was on as MotoGP headed back to the United States.

LAP 6

It was funny how things changed. He thought this as he sat out-side the Castle Mona, slowly reddening in the parched heat, chatting with Phil Read. They had never really got on. Read had a persistent habit of rubbing people up the wrong way, whether heaving bricks through nightclub windows or pointing to his backside on the grid to suggest that was all Mike would get to see of him during the race. He was a combative, arrogant sod, but he had come to his hotel and suggested they have a chat. It was 1978 and time had alchemic powers. It could heal wounds and soften enemies, but the one thing it never did was stop.

It was almost time for practice week and Mike felt his con-fidence grow as he listened to Read harp on about the problems he was having with his Honda. The longer he spent on the island the more he felt it was right. If you could do it then you should. You were a long time retired and he wanted the challenge. Just like he had in 1964, some fourteen years before, when he had encountered that olive face and thick Italian accent for the first time.

Mike was the undisputed star of the motorcycle world then. The Beatles were just making it big and a spirit of hedonism ran wild through the sport. The letters Mike received were lewd and graphic, leaving little to the imagination, and although it was a myth peddled by his father that women queued to pay for locks of his hair, they were easily humbled by his charm and fame.

And then came Ago, a more classically good-looking figure, with jet-black hair, sun-blond skin and a ready smile. He first met him at Solitude in Germany in 1964. Mike won the 500cc race that day, almost three minutes ahead of Jack Ahearn with Phil Read third, but Ago caused a stir in the 250cc class on his Morini. Read won that race, but Ago finished ahead of both Provini and Taveri. He was on his way.

Like Mike, Ago hailed from a well-off family. His father's timber yard had burnt down in the war and he had set up an earth-moving business that produced enough funds for him to run a ferry business on Lake Iseo. Unlike Mike, his father did all he could to dissuade him from a racer's life. It meant Ago had to bribe a boy with a Guzzi with the promise of a date with his attractive cousin if he could borrow his bike. Then, when he was ten, a baker, who had spotted him riding around, invited him to street race. Ago did well enough until he got to the square at Borno, which he kept circling because he had no idea how to stop.

A misunderstanding when he was eighteen changed his life. He needed permission to race at that age and his father refused to give it. One day they visited a friend of his father. He worked as a notary and noted the sullen look on Mino's face. He asked what the problem was and Ago's father explained. 'Why not let the boy ride?' the notary said. 'It's good for him to have a goal.' His father said he would not sign his son's death warrant, which provoked an incredulous response from the notary. 'Come now. It will be good for him. Let him do the sport.' Eventually, swayed by his friend, Ago's father signed the form. It was only later that he discovered the notary had thought they had been talking about bicycle racing. 'He could not understand why my father was afraid,' Ago said. 'So he convinced him and I was lucky.'

Ago was good, but his father was right to be worried. As a boy on a 175cc Guzzi, he would dice with the road trains on the Riviera, a narrow road threaded between the cliff and the lake. 'I escaped death a thousand times,' he said. He fell in love when he was still a teenager but told his girl that the bikes came first. 'I love you but . . .' The thrill and fear of riding fast overwhelmed him.

He was spotted by Alfonso Morini, who signed him to race in the Italian Senior Championships, and he made a name for himself. He had no English and, by his own admission, was 'nobody' when Morini let him race outside Italy for the first time in Solitude, but he saw Hailwood and knew he wanted to compete against him. The chance came the very next year when the Count, desperate to sign an Italian, recruited him to partner Mike at MV.

Mike liked him and taught him some dubious phrases. They would become close, but the relationship was couched in the coolness of rivalry. 'It is always difficult,' Ago explained to me in 2008. 'Your first competitor is always your team-mate. Take this year – Valentino and Lorenzo both race for Yamaha but they are not in the same box. When I arrived at MV, Mike was already a big champion. I tried to learn from him and understand what he did. I had a lot of respect for him because he was good. We were little friends in 1965 and better by the end. I liked to beat him and he liked to beat me. At first he had more power.'

Then, in April 1965, they went to Riccione. Ago's debut for MV had ended disastrously the previous week in Modena, where he had won but suffered a humiliating crash, damaging the Count's machine and raising question marks over his ability. Such was the MV's dominance that the crash was deemed more significant than the victory. In Riccione, Ago was steeled for improvement and Mike was fuming. His relationship with the

Count was always fraught, not least when he had been damned for riding like an old woman, and now Mike had been told to let Ago win. It would be good for the company to have a star Italian rider and Ago was the one contesting the domestic championship. Mike was furious, but the race was hard and fair. When Ago snaked through the back markers and Mike's brake started to fail, the result was settled. The Count had his wish, but it left a bitter aftertaste in his world champion's mouth. You win by strength and guile, he thought. 'When we went to Riccione, Mike respected me but I don't think he thought I was so good,' Ago said. 'I *had* to beat Mike Hailwood, but when he came to Italy it was just pleasure and he did not take it seriously. He was drinking and going dancing. Then I beat him and that all stopped. For a whole week. Until he beat me.'

It was a glorious time, sex and bikes and rock 'n' roll. Mike soaked up the sun outside the Castle Mona and listened to Read continue to bemoan his Honda. It felt good to be back.

CHAPTER NINE

THE PRETENDERS

The Haydens were out in force. Nicky had more pressure on him than any of his compatriots because he was on the Repsol Honda and he had suffered a long and arduous baptism. There were plenty of cynics who felt he did not have what it takes but for once he was being feted. Film stars had been drawn to Laguna Seca by the PR skills of sponsors Red Bull and Hayden's profile was being bludgeoned into the American consciousness. He had attended a celebrity edition of the television show *The Dating Game* at New York's Rockerfella Plaza where he was up against a country singer and an American footballer. The blonde had picked Hayden. 'My mom's not going to be happy, but I love a man who can ride fast,' she gushed.

Hayden also attended a drinks reception at the offices of *People* magazine. He had been voted on to the fifty hottest bachelors list alongside the likes of actors Brad Pitt and Colin Farrell. By the time they got to Laguna, Pitt was strolling around the paddock with an entourage of acolytes. In the Yamaha garage they checked their watches and looked anxiously towards the door. Where was he? Pitt's impatience began to wear thin. His bodyguards shuffled on their feet and scowled. Then the message arrived. Valentino

Rossi was not coming and, if the Hollywood actor wanted to meet the finest motorcyclist of his generation, he would have to go and knock on his door. It was a graphic illustration of how Rossi, who Forbes reported now earned £18.75 million a year, including a £2.5 million win bonus, was the hottest bachelor of all.

The return to the United States in 2005 after an eleven-year hiatus was a big deal, but a major upgrade to meet FIM regulations had not met with wholesale approval. 'They used the wrong tarmac and the track is just cracking up,' one team official said. 'It's literally melting in the sun.' Rossi and Marco Melandri, first and second in the championship, complained publicly. With memories still fresh in American minds of the disastrous Formula One grand prix at Indianapolis, where seven teams refused to race, the potential for a costly embarrassment was obvious.

That might have been why Carmelo Ezpeleta, Dorna's chief executive, refused to indulge in a show of *Schadenfreude* at the Formula One farce. 'What happened in Indianapolis was not good for our sport in general,' he said. 'Nobody benefited.'

Yamaha, who were celebrating their fiftieth anniversary by racing in their fabled old yellow livery, footed the $2 million upgrade bill. Troy Bayliss was as fatalistic as ever. 'Safety is vital, but the fact the track is a little bit dangerous does add that extra edge to the proceedings,' he grinned. Rossi was not about to let his concerns become an own goal and backed up fears with some platitudes for the fans. 'I'm just happy to be going to California where the pretty girls are.'

Rossi had reason to be content. 'For me the championship is between Valentino and Rossi,' Melandri said, echoing Loris Capirossi's claim that Rossi could win the title with one hand tied behind his back. Sete Gibernau had seemingly imploded. 'I can't deny that the championship is slipping away from me already, but I'm not going to throw in the towel,' he said at a briefing in his hospitality suite. 'I'd like this to be a turning point. I just can't understand why we can do such a good job all weekend and then not get a result when it comes to the race.' At Assen he was not helped when Juan Martinez, his chief engineer and once part of Team Rossi, spent the night in the medical centre with a searing migraine. Most put the blame for his demise on himself. Rossi had got inside his head and the pain throbbed. And so Rossi said he felt Gibernau was no longer his main rival. 'Others are closer,' he grinned. Gibernau's troubles boiled over in the pre-race press conference when Melandri called the track a 'scandal'. Gibernau responded with uncharacteristic venom, calling Melandri 'a fucking idiot'.

It was clear Honda were in trouble and the media and the public still wondered just how they could have driven Rossi out. Tsutomu Ishii, the new general manager of HRC, tried to draw a line under the affair by admitting they had made a mistake. 'If he says he is having more fun at Yamaha then it must be true,' he said. 'But losing the title has increased our motivation even more. There is still a lot more potential from this engine.' Ishii insisted that the loss of Rossi had not affected Honda's sales figures and claimed that he had been appreciated. He added that Rossi was a good rider and mentally strong. It was easy to interpret that as a critique of Rossi's replacements.

Hayden knew this was the crunch. He knew Laguna and for once he had an advantage over Rossi and the rest of the Europeans. He knew what it was like to disappear down the Corkscrew, the 300-foot blind drop that was arguably the best corner on the calendar. Just as important, he had his family with him. Earl was there with his frown, while Tommy and Roger Lee were due to ride in the support races. It was like old times.

Hayden was fast in qualifying. Home track knowledge really mattered and he was using it well. Bayliss was fastest in the first practice session, but Hayden topped the lists in the next two, qualifying and the race warm-up. John Hopkins and Colin

Edwards were also doing well and qualified on the second row. Hayden, though, broke the lap record to take the first pole position of his career, with Rossi conjuring up one smart lap to be next to him.

That morning Hayden was on his exercise bike in his motorhome and trying to banish sentimental thoughts about where he had come from, when Tommy crashed in the Superstock race. It was a calamitous exit as Tommy was due to ride again that afternoon in the Supersport race where he was vying for the title. Now he had a broken right hand. Nicky tried to offer some encouragement and hoped for the best. Briefly Rossi and the rest disappeared from his mind.

Finally, after all the waiting, the hype and gory exchanges, it was time. Hayden made a good start. Earl glanced at the foot of the screen and waited for the flashing message to come up to say his son had jumped the start. It did not come. Nicky was off to a flier.

Hayden and Edwards had used their local knowledge to steer the best course down the Corkscrew. Rossi was a canny observer, though, and had quickly learnt the track from playing his PlayStation and from following Bayliss around on the Friday. Nevertheless, there was little he could do. Hayden broke clear and the battle erupted in his wake, Edwards roughing it with Rossi, Gibernau, Biaggi and Bayliss. Rossi had second place and put in some quick laps, but Hayden responded every time. Earl took a deep breath. There was no doubt Nicky had the pace to win, but this was motorcycle racing and Tommy's hand was a reminder of how things could go wrong.

Edwards got past Rossi, his team-mate, on lap sixteen. For Rossi that was a bitter pill. He liked Edwards and respected him, but as far as he was concerned his job was to help him. This was America, though, and things were different here. They had known that when they arrived and found no electricity in the pitlane.

Third would do. Hayden could have his moment. The title was all but in the bag.

Hayden crossed the line and two-and-a-half years of pent-up frustration flooded out of him in tears and smiles. He grabbed the stars and stripes and went on his victory lap. He stopped and indulged in a burnout on the Corkscrew. Then he came into the pits, picked up Earl and took his father on a pillion ride to celebrate. There was an embarrassing jig of delight. Matt Le Blanc, one of the stars of the television comedy *Friends*, found his way into the garage. Tommy and Roger Lee roared. Nicky was ushered into the press conference on a tide of back-slapping and said, 'I was thinking about what my mom and dad have done for me. I was thinking about going to Daytona and we had buckets all over the place because the roof was leaking. The dude had spent the roof money to go racing.'

Tommy and Roger Lee did not hear that. They were getting ready for the Supersport race. They were brothers and rivals. Tommy grinned and bore it and came home sixth, good enough to maintain what would prove a title-winning lead. That night the farm boys from Kentucky partied with Brad Pitt. Then they went home to Owensboro. Within a fortnight the three brothers were appearing on the *Tonight Show with Jay Leno*, one of the most popular talk shows in America. Suddenly it seemed that Hayden had arrived.

Rossi, meanwhile, had a troubled end to his first taste of racing in America. He had decided to go into town with Uccio and the others in search of a party. They were crawling along, looking for the street name they had been given, when they saw the blink of neon blue behind them and heard the screech of a siren. Rossi pulled over. The policeman sauntered up. 'Give me your licence.'

Rossi fumbled around in the car. 'OK,' he said. 'But why?'

The policeman studied the licence and looked back at Rossi's bemused expression. 'You were going too slow,' he said. 'It's dangerous.'

Rossi and Uccio could not stop their sniggering at that and would recount the tale with glee. 'If you go fast it's too fast, if you go slow it's too slow. It's difficult to understand this point of view for sure,' he said to Edwards.

Donington was wet and miserable. It was always the latter. A grey circuit shrouded by saturated fields. Hayden was still full of it as he nestled beneath the awning of Honda's smaller hospitality unit. They had two. One was the glitzy black and orange celebrity hangout, fronted by girls with overlong legs and underdressed bodies, but the other was for the crew and selected journalists. Hayden could not stop smiling. The pressure was off. 'The whole three days in Laguna went to plan and it was like a dream come true,' he said. 'Sounds soppy, I know, but that's it. It was amazing and emotional and now we have to move on. I've always said that we Haydens work well on momentum. It took me a while to win races back home in AMA but when I did they seemed to keep coming. I know what I can do at this level and I won't be happy until I do it again.'

He didn't do it in Donington. Hayden and Melandri were among those who slipped off inside four laps. The rain was fierce and the riding dangerous. Form was drowned and a new order broke the surface. Hopkins hit the front and people briefly wondered whether this was his moment. Then his visor misted up and he crashed. Biaggi, Gibernau and Bayliss also fell in the wet. Rossi, though, was unassailable, surfing through the tidal conditions with a sureness of footing others marvelled at. Rossi's lap times fell to almost two seconds quicker than the rest. He was racing as they were surviving. As Rossi crossed the finishing line to earn yet another British Grand Prix victory, he stood upright and began playing an imaginary violin. The act summed up the spirit of a class act, a virtuoso talent who was more than capable of fiddling while others burned.

Some interpreted the celebration as an insincere reaction to the misfortune that befell his challengers, notably Gibernau. The Spaniard's exit, while leading, meant more spirit was squeezed out via the emotional mangle. Rossi, however, claimed the mime was a result of his riding being akin to fine art. At the press conference he added: 'It was the most difficult race of my career. The track was very slippery with no grip and it was hard to see anything. It was like riding a boat not a bike.'

Kenny Roberts' performance on the Suzuki was a welcome return for a man who had been in the wilderness but, while he was happy to be in the media spotlight again, he was appreciative of what made Rossi so special. 'Valentino had the confidence and bravery to take off and I didn't have anything to match him,' he said as the cameras clicked in the media centre. No one did. Even by his own lofty standards, this was an exceptional triumph, a masterclass of marrying skill and courage in weather more suited to ducks than Ducatis. The championship lead was now more than a hundred points.

Alex Barros' third place was some consolation for him as he had just been slapped with a $3 million bill from the Paris Court of Arbitration. The veteran Brazilian had been sued for breach of contract by Altadis, the owner of Yamaha sponsors Gauloises and Fortuna. He lost and was also told to pay $350,000 in costs. Barros said his lawyers were looking at the judgement, but it was a victory for the multi-million-dollar corporates. Many shook their heads at the news. Was this the sport that Hailwood and Agostini had graced? For many, Barros's plight was a symptom of the sport becoming more sanitized.

Angel Nieto thought so. He was a fiftysomething Spaniard with long greying hair and chiselled cheekbones. There was a museum in Madrid dedicated to the thirteen world titles he won on 50cc and 125cc bikes, although he called it twelve plus one for superstitious reasons. Nieto came from another age when the antics were legend and, like many of his era, he yearned for it again. For the riots at the discos and for Walter Migliorati, who would turn up on the grid with topless prostitutes, wear their knickers and then disappear to the back of the field and, ultimately, cocaine-fuelled oblivion. Like Rossi, Nieto had idolized Hailwood and had plenty of stories from that golden age.

'It was the old circuit at Nürburging,' he began. 'The 22km one. I knew I couldn't have won the 250cc race but I had a chance in the 125. I went out in the 250 race on my Derbi and on the downhill section just before the village of Adenauer, the fastest part of the track, the engine seized. There was a French rider in front of me. I can't remember his name now, but in those days we had open-faced helmets and mine came down and smashed my nose. They took me to hospital in Adenauer where they checked me over and gave me some X-rays because I was feeling dizzy. They left me in a wheelchair in the corridor. I asked them what was happening and they said they didn't know anything but were waiting for a room to come free.

'I was not having that. I spotted a door open on to a patio so I jumped out of my chair and escaped. I decided to hitch-hike. My leathers were all scuffed and my face was swollen. I didn't have a clue where my helmet was, but a German guy let me jump on the back of his bike and he took me up to the paddock. The 125 bikes were already on the grid and I saw Renzo Pasolini walking through the paddock. I said, "Paso! Give me your helmet!" I put on his helmet and ran to the grid. I can't remember if I was on pole or just the front row. By this time the hospital had called the circuit and said, "Look out, there's a madman who's escaped from the hospital and he's trying to race!"

'Well that was that. The Germans came and dragged me off the grid. Within five minutes I passed out and the next thing I knew I was back in hospital. A few weeks later I wrote a letter to the doctor thanking him because he prevented me from doing serious damage, maybe even saved my life.' Nieto stopped and shook his head. 'And the craziest thing about that story is that I wasn't some stupid kid. I was already an eight-time world champion!' Somehow this story jarred with that of Barros' court case. In the old days life and death were cheap, but now the wrong sponsor could cost you millions.

The sport still had Rossi but where was the challenge coming from? After nine rounds Gibernau, putatively his main threat, was 116 points adrift. Biaggi was a handful of points better off and Hayden worse. Edwards was doing the supporting role well, threatening second place but not his team-mate. Hopper was down among the makeweights in fourteenth. And that was when the news broke. There was no official confirmation, but Honda had made their move in the campaign to derail Rossi. Their statement that they would build a bike to crush him had backfired spectacularly, but now word was out. Next year Dani Pedrosa would be joining the MotoGP class from the 250cc series, where he was winning a battle with Casey Stoner for the title.

It was almost two years ago since Rossi, the newly crowned world champion, had led his entourage in a boisterous chant of 'Pedrosa! Pedrosa! Pedrosa!' in a Rio bar. That Caipirinha-induced homage showed the respect Rossi had for the teenager, but who was he? I wanted to find out about the boy with the metal teeth who had beaten me at pool in the Pan Pacific.

I arranged to meet him at Donington. As with any meeting with Pedrosa, Alberto Puig, the talent-spotter who had given Chaz Davies a leg-up, hovered at his shoulder. Occasionally, he would feign disinterest and read a magazine but you could see him straining to hear the questions. He guarded Pedrosa like an over-protective bodyguard, but Chris Herring, who knew both well from his work inside Honda, rejected the popular view that Puig inhibited Pedrosa. 'The fact is they're mates,' he said. 'People say Dani is a miserable so-and-so, but to him this is a job. Like it was for Lawson and Doohan. It's serious. When he goes home to

Barcelona he goes out with his mates and has a drink like anyone else.'

He did not look like a challenger but, like Nieto before him, he was the undisputed master of small bikes. Pedrosa's small frame suited the 125cc and 250cc machines and he was already world champion in both. He was now well on his way to adding another title. He had long outgrown Castellar del Valles, the village near Barcelona where his father still worked in the timber yard, and now lived in Notting Hill.

Pedrosa was sitting in front of me in a horrible pitbox at Donington because he had won a high-speed version of *Pop Idol*. It was such a romantic story that it was little wonder that many sagacious onlookers were hailing him as the next big thing. There were those who had even billed him as the new Rossi. 'If I start to think like that then I'm lost,' he said. 'You can think things like that, but you have to believe it.' Did he? A quiet smile but no answer.

His story was brief but intriguing. Pedrosa was in a shop buying spare parts when urged by a friend of his father to watch the Joven Cup on television. It proved something of an epiphany. 'If that day hadn't happened I'd be studying or working now,' he said. 'I'm only nineteen years old and I cannot complain. I'm a lucky man.'

Inspired by what he had seen, he spotted an advertisement in the Spanish press seeking wannabe motorcycle racers for the next year's Joven Cup. He went home and wrote an entry, including a personal statement of why he should be chosen. The man charged with the task of sifting through the mountain of replies was Puig, the former grand prix racer and the brains behind the scheme. 'We got 5,800 responses,' Puig chipped in. 'I wasn't surprised. After all, it was free and we were giving them the chance to race a Honda RS125. We looked at what they had done – pocket-bike, mini-bike – and why they wanted to race. We chose and tested 400 and then picked the best thirty-two to race.'

Pedrosa's talent was obvious, but the road to the cusp of the big time had already been marked with potholes. He started out in the Spanish mini-bike series until chickenpox left him unable to wear a helmet. He recovered and won the title in 1998, with his parents shepherding him around the country with his bike in the boot of the family car, but turned to mountain bike racing because of the crippling costs. It seemed another prodigy had been lost to the sport, but that was before Puig came up with his novel idea of inviting future champions to audition.

'I stopped my studies because Alberto believed in me,' Pedrosa said. 'I had no time for books and sat down with my parents to decide what to do. It was just before the 2002 season and my last school report had been bad because I was away far too often. My parents would have preferred it if I'd studied, but I thought if you are a good rider you have to do it. So I chose motorcycle racing.'

It was a decision he would not regret. That year he won the 125cc Dutch Grand Prix at Assen. The season after he won the title. Now he had graduated to the 250cc class with the Telefonica Movistar Honda team and the inevitable progress to MotoGP was all but confirmed. And if you had Rossi's seal of approval, how could you fail?

Since toasting him on a drunken night in Rio, Rossi had offered sobering advice to a man with whom he shared as many similarities as differences. From living in London to being the rising star of Honda, it was easy to see traces of Rossi in the lithe physique of Pedrosa. 'He has talked to me, but not about how to race or how to take a corner,' Pedrosa said. 'It's more about life in racing. With me he is very *simpatico*. He came to me, not me to him. His fame has not changed him, he's still a real person. I like that.'

The real mentor was Puig. The winner of a 500cc grand prix, Puig was now becoming almost a surrogate father to Pedrosa, reminding him of his failings and urging him to work. That had been an easy task with the quiet, intelligent teenager. 'Sure we sometimes have different opinions and he fights hard for his point of view,' Puig said. 'But sometimes I'm sure he listens to me and thinks, "The old man has been there himself." Dani is a very natural person, quiet, still. He understands that, with fame and money, it is easy to lose your way in life. His qualities are concentration and determination. He would be exactly the same if he was playing tennis or chess.'

When Rossi won the 2004 South African Grand Prix on his new Yamaha, the motorsport world bowed to his ability to make myths real. Almost unnoticed, Pedrosa won his first race on a 250cc that day too. That he did so after overcoming a bad crash at the end of 2003 underlined his resilience. 'My head was occupied with my rehabilitation so it wasn't difficult to keep my feet on the ground after becoming world champion,' he said. 'I had no time for parties or girls.'

Puig's faith in Pedrosa had seen him turn away from some of the other riders he had helped into the sport in order to concentrate on the boy he thought the best. That had not gone down well in certain quarters, but the proof was in the pudding and the events of one boozy night in South America. Pedrosa's time was coming.

Rossi, meanwhile, was now merrily dabbling in Formula One. He had first tested for Ferrari at Maranello a few days after that debut win for Yamaha in 2004. It had been a secret exercise. Rossi even told his mother, Stefania, that he was just going to Milan for the day. He was driven to the track in a car with blacked-out windows and told to sleep there in case anyone saw him eating in a restaurant. Rossi was quick but not as amazing as the revisionists would suggest. He had another try-out in 2005 before the Czech Grand Prix and improved. Ferrari felt he was good enough to consider for a role, and the fact Rossi penned only a one-year contract extension with Yamaha enhanced rumours that he would follow Mike Hailwood and make the switch to Formula One in 2007.

'It was a gift, a present for winning,' Rossi said of his first test for Ferrari when he gave an interview to *The Times* in his London flat. 'So I go and we make a few laps in the car and I am fast, but it is hard to go straight. On a bike the straights are easier, but in the car I had to learn. Then we do some work the next day with the tyres and I do a lap of 59.1 seconds. Schumacher has the lap record and it is 56, so I am three seconds slower. But after two tests we know it is not impossible.'

Rossi let everyone know about his options. 'I am the luckiest motorcyclist in the world. I have a lot of opportunity – I am able to stay into 2007 with Yamaha or Ducati, or change to Formula One.'

He was wallowing in the attention and the intrigue. He liked the speculation and feeding people snippets. 'On the bike I'm free, in the car it is down in a black hole, it is not so nice,' he said. 'The bike races are battles with other riders, it is strategy and it is possible to overtake. In cars, it is not a battle with the others, it is not a race, it is not as fun as the bikes, for sure. I have to make a decision in the first part of next year and it is very likely that it would not be a success. It is a big risk for me.'

His joviality was breached, however, when Ross Brawn, Ferrari's technical director, claimed that Rossi would be test driving for the Formula One team on a monthly basis. 'Bullshit!' Rossi raged. 'I saw the announcement of Ross Brawn, but it is bullshit.' This didn't sound like a man coveting a job with the most famous motor racing team in the world. 'I don't know how Ferrari knows what I am doing next year when I don't know what I am doing next week. I am totally committed to Yamaha and winning the MotoGP World Championship. That will take up a great deal of my time and I will not have enough spare for Formula One testing. I've made no decisions about anything in 2007.'

After Donington, Rossi won in Germany and the Czech Republic. He led Biaggi by 132 points. To highlight the gulf in class, Biaggi, Melandri, Edwards, Gibernau and Barros were separated by a mere fifteen. The king was peerless but there was parity among the rest. Gibernau, meanwhile, was going well in Brno until a problem with the fuel-injection system meant he ran out of petrol on the last lap. It was that bloody curse again. It summed him up. Charmed or doomed? He knew the answer.

Rossi could have wrapped things up at Motegi, another Honda test track set amid lush vines and rural communities three hours north of Tokyo. Not everyone was pleased to see him close in on a new title. Melandri had once been a friend of Rossi's but now he said things were different, even accusing his compatriot of blanking him. Rossi could not understand the allegation. 'I don't know why he said that because it isn't true. I've known him since he was ten and he is a rider of the future.'

That future took a horrible turn on race day. Rossi needed to come second to be sure of the title but was trailing Melandri as they came to a sharp right-hander. Melandri gave himself some room and then tried to square off the apex. Rossi was running down the inside and had decided to take a wide line out. The two collided and fell. Rossi hit the ground first and his right shoulder pounded the tarmac while sparks flew from the exhaust. Melandri found himself on top of an upside-down Honda. The footpeg ripped into his heel and blood instantly stained his boot dark red. The pain was instant. 'Va fan culo! Fuck! Va fan culo!'

He was helicoptered away. Honda saw an opportunity and put in an official protest, but it was rejected. It was a racing incident and the protest was born more of personal feeling towards Rossi than a desire for justice. With Rossi gone it was an opportunity for Gibernau to get the monkey off his back, but he crashed too. Capirossi won and the crowning was delayed. It came a week later in Malaysia. Rossi was only second as Capirossi scored back-to-back wins, but this had been a strange triumph. Where last year's title had evinced a colossal talent, this had been a procession with no rival. The best had been Melandri, but he turned up for the last act in a wheelchair and admitted the effort of braking had strained his thirty-five stitches. His fifth place was quasi-heroic and there was a lot of sympathy for him. He hobbled away from the track while Rossi stopped, pulled on another new T-shirt and celebrated with seven members of his Fan Club dressed as dwarves. It was his seventh world title and his fifth in the elite class. He seemed unstoppable.

I arranged to meet Melandri in Birmingham for the NEC Bike Show in the days running up to the final grand prix of the season in Valencia. It was now between him and the Americans, Edwards and Hayden, for second place. We went to the top of a bus and sat on the hospitality deck in the middle of a huge hangar, looking down at the sea of bikers swarming through the gangways like a leathery python.

Melandri was likeable. He was short and had the pronounced square chin of a Shetland pony. He had sparkly eyes, but his English was not as good as Rossi's. However, it was still clear that Melandri, who lived in a converted barn in a Derbyshire village near former world motocross champion Jamie Dobb, also lived in a curious world. He said he felt that the planet was made up of black and white tubes and that this belief in positive and negative energy sources had helped him deal with a dramatic history that had involved everything from a bloody foot to a bleeding heart. In the space of twelve months alone, this paddock philosopher had turned his back on the factory floor to top the podium and become the man most likely to dethrone Rossi.

'A year ago was the worst moment of my life,' he almost whispered. 'I was going to stop racing. Yamaha offered for me to stay with them in 2005, but I didn't like the team or the bike. I wanted a Honda or I was going back to Italy to work in a factory.'

When Pedrosa decided to defend his title in the 250cc class and delay his graduation, Melandri got his wish.

Now he was another rider on the rise. Proof of that was the manner in which he had rattled Rossi. Their relationship had soured this year, he said. Melandri did not think Rossi had done anything deliberate in Motegi, but he did think he should have been punished. 'The law is not equal for everyone in MotoGP,' he said. 'But paying for other people's errors is not a new thing for me. When I crashed I spent five minutes thinking about my whole life. I thought it was over because there was so much blood everywhere. Valentino came over to apologize but saw the mess, covered his face and went, "No."'

He said he had suffered from acute heartburn the following week in Malaysia because of the painkillers, and he hoped his resilience had sent a message to Rossi. 'We were friends when we were young,' he said wistfully. 'For me nothing has changed, but he gets further and further away. Now I cannot say we are friends. He did the same with Gibernau. They used to go on holiday with each other. Now look at them!'

I told him that Rossi had dismissed the idea that he treated his rivals in that way as 'crap', but Melandri was adamant. 'Valentino wants to destroy me because I am a new rival for him. Gibernau and Biaggi felt a lot of pressure from Valentino, but I think about playing with him. I know Valentino will try to bring me down, but real pressure was a year ago when I was riding to save my job and knew the bike wasn't good enough.'

The potential had been there since he became the youngest ever grand prix winner, triumphing in the 125cc race at Assen when only 15 years and 324 days old. He followed that up by becoming the youngest 250cc champion in 2002, when just 20 years and 74 days old, but then endured two difficult years with Yamaha in MotoGP.

When Rossi joined the factory team the previous season,

Melandri found himself exiled to the satellite team and his career stuttered to its nadir. 'My bike was so much different from Valentino's,' he said. 'I requested some modifications, they gave them to him. My bike was broken so often, maybe an engine a race, that I lost confidence. I grew sad and angry.'

Honda revitalized him, his Italian team taping over his display panel so that he would not become obsessed with lap times. His maiden victory in the Turkish Grand Prix a fortnight before we met underscored the improvement. Fabrizio Cecchini, Melandri's crew chief, had explained it best. 'The bike did not need developing; Marco did.'

Melandri accepted that. Like Gibernau and Biaggi, he was both resilient and fragile. 'They understood my situation,' he said. 'I was like a very young baby. Now I'm smiling again, and I feel a hundred per cent safe. My head is better.' He had Rossi's showy side, the diary section of his website a riotous tale of policemen, beach parties and even a rogue bull, and he was a part-time DJ. The flipside was the deep, sensitive soul, fascinated by Malcolm X. 'I'm a normal young guy on the outside,' Melandri said. 'But put on the helmet and I feel like a different person.' The tubular transition from black to white was completed a few days later when he won the Valencia Grand Prix and thus beat Hayden, who had finished second, for the right to be the next best thing to Rossi.

Rossi, himself, had a miserable final weekend but he was unbeatable over a season. Melandri, Hayden and Pedrosa were the young pretenders, but nobody could touch the king. Certainly not Biaggi. It had emerged in the dusty aftermath of Valencia that Casey Stoner, runner-up to Pedrosa in the 250cc class, would be stepping up to MotoGP with Honda in 2006. Biaggi was on his way out. His sponsors, Camel, were loyal, but Honda had suffered enough of his erratic behaviour. The dream move to Honda had died inside two years. Biaggi got off his bike, strutted through the

Honda garage without uttering a word to anyone and walked out of the back door. It was a silent, ungrateful ending.

Rossi, meanwhile, was not concerned by the pretenders. They were just that. He was the real deal. And this year had been consummate. Rossi was now looking to the past and the future, thinking about his own place in history. That had been obvious from that day at the Sachsenring in July when he had equalled Hailwood's record of seventy-six grand prix wins in all classes. He had grabbed a flag on his in-lap emblazoned with a message that suggested he felt he had been born in the wrong age and would have preferred to have fled hospital beds with Angel Nieto and partied with Mike the Bike.

76 ROSSI

76 HAILWOOD

I'M SORRY MIKE

LAP 7

The island had not changed but the way of getting around it had. These bikes were so different to the things he had known. They were brutal, bucking beasts with thick, sticky tyres and too much power. He appreciated that after going for a lap with Mick Grant. The Yorkshireman was in awe of Mike and said advising him on the TT course was like teaching God about the Bible. He followed Mike and admired the lines and the style, but was staggered by the cornering. Mike was all over the place. Then he realized. This was 1978 and the brakes Mike the Bike had known were un-responsive, dull things compared to the sharpness of modern-day science. For a moment Mike looked like an awkward anachronism and Grant knew that this island had a habit of leaping up out of Douglas Bay and biting you on the arse.

It had bitten in 1965. That was the year when Ago went to the island for the first time. The weather was awful for the senior TT and both Mike and Ago crashed their MVs at Sarah's Cottage. Mike had the foresight to get up and restart his bike. His wind-screen was broken and his exhaust was battered. Blood dripped off his nose and on to his chin. He carried on and, after straightening his handlebars in the pits, went on to win. The love-in with the public reached new heights. 'We fell off in the same village, the same place, the same corner,' Ago would reflect four decades later. 'The funny thing was that I crashed and broke my brake and gearbox levers, but he crashed and did not break anything.'

It was Mike's seventh win on the island. He was lauded, but the form of Ago, who had been third in the junior TT, also drew plenty of plaudits. Mike knew he had a true rival and the respect between them deepened. Ago was a good bloke too, sharing Mike's flamboyance and love of women, and was quickly accepted into the brethren.

It remained a colourful time. 'In Czechoslovakia the Mayor always invited us to a banquet,' Bo Granath said. 'It was political propaganda, of course, and he merely hoped to improve relations. It was like one of those Russian films where someone takes a drink and then hurls the glass into the fire. Someone took a drink and hurled it out of the window. Then I followed. Then, before you knew it, everything was thrown out of the window. The Mayor never had his party after that.'

Tommy Robb and Luigi Taveri failed to contain their mirth after the German Grand Prix. A night of committed celebration had taken its toll on Luigi's best friend, Ernst Weiss, a former Swiss hill climb champion. Tommy had arranged to get a lift to the airport with Luigi the next day and turned up on time. Luigi had tears streaming down his cheeks. He showed Tommy into the room where Ernst was staying. Next to the snoring figure was a pushbike. 'What happened?' Tommy asked. Luigi explained that someone had dumped a plant on Ernst's head. Then he had stolen a bike from a garden and promptly cycled straight down a ten-foot-deep manhole. Luigi and his wife had hauled him out, whereupon Ernst kept riding.

They were all trying to avoid the holes in the road. Ago some-times thought about death as they all did, but he said he was a born survivor. You took the hits and hoped it would not happen to you. He said it was not fear so much as heightened reality. Sometimes he would think, 'Christ, I nearly killed myself today', but this was his job and his love.

It was a good era to be charmed rather than doomed. They went to Tampere in Finland. Tommy was on the 250cc Honda and Mike was on an MZ. It was dubbed the Manchester of Finland for its industrial past but had a track rimmed by pine trees. Straw bails were thrown up against alternate trunks as an arbitrary safety cordon. Tommy saw Mike come down the hill too fast and hurtle off the track, through a park bench and into the trees. To his relief and disbelief he then saw Mike walk out, dusting straw from his black leathers and smiling. 'I cannot describe the adrenalin of those races,' Tommy recounted. 'Afterwards you spoke about the excitement of the danger. You didn't talk about the fact you could have been written off. It was always a possibility but it was never going to happen. We fought for safety, but it did not exist. You went to Spa, went flat out down the hill and you knew that if you fell then you were either going to hit a tree or a house.'

Ralph Bryans believed that Mike was charmed too. Another dangerous place in Finland was Imatra. There were token ditches between the side of the road and the trees. No barriers. 'I remember coming down a right-hand bend and I sat up and changed down the gears. Suddenly, Mike came flying past with his chin on the tank. There was dirt and stones flying everywhere. He was almost in the ditch and I thought I was about to witness the biggest crash ever. But he got away with it. In fact, he got away with it four laps in a row. I said to him afterwards, "Listen, Mike, that was a bit near the bone." He looked at me and said, "I know. I was worried the first time." ' Another time they were racing and Ralph crashed. He told Mike it was his first time that year. 'Bryans, you're just not trying,' Mike said. 'I've been off eight times this season!'

The island was a throwback to the days of Tampere and Imatra, to the road circuits framed by mortal dangers. Ago did not come here any more. 'Your life is more important than any race,' he said. But what if your life was wrapped up in the bloody riddles of the island? What if, even at thirty-eight, your life was still the race?

CHAPTER TEN

ENDGAME

This is the way the world ends. Nicky Hayden went into the ground floor chapel of the gymnasium in Owensboro. There was a chill in the air. *This is the way the world ends.* He sat down and decided to converse with God. Pulses of pressure might have raced through his head. He was riding the all-new, so-called 'Brno' Honda, developing a bike while the others had the tried and tested machine. Double the work for the same pay. And Pedrosa was ultimately the one who would get the spoils of his efforts. Pedrosa! Pedrosa! Pedrosa! *This is the way the world ends.* He promised he would do his best. Ride every lap until the last inch. He would leave his soul on the bloodied track this year because this is the way the world ends. *With a bang not a whimper.*

He was not the only one suffering at the start of 2006. It was winter when Valentino Rossi was covered in the ashes of the tobacco storm. The trouble began when Yamaha and Gauloises announced they were splitting a year before their deal was due to expire. Altadis, Gauloises' parent company, claimed a breach of contract. Yamaha said there was no longer any agreement and denied all wrongdoing. Camel's efforts to get Max Biaggi a ride with Kawasaki and Suzuki had foundered and the anti-hero was

185

now slumming it in World Superbikes. His fans had been unimpressed and demonstrated outside Honda's European office in Rome. Pons Honda, run by former racer Sito Pons, had also disappeared in a puff of Camel smoke.

Rossi was inevitably placed at the hub of this row. I was told his unwillingness to be a mouthpiece for Gauloises had not helped the ailing relationship between team and sponsor. It was even rumoured that Rossi had said he would not ride under the Gauloises banner in 2006, prompting talk of a one-man team to be run alongside the tobacco-backed factory bike. In addition Altadis's patience was stretched by the fact Rossi had stepped up his testing programme with Ferrari, bankrolled by Marlboro. It was a web of intrigue, but from behind the smoke and mirrors came a bullish Yamaha attack. 'Yamaha reserves the rights to claim pecuniary damages with respect to the wrong and disparaging statements made by Altadis and the harm wilfully caused by its frivolous conduct,' a statement said. From afar the voice of the wounded soldier drifted in. 'I've been put in this terrible situation by Honda,' Biaggi moaned to the small World Superbike press.

It would not be long before *Novella 2000*, an Italian glossy gossip magazine, printed pictures of Rossi on a yacht with his girlfriend, Arianna Mateuzzi. She was smoking and another picture showed Rossi with a cigarette in his hand. The Italian media wasted no time in claiming this was evidence of hypocrisy on Rossi's part, although the pictures at least ended their stories about Mateuzzi being heavily pregnant.

For Rossi the microscopic glare of public scrutiny was becoming an invasive pain. When he had started going out with Arianna he tried to keep it a secret. However, one Italian journalist, having heard Rossi was in a relationship, visited every hotel and guest house on Phillip Island until he found the one where Rossi was staying. He asked to see the guest book and quickly deduced who this mystery woman was. When Arianna and her friend then contrived to crash their hire car in the tunnel at the circuit there was no chance of keeping the romance private. 'Vale desperately wanted to keep her a secret,' Ali Forth said. 'But it was all over the papers and he was very upset.'

A few months before the start of the 2006 season Lapo Elkann, heir to the Fiat fortune, overdosed on drugs and ended up in a coma in Turin. The tragic affair had a salacious element too as Elkann had been in the company of a group of transsexuals. Rossi, a known associate, was inevitably drawn into the affair and, to his credit, stood unflinchingly by his friend. 'Last time I saw him he was doing fine,' he said. 'I'm glad he's going back to work because he's a very smart guy.'

This troubled vista was made worse when the MotoGP promoter was put up for sale on the eve of the season opener in Jerez. CVC Capital Partners, a private equity firm, gained conditional approval for its plan to take over Formula One's holding company, but only on condition that it sold Dorna Sports, its Spanish subsidiary. Neelie Kroes, the EU Competition Commissioner, said, 'When the two most popular motorsport events in the EU, Formula One and MotoGP, come into the hands of one owner, there is a risk of price increases for the TV rights to these events and a reduction in consumer choice.' Five days before the first grand prix, MotoGP's future had never seemed less secure.

You would not have known that on a crisp spring morning in Oxfordshire. I was here to see Bradley Smith, the latest teenager to be saddled with the responsibility of filling a twenty-five-year black hole. There had been plenty of nearly kids and false dawns and I could not visit Smith without feeling a bit sorry for Chaz Davies. He was still only nineteen but was struggling to get his Campetella team to keep their promises. This was nothing new in Anglo-Italian teams. Leon Haslam, son of Rocket Ron, had suffered a torrid time with Italjet in 2000, culminating in the chief mechanic flooring the team manager after the latter insisted taping over the detonation light that warned the machine was about to throw Haslam down the track. It duly did and the punch soon followed.

Davies was still close to Casey Stoner but they were no longer sharing the mangy pit of a converted trailer. Stoner had finished second to Pedrosa in the 250cc class and had signed to ride for Lucio Cecchinello's one-rider Honda MotoGP team. It seemed an age since they had stood together at Motegi in 2002 and watched gobsmacked as Toni Elias rounded Marco Melandri on the last lap of the 250cc race. 'Jeez,' Stoner said as he turned to his friend. 'No matter how good I think I can be, I don't think I'll ever be able to do a pass like that.'

Stoner was on the up and so too was Smith. He was a fifteen-year-old asthmatic from the sleepy outskirts of Oxford, but his case was significant because he had been plucked from obscurity by Alberto Puig, the kingmaker now plotting the downfall of Rossi. Smith had signed a deal to ride for the factory Repsol Honda team in the 125cc World Championship. It was *the* place to start.

Puig's endorsement had whetted many an appetite. He had mentored Pedrosa through the junior ranks and now Dani was on the factory Repsol Honda in MotoGP. He had also handpicked Smith for the Barcelona-based MotoGP Academy, fast becoming the conveyor belt of future stars. Smith had stayed in a dormitory at the lavish Blume Residence, a plush establishment with its own team of doctors, linguists and psychologists, a world away from scrapping for a living as Davies had done. Smith had talent, though, finishing runner-up in the Spanish championship and marking his fifteenth birthday with a ten-hour round trip to Jerez, where he won the final round. 'When Alberto first rang I hadn't even heard of him,' he gushed. He had a freckle-face, a ginger crop top and a navy school jumper. 'But then you look on the internet and think, "Wow." I know this is a great opportunity but it's going to be a big learning year. I can't look too far ahead.'

The hallway of the family home in Garsington was dominated by a glass-fronted display case brimming with silver trophies. The grand prix dates had been filled in on a calendar and stuck to the fridge in the kitchen. His mother was proud but apprehensive, his father was living a dream. Puig, he said, liked his son because he was like clay and could be moulded. Dorna also made no secret of the fact they wanted a British rider to do well in MotoGP. They were interested in selling the sport rather than the purity of the competition. 'The main areas we are interested in are the UK and Germany,' Manel Arroyo, their managing director, told me.

The impression I left Garsington with was of a remarkably mature teenager, bright, articulate and already the possessor of a slight edge. If he ever sounded starry-eyed by his good fortune he quickly stamped on it. 'When you walk into the Repsol garage it is just overwhelming,' he said. 'But when you get on the grid you get tunnel vision.'

They all gathered in Jerez for another start. Hayden had put in more laps testing than anyone else and he already knew that he and Pedrosa were not going to be a team. Pedrosa was Honda's chosen one. It grated and irked. Double the work. Half the glory. And that slipper clutch they had designed for Pedrosa. Jeez! Pedrosa! Pedrosa! Pedrosa! The anointed one was confident he could be quick straight away. So, too, was Puig. Rossi was publicly less optimistic. 'We are completely in the shit,' he had said at the final pre-season test. Sete Gibernau was now on the Ducati, Melandri on the Fortuna Honda. They were all there, awaiting the start of what would be MotoGP's greatest year.

Rossi was in a rare tetchy mood when we met. I knew this because he kept reading his magazine until he had finished the article before saying hello. I also knew that he had snapped at an Italian journalist from a women's fashion magazine when she had asked if it was true that having children added two seconds to your lap time. 'I'm not going to answer stupid questions,' Rossi barked. That he had asked a similar question of Colin Edwards the previous year was forgotten. Rossi knew that he was not going to have it all his way this year.

He did concede that he was probably not going to go down the Formula One route, although this was the year when he would be offered a seat in a Ferrari for 2007. 'Riding this sort of bike is the passion of my life,' he said. 'I have been a motorcyclist since I was two, I am twenty-seven and I think I have some more years.' I reminded him he had once told me he would retire at twenty-seven. He laughed. 'Things change. People. Life. Circumstances. MotoGP is a real race of bikes, but Formula One is not about real cars. Maybe it's different for Michael Schumacher. You know, I think 2002 was the easiest year for me, but since then I have had to fight like crazy. Like crazy. But if I do feel bored then, yes, that will be the time to go to Formula One.' Was he bored? An ivory grin at last. 'No.'

Rossi had long said he craved a true rival and, with Biaggi and Alex Barros both bowing out of MotoGP and Pedrosa and Stoner arriving in the vanguard of change, it seemed he was about to get one. He felt it too. 'I remember seeing Pedrosa for the first time and saying, "Fuck, for a small guy he rides well." He is going to be very good. A great rival is a great motivation for me. A big fight will play a part in whether I stay or go. Mostly, it will depend on what my heart says. To give a hundred per cent of myself I need to have fun.'

He was unhappy with plans to downsize engines to 800s from the following year because he liked to race big bikes. With speeds of 215mph being reached something had to be done, but Rossi felt the sport was being sanitized, with smaller engines and more electronic aids. Mostly, though, he was concerned about the moment and the modified chassis and the chatter problem. 'I was very worried because with that problem it is impossible to race,' he said. 'The bike had been good all winter and suddenly, ten days to the first race, it was a disaster. But the engineers have changed the settings and put more weight on the front.' He shrugged. Like the rest, he was at the mercy of his bike.

Before I left him to his magazine he mentioned Hailwood. He was seeking his fifty-fourth win in the elite class the following day, which would take him level with Mick Doohan's mark. 'I say that records are not important to me, but when I reached Mike Hailwood's number of wins it was quite emotional,' he said. 'Mike the Bike, for many people, was the No. 1, a legend. Now the names are more important.' He was already eying Giacomo Agostini's mark of sixty-eight elite class wins, but that was some way off. For the future. Most felt he would get there. Only Formula One could stop him. Or children. Or the year of living dangerously. *This is the way the world ends.*

It took a few seconds for the mask of invincibility to slip. Rossi qualified in ninth place because of the chatter issue. His all-conquering Yamaha suddenly looked unrideable. They came to the first corner and his yellow bike was clipped by Toni Elias's Honda. Rossi fell in the middle of the track to a chorus of approval. The Spanish had not forgotten the way he had barged Gibernau off the circuit on the last corner last year. One corner of grand prix racing at Jerez later and the roles were reversed. Gibernau breezed through with the pack. Rossi scowled, swore and raised a fist at Elias. Fack!

Now the world order changed. With Rossi remounted but last, Gibernau, second-fastest in qualifying, looked a good bet for a win. Until the next lap when a mechanical failure forced him out. At the front his team-mate Loris Capirossi set a bone-jarring pace. Only one man could go with him. Pedrosa! Pedrosa!

Pedrosa! The crowd lapped it up, a new hero in their midst and one who seemed neither doomed nor cursed. An ice-cool metronome rather than a sometimes flaky philosopher. He could not catch Capirossi, but this was a stunning baptism for Pedrosa. Nobody but Hailwood had been this young and been in the top three in all three classes. Capirossi appreciated what had transpired. 'This is my seventeenth season, I saw Dani coming and I was very impressed.' Pedrosa had trimmed the lead to 0.3 seconds before Capirossi broke clear with five laps to go. It was like watching Popeye arm-wrestle a toddler and Pedrosa admitted he wilted physically. 'I tried to recover but the front tyre was sliding and I was tired, so I decided to give up.' Hayden would have been delighted with third place but for the fact his team-mate was ahead of him and had signalled his arrival in such consummate fashion. Stoner was sixth and Rossi fourteenth. The writing was on the garage door which Elias slipped under to offer his apologies to Rossi. He took it well. 'He's young, he's Spanish and it was his first race for Honda, so there's a lot of pressure, but I told him to choose another bike next time,' Rossi said. 'I was angry for five seconds before I realized the bike was still running. Toni's sorry and that's racing, but I hope it's the first and last time.' It would not be and, if Rossi knew just how pivotal Elias would be in what ensued, he might have attacked him with his olive branch.

In Istanbul I sat down with Pedrosa in one of the dirty grey boxes that passed for team offices at the isolated track on the Asian side of the Bosphorus. Inevitably, Puig was there, as he had been the previous year when I conducted my last interview with Biaggi. The Italian had asked where to go when he came to London. I had no idea where a multi-millionaire, would-be playboy should go and for some reason suggested Notting Hill. Biaggi had written that down. Now Pedrosa lived there.

Pedrosa, like Biaggi, was never the most popular of people, but

I did not go along with the view that he was an unadulterated misery bereft of personality. The main thing I gleaned from him was he was worried about his fitness. He still weighed 51 kilos. 'I'm not a hundred per cent with my body,' he said in his deep monotone. 'I need to do more training, but it's a slow process. Month by month. Towards the end of races I feel I'm losing energy and when you start to feel tired you have less concentration. The physical limitations affect your brain. I feel I can make a big improvement. This is my learning year. The world title? No. But I do feel I'm growing up.'

The race would bear that out. Pedrosa had struggled in the wet in qualifying but the drying track suited his pinpoint accuracy. He scythed through the field from sixteenth to first in eleven mesmerizing laps and was hunting victory in third when he made a mistake and slipped off with a mile to go. He remounted to finish a lowly fourteenth but it had been a Rossi-esque ride. Rossi, himself, was fourth behind a podium that boasted an average age of twenty-two. Melandri was first, the white energy tubes giving him a halo, with Stoner just two-tenths adrift on the Honda LCR. Hayden was third and happy. 'It was a wild race with everybody super-aggressive but no bonehead stuff,' he glowed.

Stoner was also grinning away in his garage. He had been hair-splittingly close to matching Fast Freddie Spencer as the joint youngest winner of a senior grand prix at 20 years and 174 days. No longer did he doubt he could match Elias for audacious overtaking manoeuvres. 'Honda have given us perfect support, even though we're not a factory team,' he said. 'I've proved I can run at the front with these guys and I hope things get easier and easier as time goes by.' Stoner, like Pedrosa a MotoGP rookie, said he had not expected to be where he was for another year. 'It's as if Casey was born on a MotoGP bike,' Melandri said. Hayden, the only man to have finished on the podium in each round, went a point clear of Capirossi in the standings after Turkey but knew he needed to up his game. 'I've got to win more races if I'm going to be a title threat,' he said. But the slipper clutch was causing him all sorts of problems. It did not suit his style. Pedrosa was silky smooth, Hayden a dirt-tracker. They were chalk and cheese.

Others around the paddock had some damning views on Hayden. He might have been top of the standings but he was the victim of a sniping campaign. He flogged his guts for the sake of the team in testing, but what was the point if he could not give the necessary feedback? 'He prides himself on the work he puts in but he can't draw any conclusions,' a Yamaha insider sniped. More tellingly, it was a view some within Honda also subscribed to. In light of such comments, Hayden would veer towards paranoia during the dramatic denouement. An industrial accident in which a worker was killed at the Honda factory further darkened morale.

The young guns continued to fire mortar bombs at Rossi. Pedrosa got his first win in China, fending off Hayden who was lapping at record pace in an effort to prove he was Honda's lead rider. Meanwhile, Rossi failed to finish in Shanghai and then at Le Mans. After five rounds he was eighth in the championship, below the likes of his team-mate Colin Edwards. Hayden was forty-three points clear of him, followed by Melandri, Capirossi, Pedrosa and Stoner. 'Youth is the future,' Jerry Burgess mused as he headed down the pitlane. Stoner agreed. 'I'm not being cocky but I'm way ahead of schedule,' he beamed. 'I didn't think I'd be in this position for another year. I'm living the dream.' He had a cherubim's face and a docker's grit and, despite his inexperience, he was not about to let a barbed comment from Rossi about his ability to ride on worn tyres go unchecked. 'I'm not intimidated by the big names,' he said. 'Most of them have been good – except for the ones you'd expect.'

His was a steely core honed during his nomadic upbringing. With his parents, Colin and Bronwyn, he had pitched up in

Penrith in 2000 and competed in the 125cc British Championship. Later the caravan went to Spain, and now he was living in Monaco, the millionaires' playground, a world away from Kurri-Kurri, New South Wales. He had a wrecking ball subtlety and did not deal in niceties. He said he had a theory why opportunities had dried up for Chaz Davies. 'It used to get to me when people said I was a crasher. Well, I've proved them wrong this season, but when you're on the way up you have to impress. You have to go out and ride right on the edge. I don't think they do that in Britain. They prefer riders to be sensible and consistent, but now and again you're going to crash if you're on the limit. You have got to get noticed. I worry for Chaz now. I really do.'

Stoner was tough and could cut you dead with a quizzical frown. Meanwhile, Britain's latest teen, Bradley Smith, was struggling to make the top twenty in the 125 class. He was a novice but he knew he needed more. Already.

Hayden's misery with his clutch continued. He was joint top of the standings with Capirossi but he had not won a race. That statistic began to worm away at him, especially when the media repeated it with each passing round. In some quarters he was almost dismissed as a title candidate, the view being he was leading by default as he was merely staying upright while all around lost their heads.

And then Rossi started to make his move. It came, inevitably, at the Italian Grand Prix where, for the first time in years, the massed ranks of fans were contemplating the mortality of their hero. Biaggi was gone and Rossi was ailing. A bunch of kids were kicking him now that he was down, but they didn't kill him off. 'Hell, I had my foot on his throat and I let him go,' Hayden would moan months later. And Mugello was where it started.

Rossi still made mistakes. The first came on the second lap and that lost him the lead. The next came with nine laps left. Rossi braked late and allowed a cavalcade past. But he then made short work of Melandri and Hayden. Gibernau, who had qualified on pole to suggest the ending of the curse was a matter of time, found he was a toe-slider short. He felt his foot heating from friction and the dampness of blood. He lifted his foot and took a couple of laps to adjust, by which time his chance had departed over the horizon at Casonova. Now it was Rossi versus Capirossi, two Italians, a red one and a yellow one, just like the old days. Capirossi went by Rossi on the start-finish straight of the final lap, but ran wide in doing so. The champion sneaked back into the lead and held his ground. Hayden was third and the podium finishers were separated by a mere 0.7 seconds. 'It was a dogfight and the guys were out for blood,' Hayden said.

It was the period in the season when the crashes began to hurt. Stoner always bristled when people reminded him of the Rolling Stoner tag. He had justified his early crashes by saying he was flirting with the limit to get noticed, but now he was catching the eye again, somehow escaping with only a severely bruised neck from a spectacular crash at Mugello. A fortnight later they went to Barcelona and plotted. Faster, harder, better. *This is the way the world ends.*

It was an awful start. Stoner was away quickest, his neck pain forgotten in the sprint to the first corner. Rossi and Hayden were inches behind and held their shape for the first bend. They could not know that, behind them, the championship had already changed beyond all recognition. Ducati were gone. It was Gibernau's fault. He closed the gap to the apex and his brake lever touched Capirossi's rear. Gibernau's bike somersaulted into a gravel trap. Capirossi fell and barged into Melandri. He slid off and was trapped momentarily by Pedrosa's bike. Hopper jumped off his Suzuki before it careered into the tyre wall and Randy de Puniet escaped a horrific injury by a matter of feet as Gibernau's airborne Ducati whistled past him. They had fallen as dominoes.

When they restarted the race Stoner was again the fastest until he crashed. Rossi won and was suddenly third in the championship. He had now officially stopped dallying with Ferrari and committed himself to Yamaha for the following season. People speculated about the precise nature of the role he had been offered at Maranello with many saying, somewhat sniffily, that it had been a test driver's post. It was not. Rossi was offered the chance to race a full grand prix season, but refused. John Surtees, the only man to have won the world title on two and four wheels, insisted to me that the stopwatch had decided it and the bare fact was Rossi was not quick enough. In truth Ferrari were very impressed and realized the massive marketing coup it would be to have Rossi teamed with an Italian factory.

A female fan loitered outside the Yamaha truck. This was normal. In Spain there would be some fans waiting for Pedrosa too, but Rossi had a larger throng following him in every country. The woman eventually approached Ali Forth and dumped a container in her arms. 'Give this to Valentino,' she said. 'I love him so much.' Forth looked at the box and saw the No. 46 carved into a piece of wood. More alarmingly, she also saw a face looking back at her. 'It was a customized bowl with a live terrapin in it,' she recalled. 'I shouted after her to come back, but she was gone.'

There followed a worried debate. Someone suggested flushing the terrapin down the toilet, but Rossi, an animal lover, insisted it must not be harmed. He then ordered Robbie, one of his entourage, to take it back to Milan. Forth remembers taking a cab with Robbie to the airport the next day. 'I said, "I take it you managed to get rid of it then." That's when he unzipped a helmet bag and there it was. He was terrified about getting it through customs. He thought we were going to get done for smuggling animals.' In the end they got it a special passport. The terrapin made it to Milan where it still lives with Robbie.

Rossi could ill afford any distractions. The season was becoming a brutal one. Melandri was in Holland a week later for the Dutch

TT and sported a deep red shiner. His shoulder was strapped up and he winced in pain when he moved. Capirossi was even worse with a terribly bruised abdomen. Gibernau was, as ever, the least fortunate. He had been rushed to hospital after the accident only for the ambulance to crash into a bus 50 yards from the entrance. He would not race at Assen.

The trauma continued in the Netherlands where Rossi fell and broke his left foot and right wrist in practice. Elias was sent home with a mangled shoulder. Suddenly, it looked as though it might be a case of last man standing. Hayden had emerged through all this unscathed and took advantage to win in Holland. His luck seemed to have turned. Trailing Colin Edwards into the final corner, he arrived too fast and rode into the gravel trap. 'Man, those things are so deep you need a 4x4 to stop you from sinking,' he said. Amazingly, as if charmed, Hayden kept his Honda upright and looked on as Edwards ran on to the grass and was flung over the handlebars within sight of the flag. Pumped full of painkillers, Rossi had to make do with a race against his body and was eighth. 'We have a lot of work to do to improve the situation with my wrist and try to reduce the swelling and heal the bone,' he said. 'It would be better to have a month off to recover, but we are racers and we have to go straight to the next one. For sure I won't be at full fitness.' Hayden's lead over Pedrosa was now up to forty-two points and Rossi was another four adrift. Earl paced the paddock and Graziano pulled his braces.

It was survival of the fastest. At Donington Park, it was hard not to feel some sympathy for Pedrosa. Although he now exuded the *joie de vivre* of a depressed traffic warden, his frown after winning the British Grand Prix by 3.86 seconds was understandable. The sublime ride underlined his immense potential, but the joyous scenes that greeted Rossi's second place showed where the public's affection lay. Pedrosa won by the MotoGP equivalent of a country mile, parked his Repsol Honda and insisted that he was happy. Rossi rolled into the pits, covered everyone in smoke and then swore live on the BBC. 'For me and for the people, it is like a victory,' Rossi said, but even with his ice pack the people's champion could feel the heat.

Stoner, meanwhile, had shown another side to his make-up. At Assen he made a last-lap mistake that enabled Pedrosa to finish ahead of him in third place. People were hailing Pedrosa as the genius-elect at that point, whereas Stoner was undeniably fast but too erratic. It was a harsh appraisal, given he was on the LCR Honda and shorn of the latest factory add-ons from Honda. When Pedrosa got the better of him at Assen, Stoner stormed into the garage and sank into a violent sulk. 'Fuck off!' he told Cecchinello when he went to speak to him. He had words with his father. Chris Herring was in the garage and had seen enough. A blunt-speaking northerner, he told Stoner he couldn't go around treating people like that.

Stoner was still learning the ropes of working with a major Japanese factory. He sat down with his engineers after Donington and they listened to his woes for half an hour and then left. Stoner looked at Cecchinello. 'You can tell Chris that was a waste of time,' he griped. The following Monday an email came from Japan saying Stoner would be getting the works frame. 'He just didn't understand the process at that point,' Herring recalled.

The season then twisted at breakneck pace to its shuddering climax. Rossi won in Germany and celebrated by wearing the Italian football shirt of Marco Materazzi. The defender was then at the centre of a global debate after he provoked Zinedine Zidane into headbutting him during the World Cup Final in Berlin a week earlier. 'I am an Inter Milan fan and Materazzi is a great guy,' Rossi said, ignoring the plethora of lipreading experts who had claimed the tattooed hard man had insulted Zidane's mother, sister, race and psychological state. 'I asked him if I could have his shirt and I said I would wear it if I won. It was a thank you for winning the World Cup.'

Hayden won in Laguna, as he knew he had to, and the lead over Rossi was fifty-one points with six races left. It was a huge advantage, but Wayne Rainey, his compatriot, said he needed to win more races. Colin Edwards argued that Hayden could follow but not lead. Rossi, too, adopted his time-honoured stance with rivals. 'Rossi was always very chummy with Nicky, but later that season he started blanking him,' a Honda official said. 'I don't know whether it was deliberate but it was noticeable.' Certainly, one of Rossi's traits was to start whispering to another rider or even himself as soon as someone else started speaking in a press conference. He did this without fail. 'I've never seen him sit in a press conference and listen to what another rider has to say,' Forth said. 'It would be his worst scenario – having to listen to people talk tactics.'

Hayden said 'the trash-talking' should stop, but could not find the results to convince his critics. He was only ninth in the Czech Republic but managed to get under the skin of Pedrosa, who complained that both Hayden and Rossi had been too aggressive in slamming doors on him. He felt like the kid being beaten up in the playground and he was not about to let it continue. Pedrosa! Pedrosa! Pedrosa! *This is the way the world ends.*

Pedrosa felt even worse by the time they lined up in Malaysia. It was Friday and free practice when Pedrosa got it all wrong at a corner and his knee was rammed into the jagged concrete kerb. He was jettisoned off his bike and crashed down on his legs. His right knee was a mess. Someone inserted a spoon into the maw to scoop out some flesh so it could be stitched. The pain was excruciating and a red rivulet ran from the gash. He was pushed around the paddock in a wheelchair to ease the burden on the joint and his team feared they would have to pull him out of the race.

In the event Pedrosa proved fragile looks can be deceiving and he beat Hayden to third place. Rossi won from Capirossi and, as Pedrosa went away to have his knee restitched, they indulged in a mocking prank on the podium. With a pointed nod to Pedrosa's wheelchair, Rossi picked up a chair and sat on it. At one point Capirossi even sat on his knee. The implication that the twenty-year-old with angelic looks was a baby was as clear as it was misguided. Hayden, too, had sighed at the sycophancy of the Rossi phenomenon. 'It's unbelievable the amount of support he has,' Hayden told me. 'It's everyone. Fans, but also people around the paddock too. It's tough.'

The thought intensified in Australia. The race was a curious one as it was run under new flag-to-flag weather rules, meaning that there would be no race stoppage if the rain came, but racers could come in and pit. Sure enough the rain did come and the pitting allowed Chris Vermeulen to score his first podium finish in MotoGP behind race winner Melandri. Rossi was a crucial third, but should have been docked ten seconds and thus relegated to seventh because he overtook Stoner under a yellow flag. Hayden and Honda failed to understand how race direction had missed the move. The officials claimed they had not seen the decisive camera angle and were powerless to impose a retrospective punishment now that the race had finished. 'I am sure they would have docked me the time if it had been the other way round,' Hayden lamented. He found himself in a unique position. Not only did he believe Pedrosa was getting preferential treatment from his team, but he also felt Rossi was the blue-eyed boy of both the paddock and officialdom. He was fighting battles on every front.

He did at least re-sign for Honda on the Friday at Motegi before the Japanese Grand Prix, but the pressure was mounting. The clutch problem made every start a lottery and there were rumblings within Honda to the effect that it was more a psychological problem than a mechanical one. That was not true, but the clutch issue certainly played on Hayden's mind. 'Nicky definitely got the impression the HRC guys were not pulling their weight,' Herring recalled. 'They were being criticized from within the garage. That would not happen at Yamaha. Jerry Burgess would never let Rossi know his true opinion of the Japanese engineers. But there was clearly an issue with the clutch. You know they were doing things quite publicly – practising starts, pulling wheelies and nearly falling off.'

Hayden ditched the diaphragm spring clutch and used a standard version in the race. Honda were still apoplectic about the way Rossi had circumnavigated the rules in Australia. Their rage reddened when Rossi took second place behind a peerless Capirossi with Hayden down in fifth. It was a disastrous day with Pedrosa in seventh place after being bullied again, this time by Edwards who pushed him off the track. The bitterness festered.

My sacrifice, God, is a broken spirit; God, do not spurn a broken, humbled heart.

Pedrosa was the rookie of the year but he wanted more than that. He wanted to beat them all. He was fifth in the championship with a mangled knee and a season of bruising. He was deeply disgruntled.

And so they came to Estoril, an ugly track with a sea wind blowing white dust over the paddock like snow. They came to Estoril with Hayden just twelve points clear of Rossi with two races left. With Hayden having won only two races to Rossi's five. With Rossi rejuvenated. With the chatter problem long replaced by the chattering of discontent from inside and outside the Hayden camp. And that was when Pedrosa, having been picked on for so long, flexed his muscles. When he took Hayden out and all hell broke lose. *This is the way the world ends.*

LAP 8

This place dripped memories from every brick and railing. He would have liked the time to sit down on Harris Promenade and reminisce about the old days. Christ, they had some fun but it had been bloody hard work too. The pressure of being the best was a millstone, the pinched face of the Count a shadowy reminder of what was waiting if you failed to win. It was all that mattered. Faster, harder, better.

You get bound by your legacy. You are a hero, an idol and a legend, but beneath that straitjacket you are flesh and bone and weakness. He is touched that the fans remember him now in 1978, after all this time, but he dislikes the invasive glare of adoration now as then. So he shuts himself away with a paperback and his guitar.

He thinks about those who had it tougher. Like Ernst Degner. It was 1961 when the East German turned up to a race in Sweden. He was nervous and fidgety and explained to a few confidants that he was awaiting word from home, where his family was defecting under the cloak of darkness. His wife, toddler and baby were hidden under a blanket in the boot of a car with a breathing tube attached. They got through the checkpoint and made it to the West. Later, when Ernst went to race in Finland, he was a wreck because he said it was too close to Russia and so he never went out without an armed bodyguard.

The Brits had it tough too. The privateers would turn up with their rusting transits and cobbled bikes and race for a pittance. Mike left his wallet in the car one night at the Dutch TT and so he asked John 'Moon Eyes' Cooper if he could borrow £50. John gave it to him. 'I've not forgotten,' Mike would say afterwards when they met. 'I'll pay you back.' At Mallory Park John beat Mike, whose MV was struggling. Moon Eyes saw fleeting glory. Mike did his bit by balking some others to help the leader. 'Shall we call that £50 straight?' he said.

The race organizers were even harder with their money. 'They treated you like pigs,' Moon Eyes would tell me. 'You'd queue for two hours in the rain to get your start money. It was degrading. Bloody awful.'

It was different at the top. Mike had his Ferrari and lived out of plush hotels. He was a star, but it all depended on winning. Success was a voracious mistress and demanded more so the horizon moved and the sands shifted. He won an unprecedented fourth successive 500cc title in style, claiming eight races to Ago's one, but he was disgruntled. The Count's desire to turn Ago into an all-Italian superstar was an open secret and when they gave him the three-cylinder 350 to fuel his assault on the 1965 title, Mike's distinctive nose was put firmly out of joint. Ago was very much his own man, but perhaps his Italian roots made him more deferential to the Count. 'He was a very difficult person, not friendly, very serious,' Ago said of his old paymaster. 'But you have to remember that the most important thing to him was his factory. The factory had 3,500 people and the racing team had ten. Racing was just a hobby. It was not that he liked to keep Mike Hailwood or Agostini waiting, but he had a queue of people before us and racing came second. As far as the

Count was concerned, helicopters were far more important.'

Mike had experienced too much of the Count and left. He signed for Honda on the recommendation of Jim Redman, but Honda was not a trouble-free ride either. The deal was for Jim to ride in the 500cc class with Mike concentrating on the 250cc and 350cc championships. He duly won both, but the agreement hindered his hopes in the senior ranks, and Ago was now the un-rivalled darling of the Italian media, an affable hero with devilish looks and a distinctly un-Latin calm.

By the end of 1966 he was within touching distance of the 500cc title, but then Mike came back. He needed to win the last three races and he secured dominant victories in Ulster and on the island. Now it came down to the final round, the Nations race at Monza, that emotional vat of machismo. It was man against man. Ago on the MV, the bike Mike had loved and lost, and him on the Honda, a brutally powerful machine that was difficult to handle and which he labelled 'the camel'.

The two were miles ahead of the rest. They were used to lapping everybody else and fighting only each other. Mike liked Ago, despite saying that he stole all his best women, but he hated him too. Ralph Bryans sampled the duality of that relationship when he wandered into his caravan after Ago had suffered a big crash. 'Jesus, Ago's had a bad one,' he spluttered. Mike fixed him with his tired eyes and simply said, 'Good.'

The race at Monza was shaping up into a classic confrontation. Mike led, but Ago went past on the third lap. Some wondered whether Mike had deliberately moved aside to follow Ago, slip-stream him and let him do the hard graft, forcing a mistake by hanging on to his exhaust and nerves. But then Mike's own exhaust failed and he shivered to a stop. He rolled his bike back to the pits and heard the tumultuous roar from the packed grand-stands. The fans invaded the track and hoisted Ago on to their shoulders. 'There were 110,000 people there,' Ago said to me. 'I had all my Italian people with me. The track was full. We went to a restaurant in Monza that night and I tried not to think about it too much. It was overwhelming. I had beaten Mike Hailwood and I was the world champion. But then, almost immediately, I felt the pressure of being the best in the world.' The millstone was hung around his neck before the champagne stains had dried. He had climbed the mountain and now he, too, had to stop himself disappearing over the hill.

CHAPTER ELEVEN

WANTED!

'Toni, va fan culo! Va fan culo! Hey, Toni!' It was the morning after the nightmare before.

Nicky Hayden had barely slept as he tossed and turned over events. He had been given a lift back to his motorhome by his brother, Tommy, after the crash. Most felt the 2006 championship was gone. It had been wrenched from him by Dani Pedrosa. By that little upstart. Pedrosa! Pedrosa! Pedrosa! They turned on the monitor and watched the rest of the race unfold, and Hayden found himself drawn away from his anger towards crumbs of hope. Rossi was winning the Portuguese Grand Prix, but he was being made to fight for it by Toni Elias. This was the Spaniard with the ready smile and dense mop of oil-black hair who had taken out Rossi in his first race for Honda. This was the kid who had left Casey Stoner bemoaning the fact he would never be able to match the passing move he put on Marco Melandri in Japan. And now this was the man who was dicing with Rossi on a wild last lap. Rossi never settled for second best and they swapped the lead four times. The final time was coming out of the last corner when Elias slithered and shook his way to parity and a win by two thousandths of a second.

Rossi had still taken twenty points out of Hayden and turned a twelve-point deficit into an eight-point lead with only the Valencia Grand Prix to come. He would have liked the extra five points as a buffer but he was in high spirits. Estoril had restored the natural order and Rossi supped a beer and hugged Uccio. Pedrosa's gloom was mirrored by another who had dared take on Rossi. Sete Gibernau had been wiped out by an errant Stoner and was now twelfth in the standings. It had been the most miserable of seasons for the Spaniard and, if his submission to a cartoon curse was not bad enough, Ducati let it be known he was being dumped. The man who would replace him in 2007 was Stoner, a cocky kid who had fallen in five of the last eleven races.

Elias, meanwhile, had saved his career with his exploits. He had ridden on shredding rubber to a new contract. On the satellite bike he had taken on the best of the factories and won. He was making toast when he heard the commotion outside his motorhome and looked out to see Rossi hanging from a window, flicking him the finger and shouting at him. 'Toni, va fan culo!' Go fuck yourself! It was done with a smile. Rossi had evidently got over being pipped on the line. He had the bigger picture in mind as he celebrated. Elias grinned. It was hard not to like Rossi.

The same went for Hayden. It had been, as he pointed out in a glassy-eyed diatribe, 'fucking bullshit', but he handled himself with good grace in the aftermath. He wanted to punch Pedrosa, but the Spaniard had apologized. They were never friends and so the severing of a brittle alliance was no big deal. Hayden censored his anger and said he had not expected Pedrosa to take him out, that he was surprised by the lack of team orders, that he had not given up. Earl, meanwhile, showed a touch of class when he buried his disappointment to go to Rossi's motorhome to congratulate him.

Behind the scenes things were far uglier. Hayden stayed in Portugal for Monday's test but his shoulder throbbed from the crash. When he got home to Owensboro he went for an MRI scan which revealed he had aggravated an old collarbone injury. He was in pain, had seen a massive fifty-one-point lead transformed into an eight-point deficit and had his lingering suspicions about HRC muddying his mood. That was understandable. Satoru Horiike, HRC's managing director, scarcely helped when he said of Hayden's clutch problem, 'We can't fix it.'

One more bad start and the title was Rossi's. Hayden tried to ignore the shit storm. The 'WANTED!' Pedrosa posters hinted at the sympathy people felt for him, but he did not want to sacrifice his season on the altar of heroic failure. Alberto Puig defended Pedrosa, as was to be expected, but he threw a hand grenade to Kentucky by pointing out Pedrosa had a mathematical chance of winning the title and that it would not have happened had Hayden got to the front. 'He hasn't done that all year,' Puig said. The in-fighting was manna from heaven for Yamaha. Edwards said that, while it was true Yamaha also had no team orders, it was also a fact that he was not 'a retard'. Rossi also tried to stir up trouble for Hayden. 'There are two riders at Honda. One is a little rooster who is fifth in the world championship and the other is the leader who's all alone.'

Steve Westlake was the Repsol Honda press officer at the time and was staggered by the vitriol that flowed after Estoril. 'It got to the point where people were attacking Dani's personality rather than what had happened on the track,' he recalled. 'It was an excuse to hammer him. It was just a racing accident. Dani did not mean to do it.' Others felt the crash was the culmination of a bitter season. 'I think Pedrosa had been beaten up by these guys all season and that was his revenge,' a source close to the Pedrosa camp said. 'Dani and Hayden had traded paint in Germany and there was the incident with Edwards. He was the slight, waif-like figure being picked on in his rookie season. Whether consciously or subconsciously, Estoril was the result.'

The Yamaha camp's mood was improved further when one of their mechanics sat next to Hayden on the plane from Madrid to Valencia for the coronation. Hayden had been working tirelessly with his personal trainer and brothers, but his shoulder was still a problem. Hayden tried to shield his pain from the mechanic but, when told he had to put his bag in the overhead locker, had to ask the stewardess for help. The Yamaha spy stifled a smirk. This did not look like a man capable of dethroning a seven-time world champion.

Rossi's arrival at Valencia was a more glamorous affair. The Valencia football team happened to be at the airport at the same time, flying to an away match, and they stopped the Italian and asked if they could pose for pictures with him. In his public utterances Rossi championed the wonderful atmosphere at Yamaha, a double-edged comment intended to highlight the reverse situation at Honda.

I sat down with Horiike in Valencia on the Friday before the race. He was in one of the HRC transporters with its banks of computer screens. It was a sci-fi hub that suggested no stone was being left unturned, but HRC were in danger of being left red-faced and not only by the hoax email purportedly from Horiike which confessed to making a dog's dinner of the season. He was candid in the circumstances. 'During the season we leave everything to our riders,' he said, but he also acknowledged that this approach had handed the initiative to Yamaha. Regarding the clutch issue, he said he had been personally very frustrated that it had festered away for so long. Could Hayden and Pedrosa work together next season? 'Yes.' Even though Hayden had said he felt like killing Pedrosa? 'Yes.'

Rossi used his last media briefing to try to alienate Hayden from HRC. 'They have not treated Nicky like a championship leader,' he said. The use of the Christian name was again deliberate. Rossi was the smiling assassin once more, an enemy sharpening his knife beneath a cloak of camaraderie.

The role of Puig also came under increasing scrutiny. With Pedrosa's title hopes all but gone before Portugal, the theory was Puig had put his protégé's interests ahead of the team. Puig had added to the furore by suggesting Hayden had been responsible for the crash by braking too early, but even Pedrosa was not having that. 'It's hard to forget such an incident and I'll do everything I can to help Nicky,' he said.

Hayden had worked out his approach before first practice. He would give it his all and let the cards fall. He even had a gambling motif on the rump of his new leathers bearing the words 'All in'.

'You don't chew yesterday's breakfast,' Hayden said in his dusty southern brogue, 'but I still want to puke.' The Pedrosa issue still rankled. 'I can't believe what he was thinking,' he muttered. 'But I don't sign his cheques.' He sat down with both Puig and Pedrosa on the Saturday night and buried the hatchet, at least temporarily. 'We made a gentlemen's agreement,' Hayden said. There were still no team orders, 'but we said we'd help each other and behave like team-mates'. Hayden left his last media briefing with a smile, his eyes hidden by mirror shades but his heart on his sleeve. 'If I lose on Sunday then I may never get over it,' he said. 'I'll just try my hardest and see what the big guy's got planned.'

Rossi was fast. He did not like Valencia. Too many short straights and twists stuffed inside a bowl like intestines. He did not like it but he could get around it quickly. He topped the first practice and qualifying, four places and almost four-tenths of a second better than Hayden. Troy Bayliss, the Aussie brawler, was second on the grid on Gibernau's Ducati with Loris Capirossi completing a front row of hard-to-pass racers. Hayden had Pedrosa next to him and Stoner behind. He needed to win and have Rossi fade to third to be the champion, but the American had not made the podium in five races. Rossi had five wins. It would take something unexpected.

Earl was a caged lion in the garage. Basi Pedrosa watched and hoped her son would be safe. Everyone focused on the Repsol duo and few considered that Rossi, too, was under pressure. None of his other titles had gone to the wire and, having performed a fantastic rearguard action that drew the applause of everyone from Agostini to Valencia's footballers, he now had it all to lose.

Hayden needed a good start. The clutch issue evaporated and he got one. He barged past Rossi before the first corner. 'I was either going to the front or I was going down,' Hayden said. Rossi, by contrast, made a sluggish start, but had places to play with. Bayliss, the man who had once made his knuckles bleed by punching plastic, was in front and loving the freedom from World Superbikes. It was a thirty-lap race and Rossi's mind was calm. Thinking fast. Moving slowly. He knew he needed to make inroads but he had plenty of time. He was seventh by the start of the fifth lap and Hayden was second. If the American stayed there Rossi would need to pick up three more places before the end. This was his stage. This is what he loved. Speed. Too fast, too furious. Everything more difficult, everything more beautiful.

Pedrosa dutifully moved aside when he felt Hayden coming behind him. Hayden had said the only way Pedrosa could make it up to him was by helping him in Valencia. Here was the help. It went against every competitive instinct in Pedrosa but he eased off and let Hayden take second place. And then . . .

It happened on the fifth lap and was a gentle slide.

Rossi lost the front end of the Camel Yamaha and went down. There were shrieks in the press room. Mack looked calm but his blood was pumping as violently as the rest.

In the Yamaha garage Uccio, Rossi's oldest friend from the nights spent in the bars of Tavullia, thinking up bizarre celebrations and drinking deep on the dream, held his head. Twenty yards along the pitlane in the Honda garage, there were stifled cheers and pulled punches to the air. It could not be.

Rossi was thinking clearly enough to scamper to his bike, make sure the engine was still running and remount. Hayden's heart skipped several beats when he saw his pitboard. 'ROSSI P20'. But it was not over. Rossi had charged through fields before so why not again? 'I saw my board again and realized Rossi had picked up a few places and thought, "Oh boy!"' Hayden would say later.

Capirossi was crawling all over the back of Hayden so he let him through. Rossi needed to get to eighth, but it soon became apparent that he was not going to make it. The crash had twisted his handlebars, bent his footrest and broken his clutch lever. That raised the tension even more. Now it was a question of whether Hayden had the bottle to see it through. In the Repsol garage they tried to assuage their hysteria. Tommy and Roger Lee grinned and grimaced in equal measure. Earl and Rose held their palms together. This was journey's end. All the years and thousands of miles ploughed across the Midwest were leading to this moment. These 2.4 miles around Ricardo Tormo.

The soundbites from a fortnight earlier hung in the air. 'I know he hates this situation but I don't know if I can forgive him,' Hayden had said. 'We are one big team not two,' Rossi sniped. 'It is the first time I've ever hit another bike in my career and it had to be like this,' Pedrosa groaned. Fucking bullshit. Puke. Kill him. 'If Rossi makes a mistake you know, well that's highly unlikely.'

The mistake had happened though. And Pedrosa, nursing the broken finger that had added injury to the insults, had rolled over. Two corners to go. Thinking fast. Moving slowly. Everything beautiful.

Bayliss won from Capirossi but they were little victories. The future lay behind them. Hayden crossed the line, head bowed, in tears. Back in the wee small hours of a Kentucky morning, Kathleen Hayden bounced around her room. Her computer had stopped working after she saw that Rossi had crashed. She was excited and frustrated in equal measure and hoped her brother could win in cyberspace.

Hayden and Pedrosa shook hands. He had done his bit. The pair would never get on and their relationship would endure several more troughs, but a blood feud had been spared. Rossi took defeat well publicly. 'He wins with class and loses with class,' Hayden said. Rossi had plenty of reasons to be angry. He said he had tested how far he could push things on Turn 2 around 400 times, but still his front tyre had failed him. He thought back to Estoril and how Toni Elias had beaten him by six inches and two-thousandths of a second. Had he fended off Elias he would have had another five points and the championship. Toni could go fuck himself all right. Rossi had won five races as opposed to Hayden's two. Capirossi had also won more than Hayden. Melandri and Pedrosa had just as many. 'Nicky won and so he is the best,' Rossi said. 'If it is not me then I am glad it is him. With Nicky there is not the polemic and shit there is with other riders. I made a mistake at the start and I made a mistake when I slid; whenever you crash it's a mistake. But Nicky's a good guy and a great rider.' Hayden joined in the mutual back-slapping. 'It's not like I beat some kid down the street – it's Valentino Rossi!'

Bayliss wallowed in his victory. It was a high-speed V-sign to his former MotoGP employers and a well-received return. People liked Bayliss for his honesty and toughness. A few months later he would suffer a horrific crash at Donington Park which saw him almost lose a finger and then endure a four-hour operation to save a testicle. His reaction to that was typical. 'I whipped off my gloves and to my surprise my pinky was hanging by a thread. I'm no expert, but I knew it wouldn't be there for long. Luckily there was a very good hand specialist unit in Derby and they trimmed it. While I was under, the urologist worked on my groin. You could say I split the atom!'

In the press conference Bayliss beamed. 'Hell, seven days off the beer and I come up a treat.' Hayden celebrated with his family. With Earl and Rose and Tommy and Roger Lee. 'Blood's thick in Earl's yard,' Hayden said, the country boy who shunned the racers' playground of Monaco to live on the family ranch in the American south. 'My brothers are my boys. This is what I've dreamed about since I was ten years old.' Hayden rang Kathleen and wondered what he would do with the BMW he had won as the qualifier of the year. 'There's a place for it back on the lot,' Earl said.

Someone said they had seen Rossi in the garage with a cigar and a smile, but he was not fooling anybody. This hurt him to his very core. Not only had he lost the title, he had done so through a new-found fallibility. He hid behind his smokescreen of generosity and fatalism. 'Nobody died,' he said. Indeed, the king was not dead, but he had taken a hell of a beating and, for the first time in his career, Rossi was forced to begin plotting *his comeback*.

A month later a handful of journalists arranged to meet Hayden at Gordon Ramsay's Boxwood Café in London. It was a classy place with pretensions that were anathema to the farm boy. He sat down in his bright leather Repsol jacket and Gas jeans, pawed at his food and picked over the bones of a stunning climax. He certainly did not need reminding of the ephemeral nature of racing bikes at 200mph. The previous week he had watched in horror as Tommy had been knocked unconscious on a blood-stained track in Malaysia; the following week he would go to a California clinic for an operation to save his MotoGP world title defence. 'This ain't fishing,' he said.

Hayden was now big news as the man who had ended a motor-sport era. In Ramsay's restaurant he spoke of relaunching the sport in the United States and silencing the doubters. They were aims that depended on the surgeon's knife. The twenty-five-year-old revealed that he was struggling with injury during the last race of the season, when Rossi cracked and crashed. The pain stemmed from the accident two weeks earlier when Hayden had been attacked from behind by Pedrosa and left raging in a gravel trap. 'I fractured the tip of my bone and there's a fragment floating around in my shoulder,' he said. 'And they need to get the plate taken out that's been in there for two years. Valencia wasn't too bad because I had a lot of adrenalin and the World Championship was on the line, but I can't ride like this.'

He hoped to be back on the Repsol Honda in January. He was worried, but knew surgery was an occupational hazard. 'You can't do this because you want to be a paper chaser,' he said. 'It takes guts and nerve. In Malaysia I had to watch them cut the leathers off my brother and then go back to testing. It's tough on my mum, with three sons who race. When we were kids, my older brother [Tommy] crashed and had some internal bleeding. That was pretty bad. Then my little bro [Roger Lee] broke his leg this summer. In this sport you break a foot and it's like walking away uninjured.'

The celebrations had been low key. Rose had hired a DJ and booked a hall in Owensboro for a victory party, but Nicky did not drink and it was no wild night out with Rossi and the Tribe. Nevertheless, his world had changed in those few weeks. 'I had it when I was a teenager,' he said. 'I started winning races and the girls who had given me the blow-off in middle school started coming round again. But I don't want new friends.'

He did not want friends because he had his family. 'My dad worked with thoroughbred racehorses and my mum's side grew tobacco,' he said. 'I'd work in the fields in winter, cutting tobacco, stripping tobacco. I did it all apart from smoke it. It taught me not to take short cuts.' He also worked at Second Chance Autos. 'Some days they'd repo a car and there'd be an argument – that was the highlight of my day.'

It had been a long journey, but Hayden had arrived and Rossi's hegemony had crumbled. 'I could have gone to Yamaha in the past, but I'd have been fooling myself,' Hayden said. 'I didn't want to play second fiddle to Valentino and I'm not going to give a five-time world champion my scraps. Now I hope people in the States wake up to MotoGP. They didn't shut down the streets when I went home and, while I'm not in it to be a rock star, I want it to grow.'

Hayden's rematch with Rossi in 2007 was a mouthwatering prospect, especially as the sport ushered in the new 800cc era. The king was not dead, but he had been usurped. Rossi mourned his loss by coming eleventh in the Rally of New Zealand, but Hayden's plans remained resolutely two-wheeled. He looked at his plate, wondered about the size of Ramsay's portions and sipped a mineral water. 'Cars? Hell, I can't even drive a stake in the ground.'

LAP 9

Mike rang to check on Pauline and the kids. They were doing fine, but he could hear the apprehension in her voice. *The comeback* had taken over them all and its tremors were being felt far across Douglas Bay. Mike wondered if people were taking it all a bit seriously and expecting too much. He was thirty-eight and had a gammy leg. It was 1978, after all, eleven years since he had got back together with Pauline and gone to the island for his TT apotheosis.

That was 1967 and Pauline was working as the receptionist at a hairdresser's shop in Kensington. Someone in the salon was boasting about her new boyfriend. 'He's just won an important race,' she gushed.

'What's his name?' Pauline asked. 'I used to know someone who raced bikes.'

'Mike Hailwood.'

'Oh, really,' she stuttered. 'I . . . I used to know Mike Hailwood.'

The woman described Pauline to Mike when they next met, but she had changed beyond all recognition in the five-year hiatus since they had watched *A Kind of Loving* and left the island in a gloomy state after Tom Phillis's accident. 'When he knew me I had very short hair and was as green as the grass, Plain Jane, young and very innocent,' Pauline remembered. 'But five years on I was living in London, had waist-length hair, had all my nails done and was into the latest fashions. I was a totally different package and so, when she described me to Mike, he had no idea who I was.'

Mike's girlfriend said he was racing at Brands Hatch and she wanted to surprise him. Pauline had read about Mike over the years and was well aware of his reputation as a womanizer. 'Do you think that's wise?' she asked.

'Oh yes,' the girlfriend said confidently. 'He'll love it. Why don't you come along?'

Pauline said she would. She was intrigued not jealous. A stylist who had a crush on her said she could drive his new Mini Cooper if she let him come too. 'I thought it would be nice to see him again,' Pauline said. Sure enough, Mike had arranged to meet another girl that night, but luckily she could not make it. 'We were in the bar after the day's racing and I could see him looking at me,' Pauline said. 'He still didn't recognize me. Finally, it clicked and he came bounding up and said, "You've grown up haven't you?"

'Bill Ivy's parents were away and they lived in Maidstone, not too far from Brands, so that night he said we should all go back to their place. "We'll have a party," Bill said. Mike sat with me one side of him and his girlfriend the other. He was looking at her and talking to her, but fondling my knee. At every available moment, he'd whisper out of the corner of his mouth, "Give me your number." I told him he didn't need it. The night wore on and eventually it was time to leave, but the guy who had the crush on me had gone. I guess he'd got annoyed with me because he could see I fancied Mike. I asked who was going back to London and Bill said nobody was until the next morning, I'd have to stay the night. I did and spent the whole night fighting Bill off. I slept in my clothes but his hands kept roaming over. "Get off! Get off!" Before I left I said, "Great party, Bill" and slipped him my number. I knew it would get back to Mike. Two days later the phone rang and a voice said, "Hello." I said, "How on earth did you get my number?" '

They started seeing each other after that. Pauline knew there were other women and she sometimes wondered why she put up with it. 'He did not have to go looking for it,' she said. 'They would pester him and I suppose if he'd had a few drinks and it was on offer, well, he's only flesh and blood. The letters he got left nothing to the imagination. Even later, when we were married, a French girl called Monique would ring and ring. She would just not go away and so we had to change the number because she was such a pest.

'People like Mike, and I'm sure Valentino and Ago, they all have a certain charisma that girls find irresistible. In the early days when we were together, he'd be away for two or three months. I knew there were girls who were, shall we say, big fans, and I'd be stupid to think he didn't stray. I didn't like it, of course, and had it been anybody else I'd have told them to get lost. He tried to make sure I was never embarrassed and I appreciated that. I'm sure there was a lot that went on that I didn't know about, but there was a lot that went on that I did too.'

In a bar in Canada Mike noticed a woman go over to chat to a lonely old Japanese man. He told her he thought it was one of the kindest things he had ever seen. They struck up a rapport and Mike liked her. Then a flashbulb went off and they looked towards the door to see who was coming in. 'It's probably Mike Hailwood,' the woman said. Mike asked if she wanted to go and see. 'I wouldn't cross a room to speak to him,' she scoffed. Mike looked forlorn and asked why not. The woman said he was a superficial playboy. It was only a couple of hours later that Mike told her who he was.

He was the life and soul of the party but he was a lonely soul too. The women could not fill in all the gaps and now he was losing races too. It was 1967 and he needed to fall in love with racing again.

CHAPTER TWELVE
THE WAKE-UP CALL

Jerry Burgess, a thoughtful man with wiry grey curls and a crooked smile, is waiting for me in a vast, whitewashed room that is empty but for some trays of fruit and two tables with an espresso machine perched in between. This is Istanbul and Yamaha have set up camp in these cavernous offices for the weekend. Two rounds into the 2007 season Valentino Rossi is back on top of the standings. Casey Stoner has already signalled his precocity by winning the first race of the season in Qatar, where the new Ducati 800cc bike showed its peerless straight-line speed, but Rossi is top. 'There's no show without Punch,' Burgess says, the words tumbling out of the corner of his torn mouth.

I wanted to sit down with Burgess because I wanted to know about Rossi. If anyone knew what made him tick it was the sartorially challenged technical guru behind the success of both Rossi and Mick Doohan. He had also prepared bikes for Wayne Gardner, Randy Mamola and Freddie Spencer. Burgess's stock was such that Rossi persuaded him to ditch his retirement plans after Doohan's departure from the sport.

Burgess had seen it all and so I sat down and asked him what made Rossi so good. 'What sets any sportsman above his peer group?' he said as if stating the bleeding obvious. 'It's the little things driving the section of the brain that processes information. The electric pulses that send messages to Valentino, Tiger Woods and Roger Federer are far faster than in you and me. If he started playing tennis when he was three and Federer had a bike then the results would be the same but the names would be different. Until we know how fast these signals are being sent then these guys will have an advantage.'

Rossi called Burgess 'the wise man' and it was easy to hear why. His view of the MotoGP world extended way beyond new tyre rules. 'I don't think there is such a thing as natural ability,' he continued. 'I think it's about mental application. You can learn anything, or at least you should be able to. Rossi, Woods and Federer can be beaten on any day but they have the skills and focus. The guys I've worked with finish their careers and have the intelligence to compete in the business world.

'Sport is a constant correction of small mistakes, but you have to know you're moving into a small mistake before you can begin the correction process. Valentino goes around a track at phenomenal speed and can be a bit wide or a fraction off on the brakes. I don't see the mistake, but he feels it instinctively. No two snowflakes are the same and no two laps on a motorcycle can ever be the same, but the closer they are to each other the more information a rider has and so he knows what is expected of him.

'When he came to Honda he was already good. Sure. Very good. We have to thank Aprilia and the group he had around him in his infancy because they taught him the correct way. It's not like we taught him anything new or did anything other than adjust the machinery. I said when he came to us that the only thing that could stuff it up was us. The bike was good enough – Mick'd won world titles on it, so had Alex [Criville] – it was just up to us to make him feel comfortable.'

I asked Burgess whether it was hard for him to make the adjustment from the blunt brilliance of a downbeat realist like Doohan to the maverick ways of the most flamboyant figure since the Hailwood era. 'I say to riders, "Don't ever be scared about the day you retire because you know it's coming." Mick could have come back from those injuries but he had won five world titles. It was time to move on to a different phase in his life. And out of every bit of bad comes a bit of good and we inherited Valentino. That's been absolutely fantastic. Very different, yeah. He has an entourage, but Mick had the people around him that he needed too. With Valentino it's different, but we understand the depth of the Italian family system.

'People wonder if this sport can cope without Valentino. I've been there with Mick. People said the same about him. Then, two races after he had gone, people stopped talking about Mick. I've seen it happen with Spencer, Gardner and Lawson. All forgotten. There's always going to be someone new. Look at Dani Pedrosa. He's exciting.'

Burgess grew up in the hills outside Adelaide and knew plenty of immigrant Italians. He said that was partly why he and Rossi clicked. 'Australians and Italians generally get on well,' he said. 'When times were hard in Italy the opportunity was in Australia. The place is full of second and third generation Italians. My father lived in Florence for six months and our home was full of books on the great Renaissance painters. I had an Italian girlfriend for about eight years too, although you'd never know it from her name – Mary-Ann.'

He said he was the black sheep of an educated family, but he had made a success of himself and was comfortable in his ugly shoes. He was also still hurting about the previous season. 'In a sense I don't think that Valentino lost the title,' he said. 'As a company Yamaha and, to a degree, us, didn't give him what he needed. We can look at any one race and any one would have been enough to get us over the line. He got knocked off in the first race, he had chatter all year, the engine broke in Le Mans. He broke his wrist in Assen and we took our finger off the pulse. But he never stopped trying. To me it was amazing that he got us as close as we were with six bad results. He was right up there when there should have been three of four other guys challenging Nicky for the title.'

Burgess, like Rossi, did not make excuses but was happy to provide context as mitigation. He would never have said it to a journalist, but you sensed that, like many in the media centre, he did not think Hayden had been the best rider in 2006. He also suggested that Rossi and the team were paying for the way they worked so hard to turn the Yamaha adventure into gold dust. 'The fact is it was Yamaha's plan to win the championship in 2005 for their fiftieth anniversary. My philosophy is I can't embark on a project without giving a hundred per cent and the idea that we would use 2004 to find out where we were going was just not going to get us anywhere. My idea was to go hard at the beginning of the season and, if we got our ears boxed, then we would know we had some work to do. We worked like I've never worked before. We stayed on for two days testing after races to fix problems. There's a fantastic photo from the end of the season where the mechanics are sitting down glum-faced on benches in the garage at Phillip Island. "Why aren't you happy?" someone asked. I said, "They're all too knackered." They had bled for that title.

'The struggles we had in the first two races of 2005 were a reflection of the fact that 2004 didn't stop. The Japanese became more enthusiastic and we had all the engineers onside, and because of that they started to overwork our racehorse. From January 2004 to November 2005 we had no break. Valentino needs a rest. He knows how to ride a bike and you can't be out there every single day and give a hundred per cent concentration. I tried to stress we needed a testing programme of quality rather than quantity. It was not like he needed rider training. But because of who he is, a company like Michelin rely very, very heavily on his input. They want him to do the bulk of the work. It's a selfish attitude. Sometimes I have to put a hand on their shoulder and say, "No." They are killing the goose that lays the golden egg.'

There were other sides to Rossi, too, which Burgess acknowledged, particularly his ability to get beneath the skin of his rivals. 'Riders are all different,' he said as he tucked into a banana and one of the many Yamaha jobsworths looked in to see just who was responsible for the voices echoing around their empty shell. 'Take Wayne Gardner. Great rider. A world champ. But he was quite delicate emotionally. I remember there being something bad about him in the Italian press and he got very upset. I had to calm him down. I said, "It's a bloody good job we don't read the German press because we haven't got a clue what they're saying." The next time the issue was brought up he repeated that verbatim. Wayne was a worrier. You had to tell him he had beaten everybody out there for the last three weeks. It was constant reassurance. If I went to Mick and said that, he'd have looked at me with his eyes burning and said, "Don't you think I can do it, JB?" I'd have been like, shit, I shouldn't have said that. And Wayne won one world title and Mick won five. Analysing the two I'd say Wayne had an enormous amount of determination and Mick had an enormous amount of skill – he never made the same mistake twice.

'Then there's Valentino. He certainly wound Max up. No two ways about that. And even from outside looking in you could see how upset Max would get by certain things. One day he was brilliant, the next day dismal, he was already on a seesaw, but this guy and Mick they don't doubt their own ability.

'The thing with Valentino, too, is that, even if we're a bit behind, he will be happy to keep working even as we enter the race. Some riders would be reluctant to do that. To try things at that time. It's like he said to me when the Formula One thing was going on, "When you give me the bike on Sunday, right or wrong, it's up to me to make the difference. I can put some of my character into that bike. In Formula One if I make a mistake and lose some places then they tell me I have two laps to pass this guy otherwise they will pull back and do the pit thing." There was not enough emotion or chance for his character to come out. He was just another thing bolted to the car. Maybe he could have changed that in time because Schumacher had created this robot-like situation. I left him to all that. We'd tune into conversations when people asked him about Formula One, but it's worlds away from this. It was something he wanted to understand and now he does. Without question he'd have been a success and he still will be if he wants to pursue it. I know from talking to Ferrari people that they were very impressed.'

The notion that Rossi had got over the loss of his title quickly was also dismissed out of hand. 'The day he comes in and says he is happy with the bike and happy to come second is the day we start going downhill. Riders are like light bulbs. When they start to flicker you take them out and screw in another. My whole career I've worked with riders who are expected to win. Two-thirds of the grid hope to win, we expect it because we have a multi-world champion and a very good team. I look around. Dani has brains and skill. At the moment he is not comfortable with the new bike, but that will change. Casey's interesting. He and Dani have always fought together and Dani has always won out. But Casey's never had the stability. Every year was different – 125, 250, back to 125 – now he's here for good. He's got an arrogance about him and Mick had a lot of that. They're good, but I think Valentino is better.'

What neither I nor Burgess could know as we parted was just how dramatic Rossi's year would become, both on and off the track. It started with him in good form when we met in Qatar at the opening round. The new rules, limiting engine capacity to

800cc and teams to a mere thirty-one tyres, pre-selected before first practice and bar-coded, were not popular. 'It's better for the safety but it's not an easier life,' Rossi said on a Friday night in the desert. 'What it does mean is it's more on the rider to make the difference now. Last year, for every problem there was a tyre. "I have this problem." "Fuck it, here's a new tyre." That's gone.'

More worrying for the purists and for Rossi was the rise of electronic aids, which enabled Stoner to keep his throttle open and let the software do the work. The issue of traction control handed the initiative to Stoner, who was also on a bike that had a more powerful engine. The early consensus in the paddock was that Ducati would run into problems with fuel consumption. When that did not happen, rumours abounded that they were cheating. Ducati denied that they were filling their catch tank with fuel, but the gloves were off and blood was spilt. It would stay that way all year.

Rossi seemed rejuvenated in Qatar. As the light faded we sat in a Portakabin and he explained why he was wearing furry yellow numbers on the back of his leathers. 'In 2004 and 2005 we always said we pulled the rabbit from the hat,' he explained. 'Last year we lost and tried to understand why. I decided the rabbit was dead.' Now the rabbit was literally with him. Was it real fur? 'Yes, yes.' Given the terrapin rescue, it had presumably died of natural causes.

This was the Rossi of old, the one whose stunts grew more colourful in tandem with his confidence. He had been on holiday with his girlfriend, Arianna Matteuzzi, to Miami and Ibiza. He was relaxed, energized and gunning for revenge. *The comeback* consumed him. 'I had a choice to make with Ferrari last year and if I had been winning last season then it would be different in my mind,' he said. 'But now I have a lot of motivation to come back stronger. I don't want to change for another bike. That would be like going with another girl. It's my bike and my team. I will finish my career with my team.'

It had still been a difficult time for Rossi and the Italian press had reacted badly to finding their hero had feet of clay. He had been written off in some quarters and accused of taking his eye off the ball. 'People say bad things,' he sighed. 'Why? Because I am Valentino Rossi. I have tried with all my power to keep my private life private and it takes a lot of sacrifice. People knock me, but I never thought I was unbeatable. Well, maybe in Barcelona after the IRTA test when I was very fast, I did think that. After five championships in a row it is normal to relax, but we have learnt from last year. It was good for Yamaha and the engineers. Everyone now thinks we need to get better.

'I lost the championship in Estoril not Valencia. I lost when Elias beat me to the line. That race gave me a very bad feeling, a sick feeling. I didn't want the two Hondas to crash. If I'd won everybody would have said I was lucky. But I had some problems in that race and was not able to go as fast as normal. If I'd had the normal rhythm from the weekend I'd have been five seconds clear of Elias. I knew there was trouble. I was already, like, "Fuck!" '

He singled out Pedrosa as the man to beat and thought the new lighter bikes would help him. 'Sport needs rivalries,' he said. 'There were five riders fighting for the championship in the last few races of 2006, but Dani knows something more about his talent. He is very young but he is growing up. It will be a great fight for the future and, yes, it will be harder if he beats me because he is more a real rival. Like Biaggi, like Gibernau, when a real rival beats you it hurts more. Like if Milan beat Inter or Arsenal beat Spurs.' He paused. 'You know the difference between England and Italy?' I shook my head. 'In England the match lasts 90 minutes, in Italy it's one week. The tension and friction are huge.' He smiled and carried on. 'With Biaggi I never had a relationship. We were free to hate each other. I have no problem with Dani. I met him in Spain after the test and we went on TV together for an hour, and I had a good relationship with him before he came to MotoGP. There is no problem there.'

He did not even mention Stoner but felt Hayden might take time to get up to speed. 'I know from experience that the No. 1 plate is heavy. That's why I always used No. 46. But I don't think it's the pressure that's getting to him, I think it's the type of bike. At this point he does not use the bike well, but his experience with a superbike is very different from Pedrosa on the 250.'

The British were still trying to make an impact too. Chaz Davies had gone to America to join Neil Hodgson in the AMA Superbike Championship, bonded by a tainted MotoGP dream, but Bradley Smith and Danny Webb were in the 125cc series. The previous year I had flown back from Valencia the night after the end-of-season party at Spooks nightclub. I was struggling to acclimatize to having been up all night when I caught the plane. There was a seat next to me and I was hoping for the extra leg-room when Alan Smith, Bradley's father, sauntered down the aisle, dwarfed by the rookie of the year trophy in his arms. He sat next to me and poured out his heart about the way the team did not want him near his son. It was a familiar story. I remembered how Ron Haslam, the former GP racer, had told me that parents were despised by teams. Smith had a trophy but needed a good second year on the Repsol Honda. He was sixteen and, in the accelerated world of MotoGP, time would be running out if he did not move forwards.

At the other end of the spectrum was Jeremy McWilliams. The forty-two-year-old Ulsterman was the last Briton to win a grand prix, the 250cc race in the wet of Assen in 2001, and had signed to race for the new British-made Ilmor bike. The only problem was he had a broken thigh and one finger less than last year. He was nonplussed and had decided to ignore the pain from his fractured femur and had thrown away the crutches to race. 'The finger used to get in the way,' he said as we stood in the pitlane in Qatar. 'It was knackered from a previous crash and didn't close properly. Losing it isn't the end of the world. I'm better off without it.'

It was four months since McWilliams crashed while testing the Ilmor and was taken to hospital with a broken femur, collarbone and hand. When he revealed his damaged hand with its missing digit and misshaped survivors, he did so with a phlegmatic approach to risking life and limb. 'Finger injuries follow me around and I've managed to rip a few. I did this one in Brazil and this one at Cadwell Park. Most of my fingers have had surgery.'

He added that he had broken every rib in his body and laughed when saying that his wife was angry because, after the operation to remove the damaged finger, he had nothing left to put his wedding ring on. 'I'm getting better little by little,' he said. 'I don't have the strength in my leg that I want, and jumping off the left side of the bike is hard. The hand is fine, though. If I'm in the gym pulling weights I don't even notice the finger not being there.'

He said he wanted to help bring young British riders through, but feared that they were coming to MotoGP too late and that their superbike backgrounds worked against them. 'MotoGP bikes are completely different beasts and you have so many more options on set-up,' he said. 'The talent is there in Britain but superbike riders don't adapt. Whoever comes in has to go with a big team straight away. I'd love to help that person make the transition.' That was the future. For the moment McWilliams wanted to race. 'I've no regrets,' he said. 'I've ridden with bits of me hanging off but I'm still here after fourteen years.'

He was gone by race day. McWilliams gave in to his injuries and decided he could not ride. Andrew Pitt, his team-mate, started but did not finish. The team turned up to the next race at Jerez, but then announced that they were pulling out. The costs were prohibitive and they were hopelessly off the pace. For McWilliams the mid-pack career was over.

By then the MotoGP world had already entered an altered

state. It started in Qatar when Stoner utilized the Ducati's extra 20kmh on the straight to undo Rossi. The obvious advantage in terms of power rankled with some. 'Fiat versus Ferrari,' one tattooed journalist sighed. Ducati dismissed the rumours about bending the rules, citing their unique Desmosedici valves as the cause of their ascendancy. It was a win that surprised many, not least because Stoner's reputation for crashing had become ingrained, but the most telling aspect of it was his reaction. 'For eighty per cent of the time I really wasn't pushing that hard,' Stoner said to dropped jaws. 'We were fast in a straight line but we need to iron out some bugs.' But how did he cope with the knowledge that Rossi was clamouring for a mistake in his wake? 'He was just another rider,' he said. It was a no-nonsense comment that, although widely twirled back home in Italy, smacked of confidence. Surely then, he was ahead of schedule in winning his first race for Ducati and his first on Bridgestone tyres? 'Ah, I got married this year and some people said I was too young for that too,' he said. 'That was the best decision I ever made. I've no regrets.'

It was something of a non sequitur, but Stoner was certainly maturing. He had, indeed, got married to Adriana. 'I approached him at the Australian Grand Prix in 2003 before we started properly talking and asked him to sign my stomach,' she would explain to an Australian news crew with palpable embarrassment. 'It was completely decent, it was just here.' She was fourteen at the time so they waited before dating. Stoner, himself, was still only twenty-one but he was a married man beating the five-time world champion. The kid gloves were off.

Rossi was just as dominant in Jerez and celebrated by bowling over eight friends dressed as skittles. The stunt had been planned for the title celebration that never came in Valencia. Giacomo Agostini was in Jerez and the duo hugged and exchanged stories beforehand. The crowd topped 130,000 and was the usual cocktail of drunken machismo and debauchery. One group of fans arrived armed with chainsaws and a severed pig's head. Thumping rock music blared out from the tannoy in the campsite in front of the Montecastillo Hotel, the rows of stalls selling great plates of meat and shellfish warming in the afternoon sun. Colin Edwards was third behind Rossi and Pedrosa and admitted to being concerned when he realized Toni Elias was chasing him. 'I remember Elias coming from nowhere to win in 2003. I thought, "Instant Spanish hero" at the time, so when I saw my board with "Elias plus three" on, I thought, "Shit, anyone but him."'

They all thought of themselves. Of winning. Or getting the podium. Of doing enough to get a new contract and go faster, harder, better next year. It meant that the crash was almost an afterthought. It came in practice when Roberto Locatelli veered off the track at a modest 87mph and into the tyre wall. It was enough. Initially, the theory went around that he had struck a bird, but there were no feathers amid the wreckage and concern moved from cause to consequence. The prognosis was gloomy. Reports came in that he was in a coma. Later it emerged this was medically induced. He had head, facial and shoulder injuries, along with a badly broken ankle. 'Locatelli is breathing unaided without any problem,' Dr Claudio Macchiagodena said. 'There don't appear to be any signs of internal haemorrhaging and I want to be optimistic. The main problem is that Locatelli hit his head really hard.'

Locatelli was thirty-two and a former 125cc world champion. Affable and sincere, he was nearing the end of the road, but nobody expected him to depart like this. More details trickled out. His face would need to be rebuilt, his ankle would need reconstructive surgery. He had a fractured elbow and collarbone. There was also a bruised lung. 'Poor sod,' a journalist sighed over a beer in Ducati's hospitality suite. 'That's him finished.' As a person or a racer he did not make clear, but sometimes in this insular world you felt it was the same thing.

There were more problems looming in 2007. Carmelo Ezpelata invited a few of us into a Dorna transporter in Jerez to respond to crisis talk. The most influential figure in MotoGP admitted that his company was paying $50 million in subsidies to cash-strapped teams in an attempt to avert a sponsorship disaster. The chief executive of Dorna also revealed that there would be a summit meeting with team owners and manufacturers on 12 April to resolve the mounting problems.

Although MotoGP's popularity was soaring in terms of attendances and television audiences, the winter had been marred by financial difficulties. Kenny Roberts, the former world champion and now a successful independent team owner, said he had two races to make up a twenty per cent shortfall in sponsor-ship money or face withdrawing from the World Championship. The new rules on engine size had led to further costs and even Rossi's factory Yamaha team had spent the last pre-season test in a plain blue livery because of the lack of a title sponsor. They had cut a deal with Fiat, but that was down to the Italian company's plan to use Rossi's huge profile to sell cars. Had Rossi still been at Honda, Yamaha would have faced the embarrassment of beginning the World Championship without a backer.

The problems had been brewing for some time. Small teams such as WCM had come and gone, while self-inflicted wounds had bled the sport of about $50 million in corporate money. Telefonica Movistar, the Spanish communications giant, pulled out of MotoGP when HRC decided to put Dani Pedrosa on their factory Repsol bike. Telefonica, who sponsored the talent search the Movistar Cup, had hoped to sign their own deal with the former 250cc champion.

Elsewhere, Biaggi had the backing of Camel, but Honda barred the notoriously difficult Italian from racing for any of its teams.

Biaggi had been forced to take a ride in World Superbikes and Camel's money had gone. Rossi's tobacco war had also been an issue. The gradual decline of cigarette money and the huge costs of an 18-round series meant that, while television audiences were up to 320 million per race, the teams were struggling.

Ezpelata's Formula One equivalent, Bernie Ecclestone, pitched up in Istanbul too. He suggested the sport ditch the 125cc and 250cc World Championships. How could MotoGP ensure bigger crowds? 'Birds on bikes,' he said. There was an air of disillusionment as the championship prepared for another race at a track that already knew it was being shelved from the calendar.

In the circumstances Pedrosa was not the best person to go to for a pick-me-up. Pedrosa's reputation as a dour metronome was increasing and he was clearly in a foul temper when I entered the little grey box where he was waiting. There was no acknowledgement, no recognition. I had snatched a word with Alberto Puig beforehand. 'Dani is tough but there is always the Italian guy,' Puig said of Rossi. When I sat down opposite Pedrosa he fixed me with a stare and his best monosyllables. I thought, 'Sod it' and asked him about the public perception of him as a misery. I had bumped into John Hopkins earlier that day and he had said that Pedrosa would wake up in twenty years' time and regret not enjoying himself. 'You don't change,' Pedrosa said. 'I see people celebrate and do wild things, but it is not wrong to be quiet. You behave the way you feel inside and I'm not a big fan of the night-time. I like to rest.' Given that Rossi was often out until 4 a.m. on the night before a race, such comments only served to drive a wedge between those who favoured hedonists and mavericks over waifs and strained interviews.

Pedrosa had been forced to deal with the flipside of fame after his spat with Hayden in Estoril. He was terse when asked to go over that old, shaky ground. 'Yeah, yeah, he won the title and I helped him,' he snapped. 'That's finished. I understood that

I made a mistake in Estoril and it was the moment to move over. Finished.'

I ask him if he learnt anything from the reaction and having his face printed under the 'WANTED!' headlines. He looked to the floor. 'I didn't learn anything from it, but it made me realize how everything works with the press.' He added that he did not seek advice from other riders because they can be 'hypocrites – say one thing to you and something else to another'. I had always liked Pedrosa, but this was the first time he had treated me in the off-hand manner that had earned him the nickname 'Pedrobot'. It made me recall Rossi's response when asked if he was excited to share a podium with the rising star at Donington the previous summer. 'Oh yes,' Rossi had replied. 'So excited I nearly pissed myself.' Pedrosa did not care. 'Last year I was riding strongly but without experience,' he said. 'Now I have it and that counts. Last year I was not a hundred per cent ready. Now I have more control.'

He had no control over what happened two days later in the Turkish Grand Prix. Having qualified third fastest, he was brought down by Olivier Jacque, the French rider who got his braking hopelessly wrong at the end of the first lap. Pedrosa suffered chest injuries in the fall, which saw him dragged along under Chris Vermeulen's Suzuki.

It all allowed Stoner to dominate. A frenetic battle ensued in his wake, but he was 6.2 seconds clear of Elias and his Honda Gresini, while the 19-second gap back to Rossi in tenth was evidence of a gauntlet thrown down. Rossi cut an unusually bitter figure afterwards, bemoaning Elias's style. 'He changed his line and we touched,' Rossi complained. 'You need respect for other riders, but Elias is very dangerous to everybody and to me in particular.' Elias was not the sort to seek controversy but was not about to allow the slurs to pass. 'The races are like this,' he countered, repeating a time-honoured Rossi phrase. 'If he is angry what can I do? Another day these things can happen to me.' Certainly, anyone who remembered Rossi's more heated clashes with Biaggi and Gibernau felt it was a case of pots and kettles. Rossi also snapped at Michelin. 'Something happened, something unnatural, inside the rear tyre and I thought it was going to explode,' he said. 'I lost a lot of grip and was scared. The bike is working well, but Michelin need to work like us.'

And then there was Stoner showing that at last Rossi had a rival who would just refuse to be intimidated by the sport's megastar. 'He gifted me first position,' he said in reference to Rossi's first lap error. 'We're not far from the perfect racing bike,' he added. And then the backlash. 'Last year there was a lot of bad press about me crashing and I think they [LCR Honda, his former team] thought I was too inexperienced and didn't know what I was talking about. Here they listen to me.' He was ten points clear of Rossi and everybody was listening now.

It was clear the Ducati's power was going to be the dominant factor on tracks that had long straights like Shanghai. The theory that corner speed was the key to the title was being severely tested. With it, Stoner's efforts were being casually belittled. Fiat versus Ferrari. Few people bothered to refer to the fact that Loris Capirossi, his hugely experienced team-mate, was struggling to wrestle the same sort of results from his Desmosedici. And, as Stoner said, you had to get the thing around corners too. By the end of a weekend in China, reputations were being carved in stone; Stoner as the best of the young guns and Elias as the most calamitous, irritating Stoner in practice and then charging into the first corner and almost scuttling Nicky Hayden, whose title defence was as good as over after four rounds.

Stoner's spiky nature meant people naturally looked for flaws. One Ducati official said it was a case of nobody liking hot-shot kids coming through, and there being a natural jealousy of anything that upset the established order. Certainly, there was a widely held expectation that Stoner would come crashing back down to earth when he came to Europe. Then his Desmosedici and his Bridgestones would be found wanting.

In fact, when the MotoGP circus did arrive at Le Mans and the rain came, Stoner was an impressive third behind Vermeulen, winning his first grand prix on the Suzuki, and Marco Melandri. Rossi had looked well set for a win in the dry, but the rain wrecked his day as his second bike was set up for damp conditions rather than a monsoon. He struggled home in sixth place and Stoner's lead was up to twenty-one points.

Rossi was now falling out of favour at home, where they demanded he win. It felt like death by 1,000 short cuts because the new bikes did not offer as much room for rider skill to make up ground and the electronics were further negating talent. The podium was full of twenty-one-year-olds. Rossi was beginning to look a little old and so he turned up for the Italian Grand Prix with a helmet adorned with a big red heart to prove that he had not lost his. And he won. Stoner, though, was looking increasingly inviolable. As they headed for Barcelona I remembered a story Chaz Davies had told me about the race there in 2003. Back then the friends were still sharing a bunk bed in the back of a Cinquecento-sized trailer. 'I was in the 250s and Casey was in the 125s,' Davies said. 'It was early on Friday morning. We were laying in bed, half-dressed, playing on the PlayStation. Casey was halfway round a lap when suddenly we heard the sound of bikes revving. "Shit!" he said. "What time is it?" Sure enough we'd lost track and he should have been out there for practice. You've never seen anyone get dressed so quickly. I was pissing myself.' These days, though, Stoner was on time and the only alarm bells going off were in Rossi's motorhome.

LAP 10

The comeback would rest upon Mike's ability to relearn the island and the reliability of the Ducati that Steve Wynne had loaned him. The first time out on the gleaming red bike had provided a grim portent. Mike the Bike coughed and chugged his way to a gentle stop outside the Crosby pub a few miles into his first test. He was never a technical man and had little idea what was going on below him, so he allowed his frustration to boil over. He swore and thumped his fist and pulled at stray wires. The bike did not start and he hitched a lift back with a man on his way to a cricket match. In the pits Ted and Nobby groaned and wondered what had happened. And then they levelled the bump in the road. His leg suddenly straightened, the hair thickened and the lines around his eyes faded. Mike climbed on to the 500cc Yamaha that he would ride later in the week and tore off. Ted held a stopwatch and waited. By the time Mike returned he had broken Phil Read's lap record. He still had it. The old bugger still had it.

Nine years earlier they were wondering if he still had it as his duel with Ago reached its zenith on the island. He had been beaten to the world title in 1966 and the bellicose nature of the Honda was proving an enduring struggle. John Cooper knew that after asking if he could borrow it to ride at Snetterton one Sunday. Mike was due to race the following Bank Holiday Monday. 'Sure,' he said. 'And when you fall off draw a yellow line round the body so I know where it happened.' Moon Eyes grinned but was confident Mike was exaggerating.

He soon got his answer. 'That Honda was unbelievably bad,' he said. 'You can't imagine. God, it was frightening. You just couldn't steer it. I was pretty good at riding round problems, but God, you couldn't keep it in a ten-acre field. Mike was good like that. He didn't know about the bikes. He just said prepare it and he'd ride it. They were all the same to him.'

Pauline knew it was getting to him. Losing the 500cc crown had hurt him and he did not trust his bike. It had all the power in the world but he wanted the handling of the MV. It was a battle similar to the one that would be replayed forty years hence between Stoner and Rossi and Ducati and Yamaha.

Ago won at Hockenheim and then it came to the island and *the* race. Mike had already won two races on the island that week, surpassing the great Stanley Woods' record of ten TT wins. 'Where do you go from here?' a young Murray Walker asked him.

'Down,' he said into the oversized microphone thrust under his nose.

'Are you going to switch off before you go down or keep at it for a couple of years?'

'I think Honda are coming back next year so I presume I'll be riding again next year.'

'What do you expect from Ago on Friday?'

'More.'

'Why?'

'I think the MV is easier to ride and I know he will be trying harder. I think he is saving himself.'

'I presume it is a masterpiece of understatement to say you are anxious to win on Friday.'

'You could say that.'

Come Friday Mike was nervous. He bit his fingers until they bled and asked Ted to join him in his room that morning because he did not want to be alone. He had two chicken sandwiches and a cup of tea, patted a blushing chambermaid on the rear, and cursed Ago. He said he wished he would bugger off home as he looked out of the window to the hotel that was now dubbed Casa Agostini and where the payphone was shrouded in a graffiti garland of messages from adoring girls. Ted knew his friend had suffered a restless night, while Ago always seemed unnaturally relaxed and would no doubt take his usual catnap for ten minutes just half an hour before the race.

Ago sounded the horn of his yellow Porsche as he passed the Casino Hotel. He was confident. 'To win on the Isle of Man you need two or three years to learn it,' he told me. 'It's impossible to win straight away. Today Valentino, training for a grand prix, makes maybe seventy or eighty laps in practice before the race. On the Isle of Man you make maybe six. Tell Valentino he can only make six laps beforehand and he would think you're crazy. But in 1967 I knew the circuit and I had the experience. I was ready.'

Mike rose and roused himself. This was it. It was a whirlwind until they were on the line. Mike started well and broke the lap record. The drinkers cheered. But Ago was good and grittier than his pristine image. He took his MV closer to the limit than ever before. The engine roared its disdain. He was inches from a stone wall. He was a boy riding on the Riviera overtaking road trains. He was a boy escaping a thousand deaths. And he lapped at an average of 108.4mph, faster than Mike's 107.4. He had a twelve-second lead.

Mike was good and Mike was quick. He responded and the race was on. Ago had two signers on the course telling him the times. At the start a man with Brylcreemed hair and a doctor's coat whitewashed numbers on a giant blackboard. The gap changed. 'It's normally eight seconds, some places it's three, others four,' Ago said. 'It is *a* race.'

It is a race ridden almost in isolation. The bikes set off at intervals on the island and so the duel is fought in ignorance of each other. They cannot see but they sense what each is doing. They are flirting with each other and disaster. 'Mike was a great rider who rarely rode at a hundred per cent,' Tommy Robb would say. 'He was so good he didn't need to. But the one time he did was in the battle with Ago on the Isle of Man.'

The lead ebbed and flowed and then briefly they were together. Mike was fuelling at a pitstop, the No. 1 with its white border lifting his black leathers, when Ago roared in for his stop. Mike did not look at the broader shoulders and the No. 9. He knew who it was. They had been together in splendid separation for the whole race. And now Mike had a problem. The twist grip on his handlebars was coming loose and leaving him in danger of clasping thin air. He wanted a hammer. A bloody hammer! Someone! He got one and beat the grip. Tick, tock. One of the mechanics tried to tie a handkerchief around the grip. The Old Man was there. He leant over and, discerning the problem, shocked Mike by telling him to pull out. It was madness to go on. Mike glared. Yes it was mad. But the delay meant Ago's lead had risen from two to 12 seconds. There was no time for considered thought. He raced off.

Mike ate into Ago's lead but the Italian was reckless. He would not be beaten. 'I thought that nobody could beat Mike on the Isle of Man but I was beating him,' he said. 'We were black and white, black leathers tinged white from touching the walls. We were over the limit but we had to be. He wanted to win and so did I. It was very important for me. For Agostini to beat him was so important.'

But then, a few miles from the triumph, Ago's chain broke and he started to cry. He didn't stop. Mike's face was bleeding and the soles of his shoes were worn away but he was now in the lead. He was belligerent and bloodied, the 'Pommie Bastards' T-shirt beneath his thin black armour a pledge of aggression. He won the greatest TT and sought out Ago. 'He said to me, "Ago, you are the winner," ' his rival remembered. 'That was nice, but I still cried all night.'

Mike was tired and drained. He gave a reporter a contemptuous look when asked if he had slowed down on the last lap.

'Oh yeah, right down.'

'How do you feel?'

'Knackered.'

It was a brilliant day, arguably the greatest ever at the TT, and Mike had prevailed. They went to the official dinner and Mike taught Ago to say, 'Fuck my old boots.' Later, marinated in vodka and lemonade, he stripped to his underpants and jumped in the casino's swimming pool with some girls. The security men told him to get out. 'Come and get me,' he grinned.

But nothing stayed the same in this world and it was only a few months later when Ago had his revenge. The world title was in the balance. They had each won four races when they went back to Monza. It was another Ago love fest, but Mike was superior that day. He opened up a commanding 17-second lead and then, three laps from home, his crankshaft broke. He propped the bike against a wall and Ago flew past. On the podium Ago pulled Mike on to the number one position, but the defeat cut a slashing wound. 'He was so close to it and he felt it was his,' Pauline would say. 'He went pretty quiet. That's what he was like when it went bad. He didn't say much. But you got him a drink and he picked up. Everyone was staying at our hotel and it ended up being a good night. By the time Mike threw Bill into the ornamental pond he was OK. He just thought he would have another go next year.' He thought wrong.

CHAPTER THIRTEEN

DEATH AND TAXES

Death is everywhere on the Isle of Man, in the cavernous cemetery and down each walled lane of the fabled circuit. Back in the 1960s the *Daily Mirror* labelled it 'Blood Bath Island', which caused a lot of bitterness among the islanders. Guy Martin, a fast-talking, tea-drinking ego-basher, had an eye on the top prize as the centenary celebrations began in 2007 and he explained the addiction. 'Racing around a track is like going round Morrisons' car park in comparison,' he said. 'Go to the Isle of Man and your bike sucks the rabbits out of the hedges. There's nothing like it. It's that near-death thing.'

Martin was good value. Sometimes the MotoGP could become a bit clinical and, while the racing was still savage, the TT was a symbolic passport back to the days of Hailwood and Agostini, when men were men and deaths a weekly occurrence. It was the danger that sucked rabbits out and people in. Add hair and leather and attitude and you had a potent testosterone-drip. It was scarcely surprising women still flung themselves at Rossi, or that when Colin Edwards had once reprimanded a journalist for asking questions about sex, John Hopkins had said he would happily take his place. 'Man, I love the puss,' he drooled.

Martin was pretty dismissive of track racing although he did it too. 'It's just a dick-measuring contest,' he confided. 'It's all about who's got the biggest motorhome or the blondest girlfriend.' He was similarly unimpressed by his TT rivals in the North West 200 which served as a warm-up event. 'A lot of them were talking all winter, but came over and did bugger all,' he said. 'They went home to polish their camper vans while I went back to work.'

The twenty-five-year-old had surprised many by making a close-season switch from Yamaha to the unproven Hydrex Honda team, but he had never been the most conventional of figures. He was a man who could wax lyrical about the pleasures of tea just as readily as he could about the 'buzz' he got from racing on rock-rimmed roads. 'Go through history and tea plays a major part,' he said. 'You had the British troops using it to camouflage them-selves in India because they realized their red jackets made them stand out like a pair of tits on a donkey. It's part of what Englishness is all about. I've been on teams where they all whoop and holler and go in for high-fives and chest-slapping. I had to say, "Look, fellas, we're English and let's just be content with a firm handshake." I hate all this Americanized stuff.'

Martin was gunning for John McGuinness, a modern TT legend with eleven wins. Two weeks earlier, at the North West 200, Martin had forced McGuinness wide at a chicane and thus denied him a double victory. 'Nothing wrong with it,' Martin said of the move. 'It was just something out of *Days of Thunder*.' He did not care much for officialdom and told how, after a row with a race director at Rockingham, he had slammed the official's laptop shut on his fingers. He signed the cheque for his fine but cancelled it when he got home. A ban ensued, which is what forced him to the open road in the first place.

For all the joviality, Martin knew the perils of the TT. It was there in the record of 223 deaths. It was an event that split opinion, divided an island and wrecked families, but those who were addicted to its dangers were packing the ferries. The hundred years war continued apace with the dissenters going hell for leather against the defenders.

McGuinness loved the Isle of Man too but knew why many saw the TT as an unjustifiable waste of human life. He had his eleven wins but would not indulge in pre-TT braggadocio because, 'This place will leap up and bite you on the arse.' Mick Grant had thought the same thing twenty years earlier.

McGuinness knew it because four years earlier he was riding near the village of Crosby at mind-boggling speed when he came upon a crumpled bike. 'I knew it was David straight away because he'd been ten seconds ahead of me,' he recalled. 'If an aeroplane had crashed it couldn't have caused more damage.'

This was the scene of David Jefferies' death. That McGuinness was a close friend and was back again underscored the lure of lapping the 37.7-mile course at 129mph. 'It does play on your mind,' he told me. 'After David's crash I thought, "Bollocks to this, I'm not going back." That lasted for a couple of days, but David's mother was one of the strongest people in saying I should carry on.'

And the TT always did. Despite the death toll and the anachronism of Mad Sunday when punters could ride on the course and indulge in boy-racer fantasies, it was oversubscribed, even if some still saw it as a twisted mongrel of a motorcycling race that reinforced stereotypes. 'People think we're greasy-haired Hell's Angels and petrolheads, but I'd like to think I'm a professional athlete,' McGuinness said not unreasonably.

However, Andrea Coleman, widow of TT legend Tom Herron and co-founder of the Riders for Health charity, said, 'There is something special about the biking fraternity, but the negative image some people have is amplified by the TT. It is a wonderful place – I lived there for a while – it's atmospheric and the talk is all about crankshafts and tyres. But people you know die. It's like living through the war.' The camaraderie of the TT was shown by the story of how Coleman had met Herron. 'He'd crashed and was in hospital and, although I didn't know him, I still went to see him.'

The late Barry Sheene was a committed critic. 'I rode there once and thought, "This is not racing, it's a suicide mission."' Rocket Ron Haslam was more enamoured. 'I remember jumping over Ballaugh Bridge and going so high I could see inside the commentary box,' he recalled. 'The bloke inside was going mad.'

The event lost its World Championship status in 1977, in part because of protests from the likes of Sheene and Giacomo Agostini. It had suffered peaks and troughs but McGuinness believed Jefferies' death had provided a wake-up call. 'After David's crash the whole place was on its arse, but they got new management in and it's a new era. If you like motorcycling racing, then the TT is it. Tennis, football, cricket fans should come and watch bikes going 180mph six feet in front of them – if that doesn't blow your skirt up nothing will.' He did have reservations about Mad Sunday, though, and the idea that anyone could do what he did. 'I might take a flask of tea, sit on a bank and watch the one-day heroes,' he said. 'They had a big bike in 1979 and so they think they're it. It's like a football crowd – there'll be some fucking idiots in there.' Somehow, though, the risk of death would always be life-affirming. 'When I set the lap record last year there was such a buzz you could have lifted the island out of the sea,' McGuinness said.

On Friday 8 June McGuinness won the senior TT race from Martin, but an accident that killed a rider and two spectators led to more banning calls. On that same day I waited in a transporter in Barcelona for Roberto Locatelli. The Metis Gilera PR girl gave me a Coke and said he would be here soon. He could not rush anywhere after what happened. After seven days in a coma he had woken to the drained eyes of his family and tried to make

sense of the tubes and dulled vision. He could not remember anything but, as the week of living dangerously came to an end, and
as he coughed up more blood, he knew that he had to get back in
the saddle.

It took the Italian just fifty-five days to make an aborted
attempt to ride in another grand prix following his horrific crash
in Jerez in March. Now he was back for the Catalan Grand Prix,
back in the country where he was almost killed, shunning any
suspicion of mortality with a scarred smile. He would not win,
but even by the Lazarus-esque resilience of elite motorcycling, it
was the comeback from hell.

I'd wanted to interview Locatelli as soon as possible after his
accident, but it had taken a while. Only now could he talk easily
after weeks of frustration because of his mangled jaw. He hobbled
to a chair in the hospitality unit and admitted that his vision was
causing him problems. He said his right eye did not move and he
needed to keep exercising the muscle. His left ankle, where the
bone seared through the skin and left witnesses wondering if he
would lose his leg, was a sickly sight. The day before we met the
former world champion was way down the 125cc time sheets, but
the miracle was that he was there.

Locatelli's problems and the news filtering in from the Isle of
Man provided a reminder of the inveterate dangers of his sport. It
was also here, a year before, that six riders had been put out of
action in that first-corner crash. Locatelli's return lanced the boil
of concern and the risks were shelved once more. But why come
back? 'This is what I do,' he said. 'The track is my passion, it's my
work. People told me to stop but I want to go racing. In the
medical centre in Spain I was bringing up blood and it was very
dangerous, but I have no fear.'

Locatelli said coming back from the brink was not a choice.
'This is the biggest challenge of my life. The medical people say
it will take a long time, but nothing stands still. After two hours

of practice my body is sapped of energy. But it is results that matter.' The implication was that he might be axed at the end of the year. As a thirtysomething in a class dominated by precocious youths, he needed to prove that he was not a broken man. 'My ankle still hurts,' he sighed. 'It normally takes people four months to get movement back – it took me thirteen days.'

The comeback was overseen by Dr Costa, whose poetic sensibility ran riot in the aftermath. 'The doctors have watered the tree of life, but the buds of the branches have grown thanks to Roberto's strength,' he said. As soon as Locatelli could type, and still unable to speak, he penned a message to his fans on his website. 'You'll think I'm mad [for returning]. After all that's happened I think so too, but the races are all of my life.' He added the caveat, 'But at the moment my main aim is to stand because the fractures do not let me.'

He had raced for the first time the previous Sunday, in the Italian Grand Prix, where Rossi trimmed Casey Stoner's lead to a mere nine points. 'I don't remember anything about the day of the crash,' he said. 'The first problem was my leg because I put it on the ground. Then my head went and I was bounced around. I wanted to see it on television because I wanted to understand what had happened. It was just impossible to turn right. This was a crash that broke many parts. Being in a coma for a week affects your body – it all stops. Now every night I dream that one day I will be a hundred per cent.'

The MotoGP race in Barcelona explained everything. They did it for days like this. Rossi was on pole, but Stoner did not care too much about the grid as long as he was on the front two rows. He knew he had the flat speed to make up ground. He also had the Bridgestones and Rossi's public utterances meant he was well aware that the Italian was growing disillusioned with his Michelins. Even in Barcelona, during a mesmerizing race, Rossi was struggling to drive out of the left-handers, underscoring his doubts about his grip. Nevertheless, he showed he was far from the ailing force many in Italy were painting him as.

He made a mess of his start and dropped from pole to fourth. That may or may not have been down to the late night he had enjoyed in the president's box at Barcelona's match against Espanyol at the Camp Nou the previous night. Dani Pedrosa led briefly but Stoner showed his power on the straight and the race set into a pattern, with the leading three and Hopkins breaking everyone else. The last third of the race was a thriller because Stoner had to contend with enormous pressure from Rossi. His coolness in those latter stages debunked the crasher myth and would even draw warm praise from Rossi. 'Every lap I had to invent something new to get past,' Rossi said. They exchanged the lead twelve times in the last eight laps. 'We were overtaking in places you do not normally overtake.' None more so than a dive down the inside on the last corner, New Holland. Yet when it came down to it those heroic endeavours were not enough. Rossi was 0.069 seconds adrift at the flag. 'Casey rode like a god,' he conceded and you could not help thinking that Rossi was doomed if he could ride this well and lose.

It was good to see Britain's Bradley Smith finish sixth in the 125cc race and even better to witness Locatelli's twelfth in the 250cc class. Stoner, though, looked almost unstoppable. He then revealed he had needed to go to the toilet since the first lap. Suddenly, he was controlling everything.

The former champions were struggling. Nicky Hayden was eleventh in the riders' table by the time they came to a rain-lashed Donington Park. 'I'd be lying if I said things weren't strained,' he said of his non-relationship with Pedrosa. Valencia had evidently not healed the rift at all. 'We don't speak to each other and that's the first time I've had a team-mate like that.' Pedrosa confirmed the situation in his more pithy style. 'Things are not the same.' The blue-eyed boy of Honda, backed and protected over the Hayden debacle, now turned on his pay-masters. 'The frustrating thing is not seeing Casey win,' he insisted. 'It's expecting a good bike.'

The murmurs of discontent rumbled on. The Ducati had been stripped in a search for technical infringements and nothing was found. Livio Suppo, the Ducati team manager, an Italian with a goatee beard, said the change in the status quo was down to the rider. Even Colin Edwards, Rossi's team-mate, came up with a simple response when asked why the Italian was not heading the standings. 'Two words,' Edwards said. 'Casey Stoner.' He then added a few more. 'And he's as fast as hell.'

Donington was a low point of the year. Stoner joined the chorus of disapproval about the lack of grip on the surface. 'It's one of the worst circuits in the wet,' he said. 'It gets hairy out there and something should be done. You don't seem to get any grip, which is why riders are crashing.' Whether it was those words or the media image of Stoner as an upstart that prompted him to be booed when he turned up for the Riders for Health charity auction on the Thursday is debatable. He was stunned by the response. He was a twenty-one-year-old kid setting the MotoGP world alight and yet he was being heckled. He probably wished he had Mike Hailwood's old T-shirt, the one that said 'Pommie Bastards' on the front. Later it got worse when his motorhome was attacked and rocked from side to side. The only consolation was the same thing happened to Rossi, whose motorhome was also daubed with graffiti come the morning.

Stoner was certainly being portrayed in an unfavourable light. He criticized the new Assen layout too and was pilloried, even though others riders had said worse. Edwards had even labelled it 'shit'. The difference was people loved Edwards for his crude wit. 'If anyone else can ride this bike faster I'll give them a blowjob,' he had once said. And then, asked to describe the technical diffi-culties in riding the new Aprilia, he had mused, 'Imagine cutting the balls off a bull, waving them in front of his face then trying to get on his back and ride him.' He was also an elder statesman and could get away with more, but it was harsh to slate Stoner for being a boy wonder who did not do one-liners.

Rossi, too, had plenty of excuses. After Donington he suggested it might have been a heavy rock concert that had undermined his chances. 'Maybe the problem is not the aeroplanes but the concert here by Marilyn Manson a couple of weeks ago. They put the hot dog stalls on the track.' The 85,000 cheered Rossi and booed Stoner, but they were peas from the same pod in most ways and they differed in style rather than substance. Rossi, though, had crashed twice over the course of the weekend and ran on to the grass in the race. He was twenty-six points adrift. Time was running out.

The relationship with Stoner unravelled in mid-season. He had called Stoner a god but Rossi had no intention of being friends with a man who was beating him. 'I don't think he's got a very good relationship with me at the moment,' Stoner admitted. 'It's been a great season so far for us and to be beating Valentino at this stage is a huge bonus for me.' He expected Rossi to stick it out for the season and indulge in some mind games. 'His strategy is always to put pressure on people from the rear and keep plugging and try to make other people make mistakes,' he said. 'Really, that's not going to work with me.'

If Rossi and Stoner and Yamaha and Ducati were gearing up for a battle royal, Honda had become a bit-part player. They had won the title with Hayden and had the advantage of the American having widely tested the so-called 'ghost bike' in 2006. Now they turned up with a revised design that made matters worse. The main problem was a lack of front-end feel. By this time, Pedrosa was in a depressed fog and Hayden was riding for pride.

Rossi kept in touch by winning the Dutch TT, but when he crashed in Germany and Pedrosa won the Italian media went for him. Rossi was jaded and fading. He had always done his best to keep his personal life hidden in London, going to the Chinawhite nightclub in a fake beard and dining at Locanda Locatelli, a celebrity hangout in a discreet hideaway unbothered by the paparazzi. 'He wields more power in Locando Locatelli than Bill Clinton and Tony Blair put together,' Giorgo Locatelli, the owner, said. However, the media now wondered whether his private life was affecting his professional one. Rossi had split from his long-term girlfriend, Arianna, and had been linked with Elisabetta Canalis, an Italian model and small-time movie star. Rossi accepted he should have let it be known that Canalis attended the Italian Grand Prix as a paid guest of Yamaha, rather than let the rumour mill grind into action. 'It was a mistake to learn from,' he said. 'The worst was for Arianna. She knows Canalis had nothing to do with our split because we'd already broken up by then. I was sorry about that because she was a "real" girlfriend.'

There had not been many. Martina Stella was the only other woman who had received official acknowledgement and some wondered whether he was still pining for her. An article in *Vanity Fair Italy* shed some light on Rossi's women. Asked how many he had had, he replied, 'I don't know! I never counted them!' Was it more than fifty? More than a hundred? 'No, no!' he responded vigorously. 'A lot less than fifty!' He said there was no conflict between having a steady girlfriend and wearing his WLF ('long live pussy') logo. 'It's been there since I was seventeen,' he said. 'The time of your life when the magical feminine universe opens up to you! And that is a very nice passion. Yes, passion is the right word. I was about to say "pastime" but that's not so good.'

He then anthropomorphized his bike. 'I've never seen my bike as a piece of iron. Yes, we could say she's a woman. And, just like a woman, she can be naughty, you can argue with her. But she can also greatly reward you. I talk to my bike, especially at night, in the box. And always before a race – I kneel beside her and cheer her on. Because from then on it'll be just me and her. At the end of the race, I always thank her.'

The tilt at the title came undone at Laguna Seca, where Stoner rode brilliantly all weekend, topping the time sheets in every session and breaking the lap record on the way to his sixth victory of the season. Rossi was fourth and half a minute adrift. Stoner was riding magnificently and Rossi was hamstrung by his tyres. He was now fourty-four points behind and, while he had whittled away a larger deficit in his battle with Hayden, this time it was different. Stoner had stopped crashing and had the cut-throat nature to stamp on Rossi's throat now he had him down.

Stoner celebrated with Chaz Davies. The Briton got his chance to finally ride with his friend in a MotoGP race after being called up as a late replacement for the injured Alex Hofmann in the Pramac d'Antin team. Davies had mechanical trouble during the race, but put in a fast lap that was almost identical to the best of Edwards on the factory Yamaha. It was a small sign that the talent was still there, that the kid who had taken on the Aussie in skanky mustard leathers was up to the elite. There was also a reunion for the Haydens. Nicky's misery continued and he failed to finish, but Roger Lee was given a wild-card entry and finished tenth. With seven rounds left, though, the title seemed to be heading towards an inexorable conclusion. And then Rossi's world was blown apart.

When he pitched up in the Czech Republic after the summer break, Rossi cancelled his daily briefings and all the interviews that had been arranged months beforehand. The news hounds were in Brno as well as the racing press because they wanted their pound of flesh. The Italian tax agency, by contrast, wanted at least £40 million. It was alleged that Rossi's main business and financial interests remained in Italy, even though he had told the media and the tax office that he was living in London, thus making use of a loophole that allows non-domiciled residents to declare only income accrued in Britain. The taxman wanted to know what had happened to the lucrative sponsorship deals and bonuses which made Rossi the highest-paid Italian sportsman. Vincenzo Visco, the deputy economic minister, weighed into the scandal, saying, 'I'm sorry for Rossi and I'm a huge fan of his, but the law has to be obeyed.'

Rossi was placed under investigation over possible undeclared earnings for the period 2000 to 2004, but the state was reportedly seeking a total of €120 million, including fines and interest. It was a sensation in Italy and front-page news. Rossi even took the extraordinary step of recording a message and delivering it to RAI, the Italian broadcaster. It was screened on the country's most popular channel. 'I've been crucified and condemned even before the necessary checks have been carried out,' he said. 'I have been living in London for seven years, not a Disney city or a tax paradise on a small island. The professionals who handle my income declarations have assured me that they have respected all the rules, as I have asked them to do. The story will be over very soon.'

The fallout was quick. Gibo Badioli had become a familiar figure in Rossi's story. A middle-aged man with a shock of white hair, he might have passed for Richard Attenborough but for the upturned collar of his denim jacket and thick black shades. He used to sell bar stools to restaurants up and down the Adriatic coast, but was a friend of the Rossi family and became his manager. His hard-line approach to any business deals had already seen him clash with Rossi, who gradually realized that Badioli was alienating people by throwing up a wall. Now he was gone. No reason was given. Rossi soon ditched his management company too. Great White London, named after Badioli and with a registered office in Sackville Street, disappeared from the paddock. Marc Canela, the Fiat Yamaha team coordinator who had been installed as Great White's chief executive that May, resigned. Rossi had adopted a policy of *omerta* and so did not explain the moves, but when the dust settled he merely said of his parting with Badioli, 'I'll just say that to me human relationships are one of the most important things. All can draw their own conclusions.'

Everybody did. It emerged that Rossi had been collared because he was seeking broadband coverage in Tavullia and sent a letter to Telecom, one of his sponsors. The taxman's suspicion was aroused and he followed the paper trail to Rossi's home town, where he found *Tatilla*, Rossi's yacht, moored 10 kilometres away. He found that insurance had been taken out in Pesaro for eight motor vehicles owned by, or registered to, Rossi's relatives or companies. They included two BMWs, two Porsches and a Mercedes Sprinter. Pictures of the cars and the yacht were printed in the Italian press. The golden boy was tarnished.

The Catholic church even entered the fray. In a sermon Father Claudio Miglioranza said, 'I am astonished by the popular re-action. Do not let yourselves be influenced by the face of this good boy. Do you not want to believe that the Doctor has a tax bill for €60 million?' Journalists called Graziano in Italy, but he said he did not know where his son was. Loris Capirossi, Stoner's team-mate, was also accused of not declaring €1.3 million on top of a previous €13 million, while high-profile figures such as Fabio Capello, the England football manager, and Sophia Loren, the Hollywood actress, would also be investigated in the ensuing months. Rossi's case, though, was the talk of a nation.

It made for an uneasy atmosphere and Rossi rode poorly in Brno. This time he did not blame the Michelins or his machinery. He had a £40 million price tag on his head and he was suffering. Few doubted that his mind was wandering. It was later reported that Rossi's tax returns were a thing of wonder for a man who was on the Forbes rich list. In 2001, the year he first won the title, it was reported he paid £629 in taxes in Britain.

The excuses were being killed off one by one. Even a new engine with pneumatic valves rather than the traditional metal springs could not mend his fallibility. Stoner won in Rossi's back yard in San Marino and the lead was eighty-five points. Massive. Unbridgeable. Girlfriend trouble, taxman trouble, racer trouble. Rossi, the peerless figure of his generation, was cut adrift by many who had idolized him. In the paddock one Italian told me that, even in Tavullia, they had started to snipe at him. Taxes and death. Everyone had to give in to them. Rossi was not immortal.

He turned his attention to tyres and, with Davide Brivio taking over Badioli's role, talks began about switching to Bridgestone for 2008. In Portugal he delayed the inevitable, but his remarks during the weekend were staggering for Rossi. 'The championship is almost out of reach, especially when Stoner is so strong,' he said. 'We will put all our energies into holding on to second place and thinking about the development of the package for next year.' I remembered Jerry Burgess telling me that the day Rossi accepted second best was the 'day it's over'. Rossi also sounded dulled. He was no longer the man bemoaning the lack of human skill needed to race a Formula One car. 'It's a bit boring,' he said in reference to the more processional MotoGP races and electronic aids. 'It's difficult for me. It is even more difficult to fight when you know it is not possible to win.' You could almost hear the sniggers from the back of the grid. 'Welcome to our world.'

The decider was an anti-climax. Motegi was a quiet race that seemed a million miles away from the hurly-burly of the big European rounds. It was also a race in which riders had to pit to cope with a drying track. Rossi looked assured enough in the wet but struggled for feel with the Michelins after he had come in. There followed much mud-slinging between Yamaha and Michelin as to who was most culpable. Stoner was only sixth but it was enough. He had beaten Rossi and was the world champion.

Rossi was magnanimous with his post-race verdict. 'Congratulations to Casey,' he would say to the scribes in his box. 'I am very flattered that he made a dedication to me on his victory T-shirt because if someone else had to win then I'm glad it's one of my fans. He's a great rival and I hope we can continue that rivalry into the future.' In fact Stoner was not a fan and had been disgruntled that Rossi had not shaken his hand on the victory lap. Rossi claimed that this was down to the fact Stoner was on the other side of the track when he passed. He had shaken hands with Hayden in 2006 after all.

Stoner used the spotlight to take on his knockers. 'First it was the power of the Ducati, then the Bridgestone tyres, blah, blah, blah,' he said in his garage. 'Well, I reckon we've proved a lot of people wrong this season. This is unreal.' His father, Colin, fiercely protective of his son, said, 'When he was four, a Japanese magazine asked him what he wanted to be and he said Mick Doohan.' He was only the third Australian to win the title after Doohan and Wayne Gardner. Only Freddie Spencer had won the championship at a younger age. Stoner thanked Alberto Puig for giving him his chance – 'we were camped out in Alberto's backyard for a couple of years, we were like the gardeners' – and recalled how there had been no shower in the caravan when he came to England as a fourteen-year-old. 'It was hard in Europe because they wanted European riders.' Colin Edwards, who had no axe to grind with anyone, gave his appraisal. 'Casey can stand toe-to-toe with Valentino,' he said.

Chaz Davies watched the race on television at his girlfriend's house. He would have been racing there with the satellite Ducati team but had got injured in a two-day test, a reward for his good showing in Laguna. He was not surprised and flew to Australia the following week to stay with Stoner before they raced at Phillip Island. 'In some ways it was unreal given what we'd been through,' he said. 'But I knew how good he was. I would put him up there with Rossi. Most people wouldn't, but in terms of who can go faster round a track I'd even put him slightly higher. The thing with Rossi is he has the consistency and a way of adapting that puts him ahead at the minute, but Casey can get there.' Stoner would cope with the brickbats too. 'He's an Aussie,' Davies said. 'Not too interested in what other people think. He has a lot of self-confidence. He knows he can beat Rossi. The trouble is there are not too many people who don't like Rossi, so they will side with him whatever you say.'

It got worse for Rossi. The new generation had got him and Romano Prodi, the centre-left prime minister with a bugbear about tax dodgers, was closing in. At Valencia he fell in qualifying and suffered a minor break of his right arm. He rode in the race but the engine failed. Then, to cap the worst year of his career, Pedrosa won to take second place in the standings off him by a point. The deposed king was now not even second best. He went home to Tavullia to lick his wounds. His day of reckoning would come.

LAP 11

This was why he did it. This was why he was here. Sure, it was still scary and the scabbing of old wounds was scraped away with each lap, but it was also a mind-numbing fix. The blur of the walls and the fields and the tarmac, the sheep and the people and the ghosts. Mike breathed in deeply. Suddenly, he did not feel like a thirty-eight-year-old with a gammy leg. He lapped at 111.04mph in the penultimate practice session, faster than Tom Herron and faster than Phil Read. And he had not been pushing to the limit. He sought it, tasted it and drew back. There was more to come and he was already flying as the years toppled.

The beginning of the end came as early as 1968 when Mike was only twenty-seven. The previous season had been hard. With Jim Redman injured, it had been left to Mike to shoulder the burden for Honda in the 250cc, 350cc and 500cc classes, with only Ralph Bryans, a 125cc specialist, in support. The beastly Honda, the unmanageable camel as he called it, and the championship finale at Monza had exhausted him. Then, at the start of 1968, Ralph was summoned to Japan to meet Honda's top brass. They delivered their bombshell and he went home. Mike arrived from South Africa in ignorance of Honda's plans. He was taken out for dinner, where he was also told Honda were quitting bikes to focus on Formula One. He was offered £50,000 not to race for anyone else that year. Or he could take a much smaller sum and be free to ride in grand prix races for others. Mike took the money. He could still race in national and international meets, but he was gone from the elite. Gone at twenty-seven. 'He thought he was going to Japan to talk about next year's contract and he was quite taken aback when they said they were pulling out,' Pauline recalled. 'It was not the way he would have chosen to bow out.'

He went back to cars. Mike's dalliance with four wheels stemmed back to 1963, when he had finished tenth in the British Grand Prix at Silverstone. He would make some of his very best friends in Formula One but he bristled at the inveterate snobbery and aloofness of the hangers-on. In 1964 John Surtees, another old biker, won the Formula One title in a blue and white Ferrari. It was a hugely controversial crossover triumph. Surtees trailed Graham Hill by five points going into the last race of the season in Mexico. Hill was then taken out by Lorenzo Bandini, Surtees's team-mate, and Jim Clark, who suddenly stood to win the championship, was seven laps from the crown when oil began leaking from his Lotus. Bandini then moved over to let Surtees through into second place to give him the crown by a single point.

Surtees, the only man to win world titles on two and four wheels, has an intriguing take on what happened that day in Mexico City. 'Frankly, I was astounded by what Graham did,' he said when we met at his office in Monza House on an industrial estate in 2008. 'He decided that the only way to get out of the hairpin was to take a certain line, but it left the door open and Lorenzo said, "Thank you." Lorenzo had the corner because he was on the inside. Purely because I had appeared on the back of Graham, he momentarily forgot about Lorenzo. It wasn't controversial from my point of view. We're not pre-programmed machines, we're humans and we all make mistakes.'

Surtees became Mike's boss in 1971. By then the pragmatic, sometimes cold figure was running Surtees-Ford. Mike was fourth at Monza for him the year Michelle was born. The following year he was the European Formula Two champion and was eighth in the Formula One table. He was not scorching the earth as he had done in bikes, but he was good.

Driver and boss were chalk and cheese. Surtees had been forced to step over sick stains on the carpet after a party at Mike's in order to get his signature. There were reports of Mike sleeping with women the night before races and turning up with thick stubble and a thicker head. Surtees was cast in the guise of the puritanical headmaster, Mike as the profligate son. 'It was not the easiest of relationships,' Pauline said. 'Mike had to choose his words carefully and I've still got letters they exchanged. Mike was always trying to get John to relax and he congratulated himself in managing to mellow him a bit by the end.'

Surtees had a razor-sharp mind, however, and could overlook some of Mike's waywardness if he maintained his professionalism on the track. 'He was quick and he was not flying off the circuit,' Surtees remembered. 'It was just a question of understanding Mike and moulding the car to him.' Surtees had already played a key role in the Hailwood story by recommending him to MV when he left the Count. Later, he also went to Japan and tried to ride the beastly Honda. 'I felt it was a good bike but there were some basic things wrong with it,' he reported. 'That made it difficult to ride. What you have to remember about Mike is that, first and foremost, he is a rider. He related to the machine as it was. He had no idea about what was happening underneath him. Mike was not the person to put on a new bike.'

So he ploughed on with his second career while Ago helped himself to a place in folklore. With Mike gone there was no chal- lenge to Ago and the MV. The rival bikes were not in the same class and Ago was both revered and resented for having it easy. He cruised to dominant titles for the next five years, taking his total to seven. 'I won the world title in 1966 on the MV Agusta and they said, "Hey, that's not bad." Then I won it again and they said, "That's good." I won again and again and suddenly it was, "This guy is a big legend." I became something. Someone.'

In Czechoslovakia Ago went for dinner with a gorgeous, svelte twenty-four-year-old. It was only much later that she told him that her husband was a fan and had wanted her to spend the night with him while he waited in the bar. On another occasion in France the phone rang during a liaison with another girl. It was her boyfriend asking if she was going to be much longer.

His image as one of Italy's most eligible catches was assured when he starred in a series of films. Forty years on and the posters from the films, with colourful portraits of him and his leading ladies, still adorn his basement. Eventually, he was given the option to make a career as an actor. 'I started with photo romances, books with pictures, always centred around a girl and a motorcycle race. Then came the films. I made three but I was not Alain Delon. Nevertheless, I got an offer from Pietro Germi, a very famous director in Italy, to be the protagonist in his new film. Germi was very well known for films like *Divorce, Italian Style* and *Seduced and Abandoned*. Everyone went to him and begged him to let them be in one of his films. I was the first man to say no to him. He said he needed me from March to August, but that was the racing season. Germi said, "I know that, but it is more important to make a film." I told him he was wrong. He was very surprised. "I am not an actor," I said. "I am a racer." '

So he carried on racing and winning and seducing until the tale began to twist and turn and threatened to leave him bleeding and bereft on the cutting-room floor.

CHAPTER FOURTEEN

BAD BLOOD

Don Pepe's restaurant, a salmon-coloured villa a short ride from the Jerez circuit, had witnessed some of MotoGP's finest food fights. The teams all used it and, once a year, would shuffle through the foyer, bedecked by Iberian ham stalactites and vast cabinets housing iced fish. Conversations about bikes and riders hummed around the wooden walls. It was the start of another year in the cycle. Another beginning.

It was good to see Gav and Matt again. Gav was now Dorna's director of communications, a hugely responsible job and one he did well. Matt had left Dorna and was working for the BBC, doing reports for *Football Focus* as well as interviewing and presenting in MotoGP. Nick Harris was also there, having organized the media trip to the IRTA test. There was a woman from the *Daily Telegraph* who wanted a lifestyle piece and there was a man in a leather jacket from Radio One. We made an incongruous bunch.

Nobody batted an eyelid when James Toseland walked in. To the Repsol Honda mechanics in the corner he was just another no-hoper from World Superbikes. To us, he was the great new hope. After Chaz Davies, Leon Haslam, Chris Walker and Neil Hodgson, here was the real deal, a two-time World Superbike champion who had got a decent seat with the Tech 3 Yamaha team. He was a down-to-earth Yorkshireman who had no airs and graces. When you got to know him a little, he also had a dry sense of humour, which was no mean achievement given what he had already put up with in his life and career; the suicide of his mother's partner when he was a teenager had left mental scars, but meant he dripped perspective.

I once had to step over him as he sat in a collapsed heap in Spain, his leathers undone to the waist, eyes starched open through dehydration, to interview Hodgson in the back of the GSE Ducati truck. Now Hodgson was ploughing a decent but unspectacular career in America and Toseland was the superfit racer who had wowed Middle England by playing a self-penned piano piece on BBC *Sports Personality of the Year* a few months beforehand. That had got him fourth place in the public's vote, a hitherto unheard of feat for a motorcyclist. He was under no illusions as to why he was so popular, though. 'I was tenth before the piano,' he said. 'Had sod all to do with racing. I actually wanted to sing too but they wouldn't let me. Might have won.'

Toseland bore daft questions better than most and it was little wonder his manager, Roger Burnett, a former racer who now ran a PR company, was beaming away. He knew that good looks and a background in classical piano gave Toseland the chance to make it as a crossover star. The future was bright. Hodgson, another of his men, had gone to MotoGP when he was at the tipping point. 'The difference is he went then because he had no choice,' Toseland said. 'I did. I could have stayed. I'm young enough. I wasn't desperate.'

The woman from the *Telegraph* liked him too. He was like an HRT patch. Toseland had a square jaw, bottomless brown eyes and *Top Gun* hair. He was a curious mix of pragmatism and emotion, admitting to waving to his lucky tree as he drove down the M1, but resisting the overtures of a tattooist friend to cover him in ink.

It would be at the final test of the winter that he made others sit up and take notice. MotoGP has always treated World Superbikes with a snobbish disdain, but its two-time champion was second fastest under lights in Doha. Valentino Rossi expressed his surprise. Toseland was also privately shocked to have led the test until its dying embers and a blitz from fellow rookie, Jorge Lorenzo, putatively Rossi's team-mate but riding on different tyres and with a wall down the centre of the garage.

Even as we met in Don Pepe's several weeks before that test, Toseland was brimming with enthusiasm and ambition. 'I exceeded my expectations of what I thought was possible years ago,' he said. 'Never in my wildest dreams did I think this would all be possible. I could have stayed in World Superbikes and kept on winning, no problem. I had a great life, a great career. I'd walk down the paddock and it would be, like, "Hi, hi, hi, hi, hi." Here I get two. It's different, but it was time.'

Toseland reasoned that Casey Stoner and Ducati were the team to beat, although he was not about to underestimate Rossi. 'I admire him for his ability and his success, but he's not out of reach.' Toseland was twenty-seven, the age by which Rossi had once declared he would be retired, but he was as excited as Chaz Davies had been when he had made his bow in GP racing as a fifteen-year-old. Like Chaz and Casey at the Sachsenring that year, he was a kid in a sweetshop. 'I never ever think I've made it,' he said. 'I don't understand that way of thinking, it just doesn't register. I'm just doing something I love and I know I'm fortunate.' So was Bradley Smith of the next generation. He had now graduated to Aprilia and said he could not sleep because of the adrenalin. He would actually go one better than Toseland at the Doha tests and top the time sheets. 'I cannot even tell you how excited I am this season,' he said. 'I have got to be looking at regular podiums now.'

It was a good night in Jerez. Don Pepe's steaks were big and bloody. The Rioja flowed. Back at the hotel we had a drink in the bar and then I went to bed and wondered what I should ask Stoner the following morning.

It was a hot and bright day and we were glad to be shepherded into one of the anodyne anterooms behind the media centre at Jerez to await the champion. He still looked like a boy when he arrived. He wore stonewashed jeans, a red Ducati jacket and white trainers. It was obvious he hated doing this and he left nobody in any doubt as a few polite questions were proffered to break the ice. His life had not changed, he said, apart from that he and Adriana had less time to themselves. There was a lot more media to do after winning the world title. Did he enjoy that side of the job? 'No.' This was typical Stoner, blunt and honest and almost antagonistic. Mini Mick, as he was sometimes called in the paddock, a reference to Doohan's bloodless nature as well as his relentless riding skills. I asked him if he would mind repeating how he came to leave Australia as a teen to seek his fortune in the UK. 'On a plane,' he quipped. The Ducati PRs laughed.

Although he did not like the media, Stoner was too candid to be a poor interviewee. Ask him a question and he gave a true answer. So he did tell me about his early days in England. 'We met some really good people in the UK, but we also met some people who have just tried to stamp us into the ground,' he said. 'Whatever we do we don't get the credit.'

It was a recurring theme and it was evident he was still irritated by a perceived lack of respect. He had a point too. In 2007 he had destroyed the opposition, won ten grands prix and finished a staggering 126 points ahead of Rossi. Only Fast Freddie Spencer, the legend from the Bible Belt, was younger when he won the title in 1983, but Stoner, now twenty-two, believed his achievement had been overshadowed by the belief that his Ducati gave him a huge advantage. 'It's been frustrating because everyone said my results were down to other things,' he said. 'It was traction control or the tyres or the bike. It pissed me off. Now the Japanese factories have been trying to bring in new rules to squish us down. You think about the amount of manpower they have compared to an Italian manufacturer and they are running scared. They are trying to use politics to bring down Ducati when they should just work harder.'

This was colourful stuff. Stoner clearly needed to get it off his chest. He was the champion and it irked him that Ducati and Bridgestone were seen as the reasons. Now Rossi had switched to Bridgestone, demanding the same tyre composition that Stoner used, and the playing field was levelled. We would see who was the best in a fair fight.

Rossi did not escape the high dudgeon. Like many before him, Stoner found that the Italian shutters went up as a defence mechanism. 'At the beginning of last season it was fantastic and he was giving credit, it was a real good time,' Stoner said. But no longer was he riding like a god, no longer was he the devil. 'By the end of the season he never spoke to me. He did not like the fact that I was able to come in and win.'

Stoner set the fastest time in Jerez, bagged a BMW for his trouble and said, 'Not bad for ten minutes' work. I expected my time to get blown into the weeds.' Rossi was unable to do anything about it and Stoner insisted his bike was even better this year. 'Despite what anyone else thinks, we were struggling for bottom-end acceleration last season,' he barked. 'We've changed the chassis so that the bike's easier to ride coming out of turns. I'm not expecting to win the title but I'm working hard.'

He had recovered from the damaged shoulder he suffered in testing at the end of 2007 and was still happily married. He was also the Young Australian of the Year. 'The award usually goes to guys who've worked with underprivileged kids or in the community,' he said. 'I felt a bit shallow because I'm just a motorcycle racer.' That was the other side of Stoner, the humble kid who was Chaz's mate and who had been awestruck as they stood and watched Toni Elias round Marco Melandri five years earlier.

So he had got some credit? 'Yeah, but so many people in the press and paddock just want to put us down.' I moved next door to the media room, transcribed the tape and penned my piece. It began, 'Casey Stoner is an angry young man.' Given that he had taken pops at the British, the Japanese and an Italian in the course of a single interview it seemed fair enough. It concluded, 'The anger is coming to the boil at just the right time.'

It sums up much that is wrong with sport that the next time I arrived at a track it soon became clear that I had committed a mortal sin by suggesting Stoner was bitter about his treatment. I found the Italian Ducati PR woman.

'I hear you're not happy with the piece I wrote.'

She shook her head and looked at the floor. 'No, we were not happy.'

'What was wrong with it?'

'You say he is angry. But he was in a very friendly mood that day. He was serene.'

'But all the quotes are accurate. He said people were trying to squish him down and that Rossi did not speak to him.'

'You said he is spitting blood.'

'It's an English phrase. It does not mean he literally spat.'

'I don't understand.'

I suspected Stoner couldn't have cared less. He was hard as nails and, like Davies had said, did not really give a stuff what anyone else said. As far as I was concerned he shot from the hip and did not come out with the usual PR-schooled drivel about tyres and sponsors. However, like most riders, he was surrounded by people whose job it was to care. Or maybe it was as one insider who had been in the sport for decades told me, 'Racers are the most insecure people in the world – doesn't matter if they're a world champion or a club racer. They're all totally paranoid.'

Rossi had already planted a seed or two in Stoner's mind by insisting on the same tyre at his first test on Bridgestones. The implication was the tyre was the magic ingredient that had taken Stoner to the title. Plenty of people were happy to go along with that theory, regardless of Loris Capirossi's struggles with the Ducati, and so the simmering discontent within Stoner, denied by his team but obvious to all but the one-eyed fan, was vented.

Rossi was up against it, though. He had called a summit meeting with Yamaha after the final round of 2007 in Valencia and grievances had been aired. It was there that Masao Furusawa, Yamaha's technical chief, admitted mistakes had been made. 'The bike is just a tool but the rider could hardly manage it in 2007,' he later revealed.

Jerry Burgess and his crew were working tirelessly to get the bike in perfect synchronicity with the front tyre. For Rossi it felt like starting over as he needed to relearn the tracks on entirely different lines. The front tyre was also harder, which meant feel was a problem, something Rossi prided himself on. They tried numerous settings to see what best suited that tyre. Rossi's racing position was changed; so were the wheelbase length and the flexibility of the chassis. The good news was the pneumatic valve engine was working.

Rossi had also come to a settlement with the Italian tax agency. When all payments were made, he was £26 million poorer, but he knew it could have been a lot worse. He called a press conference in Pesaro and said he had paid up for peace of mind and would be moving back to Italy. There was no acknowledgement of wrongdoing. 'I already had the intention of returning to Italy,' he said. 'This has only speeded things up. In a few more months the thing would have happened of its own accord. I feel I have cleaned my conscience. In all these months I have never felt alone.'

He was not alone at the press conference either. Graziano was there and so was Francesca Mainardi, his accountant. His tax advisor, Victor Uckmar, had told him he would win any legal battle, but Rossi wanted to put the affair behind him. 'I don't even want to know how it might have finished if I had chosen to fight it out, but I do know that it's much more important to be serene in order to ride my bike better. I will keep trying to go better.'

It was typical of Rossi to be able to adopt a serene mien in the face of having coughed up £26 million. He looked confident and assured. For the first time, he also suggested publicly why he had dismissed his backroom team. 'When you are young, sometimes you let yourself be guided by the people who are working for you,' he said.

It was a bizarre scene. Rossi had been hunted and watched for five years but he was now paying the price and that changed everything. Vincenzo Visco, the junior finance minister, said Rossi had created a 'more or less fictitious' home in London, but tempered that by reminding everyone he was a fan. The press conference became yet another audience. Massimo Romano, the Pesaro tax chief, smiled broadly and lauded Rossi as 'an example of straightforwardness and correctness'. Rossi had transformed himself from a fallen hero, both on and off the track, into a man who did the right thing and Italy fell back in love with him.

'Shame! Shame! Shame!' The cries from tax employees unhappy with a pay offer echoed into the hall. The angry proletariat bristled at the incongruity of the tax agency cosying up to a figure accused of costing them millions, while their modest demands were dismissed. 'Shame! Shame! Shame!' echoed the voices, but they were ignored, along with the leaflets they handed out to journalists claiming Rossi had got a ninety per cent discount.

By the time they got to Qatar for the first race of the season nobody was talking about Rossi's legal issues. Sensibly, he had taken a huge hit and drawn a line in the sand. Now he could focus on the season, but the clever money was still riding on Stoner and Ducati. Capirossi had departed to Suzuki and Melandri was on the other red brute. Lorenzo, the kid who had taken Davies' record for being the youngest GP racer of all, was now partnering Rossi. Nicky Hayden and John Hopkins were still there and needed big seasons. Dani Pedrosa's learning years were behind him and Michelin were making confident noises about rivalling Bridgestone. If Rossi truly was on the slide, as many back home believed, this was the cast list to prove it.

Qatar was novel because it was the first race under floodlights. For Carmelo Ezpelata, the Dorna chief executive, it was something of a coup. Although he repeatedly told people MotoGP was not in competition with Formula One, he nevertheless felt a tinge of satisfaction in beating them to a night race. Formula One would follow suit in Singapore in September, but MotoGP had the jump start. 'There's a lot of politics there,' said an official from Musco, the American company charged with the task of setting up 3,600 lights to illuminate an area the size of 70 football pitches.

Ezpeleta was candid about the reasons for the night race. 'This is not about crowds,' he said. 'It's about television and selling Qatar to the world. We've been in discussions with the prime minister ever since we signed the contract to hold races there.' To many it was not about sport. Times were hard, King Kenny Roberts had been forced to take his team out of the championship and now they were in a desert for a weekend that reeked of artifice.

The riders gave it their cautious approval. 'It would be better to move this night race to a period when the temperature is a little higher because at the moment it's very cold here,' Rossi said after testing. The 11 p.m. start had also failed to impress Pedrosa.

'There are a lot of shadows and it's very tiring on the eyes,' he complained. Stoner, who beat his own race lap record by more than a second in testing, said the floodlights meant racers had to trust their ability. 'The most interesting thing is that with the lower visibility you have to have more confidence in what your instincts tell you.'

Toseland was on a high after his magnificent test but, as the nerves kicked in, he admitted the novelty factor was trying. 'I feel like I've worked a night shift,' he said. 'Getting your body fired up when it wants to shut down is very difficult, but the only real problem was the humidity. It made it a bit hazy and I had to wear a rain mask because I was getting some moisture on my visor.'

Even before the opening race of the year there was plenty of intrigue and innuendo. Pedrosa ditched his No. 26 plate for the No. 2, a pointed reference to having beaten Rossi to the runner-up spot. Then, in Friday's practice session, Rossi shut off the throttle in mid-corner forcing Pedrosa to plunge head-first into a gravel trap at 150mph. For Pedrosa it was more bully-boy behaviour, but Rossi put it down to the Spaniard going into the corner too fast. It may have been an innocent accident, but in the knife-edge drama of that moment it showed how much these riders wanted it. The years of toil and squabbles and backbiting and tyre wars had brought them to this point.

There was an all-Michelin front row to cast doubt over Rossi's insistence on switching to Bridgestones. And then in the race it seemed little had changed. Stoner bided his time before hitting the front and eked out a huge five-second lead by the end. The winning combination was back and Stoner had rammed a few more words down various gullets. Rossi, meanwhile, found himself embroiled in a bitter scrap for, in his terms, minor placings. With Lorenzo producing a stunning debut to wrap up second place, Rossi suffered the humbling experience of not even being top of the team.

Pedrosa also beat Rossi to the line as did Andrea Dovizioso, whose fourth place was the best debut by an Italian since Max Biaggi a decade earlier. Hot on Rossi's heels was Toseland, who had played the percentages in the latter stages and decided not to risk wiping out Rossi with a last-ditch passing move. Given the criticism that would soon come his way, it was a politic decision, but it was a lustrous start, backed up by Scott Redding, another British teen with a dream in the 125cc class who had qualified second on the grid and then battled for a podium spot.

Nobody talked about the night afterwards. The logistics of installing 1,000 poles and drilling through 12,600 metres of desert rock and earth were lost amid the emotion of the race. Dovizioso went back to his garage and burst into tears. He was still blubbing ten minutes later as the vivid memory of dicing with Rossi and then beating him exploded in his brain.

I caught up with Toseland three weeks later in a room in a castle. He looked terrible but explained he had been receiving oxygen since he arrived in Jerez because of a chest infection. He was sweating and his face was ashen. 'I feel shit, kidder,' he said. It was two days until the Spanish Grand Prix and I thought he should be in bed, but Toseland said he had to fulfil a commitment to launch a new website. So here he was, streaming by the canapés, as a blonde violinist in a figure-hugging black dress circulated around confused journalists. Toseland said he had spent two hours sleeping in Dr Costa's medical centre after practice. His temperature rose to 39.5 and he was pumped full of antibiotics and put on a drip. 'It's bronchitis, mate,' he said. 'I'm not really in the mood.' He still played 'Walking In Memphis', though.

He was not the only one feeling off-colour in Jerez as the civil war between Spanish wunderkinds Pedrosa and Lorenzo blew up. The pair had never got on. There was too much of Rossi's theatrics in Lorenzo for the more sombre Pedrosa. So at the pre-event press conference, Pedrosa refused to even look at Lorenzo. This was manna from heaven for Lorenzo, who loved to stir the pot and act as an intravenous irritant by getting beneath Pedrosa's skin. He made use of an interview on Spanish television's breakfast news programme, booked to promote the autobiography he was launching at the age of twenty, to highlight Pedrosa's poor sportsmanship. Then, having pipped Pedrosa to pole position on Saturday, Lorenzo made a beeline for the Repsol Honda elf at the back of parc fermé. 'Hey, why didn't you shake my hand?' he said. Pedrosa, affecting the disinterested air of a superior, fixed him with a stare. 'Why would I want to?' he snapped incredulously.

It was left to King Juan Carlos to force a handshake that was every bit as false as the one that had been stage-managed between Rossi and Biaggi back in 2001. After Pedrosa's victory in the race, with Rossi second and Lorenzo third, the big, burly royal with the thinning demi-mullet got hold of them both and physically pulled their hands together. The cacophony of approval failed to paper over the cracks but did make the front page of the daily paper, *ABC*, the next morning.

The burgeoning dispute filtered down to the junior ranks. Before Pedrosa, the man Lorenzo loved to loathe was Hector Barbera, his erstwhile team-mate in the 250cc class. Alex Debon, another rider and Lorenzo's close friend, now filled that role. After the race on Sunday, Debon was rumoured to have found Barbera and headbutted him. One source said there were blows and blood and the pair had to be pulled apart. Lorenzo, the new showman on the grid, no doubt loved the drama.

It got better and better for him too. In Portugal he not only won his first MotoGP race at his third attempt, but he overtook Rossi at the slow chicane with a move of imagination and audacity. Then, as Rossi's Bridgestone tyres failed him, Pedrosa breezed past and took second place. After three rounds Lorenzo, twenty, and Pedrosa, twenty-one, were tied at the top, fourteen points clear of Rossi, with Stoner another seven adrift. Rossi was in the midst of the longest losing streak of his career. It was seven races now. The knives were being sharpened, obituaries prematurely penned.

The season made one of its inexorable lurches in China when Lorenzo fell to earth. It was Friday and the cavernous stands were all but empty when Lorenzo's Yamaha buckled beneath him and he was thrust high into the air over his somersaulting machine. He landed hard on his feet and the damage was instant. One ankle was badly broken, the other had severe ligament damage. Lorenzo was already recuperating from surgery on his right arm. Suddenly, the rookie who had shaken up the world looked a brittle shell. He persevered and salvaged a heroic fourth place. Rossi got the win, but it came with footnotes about his injured team-mate.

There was a lot of bad blood around in those early races and Toseland was the cause of much of it, although the criticism about his over-aggressive riding merely made him smile. 'They're having a laugh aren't they?' he said. Hayden, a shadow of the championship contender of two years before, was not laughing when Toseland held him up in qualifying in Portugal. It was one of those unfortunate things that happens to all riders on hot laps, but Hayden, desperate to get back to the top, took it badly. Toseland went to Hayden's garage to apologize. 'I shook his hand and said, "Sorry, pal, I was on a race tyre." He looked at me and said, "That's a lot of sorrys in the last two weekends." That got me. "Not to you, pal," I said, "I've not come across you." '

Later Toseland went to Hayden's motorhome to apologize again but had the door slammed in his face. Toseland shrugged. Sod him, if that was his attitude. Later that night Hayden had calmed down and sought out Toseland. 'I was acting like a baby,' he admitted. Toseland raised his eyebrows when he recollected all this. 'Then Stoner chirped up at the next race and says, "I've been watching the last two races and have come to the conclusion . . ." Come to the conclusion! He sounded like a bleeding safety officer! Give me a break.'

Tempers were fraying and it was a thinning thread that kept the riders tethered to normality. Stoner had just cause to be tetchy after his start. In Estoril he did show a touch of class by reacting to a disappointing qualifying session by shaking hands with every member of his crew in the garage and offering them words of encouragement. 'There's still time to get this right,' he said. It was a rallying call that spoke volumes about him. But then came the race and a TV camera, attached to his Ducati, came loose and began flapping around. He shoved it back into the fairing on the straight and cursed his luck. 'I didn't know what the hell it was and I was worried it might be something to do with the bike's electronics. If I'd had known it was the camera I'd have ripped it out!' A sheepish Dorna official drew the short straw and had to go and apologize afterwards. Maybe it was the disappointment over that and the wrong tyre choice in China that led to 'Lorenzo-gate'.

Toby Moody, the Eurosport commentator, had gone down into the Ducati garage to speak to Stoner after the race in Shanghai. He asked whether it was right that someone with 'knackered ankles' should be allowed to ride a 230bhp bike when he might not even be able to turn it properly and hence endanger the likes of Stoner. Moody was shocked by the vehemence of the response. 'Are you kidding me?' Stoner said. 'He's perfectly OK. He qualified in fourth place, for crying out loud.' Moody had obviously pricked a nerve. 'It's all an act, this rolling around in the gravel trap for five minutes, you know. They've got him in a wheelchair and they're pushing him around the paddock. It's a joke.' Moody said Stoner ranted on for a while. That was fair enough. Each to their own opinion. But when Moody repeated the story in a blog the Ducati PR team swung into action again and expressed their disappointment.

It made for an intriguing backdrop to my first major interview with Lorenzo in the forecourt at Le Mans. Sure enough he turned up in a wheelchair. He had a crew cut, narrow eyes and a pencil mouth. He responded to questions about his ability to rub people up the wrong way with a healthy dose of melodrama. 'Even Jesus Christ, the kindest man to walk the earth, wasn't to everybody's liking. How can I expect to be? It's impossible.'

Later in the year, when Lorenzo's season would reach its nadir with five crashes in three rounds, and he would wear a special silk glove to reduce friction on his wrist and fingers, he conceded much of sport is played out in the head. How could you deal with setbacks? 'Be water, my friend,' he said in reference to Bruce Lee's metaphysical musings. Be water and 'empty your mind, be form- less, shapeless, water can flow or it can crash, be water, my friend'.

He was the most colourful character I had interviewed since Rossi, lending some credence to Stoner's allegation of acting by saying he craved to be a thespian. He was taking acting lessons and had hired Russell Crowe's Gladiator costume to celebrate his 250cc title the previous year. He had also dressed up as a boxer on a victory lap and planted his own flag in the ground after each win to claim it as Lorenzo's Land. Unsurprisingly, his autobiogra- phy, My Story So Far, lent itself to grandiose statements and deep thoughts on all matters.

What did he want to be? He said he would like the wealth of Bill Gates, the looks of Brad Pitt, the arrogance of Eric Cantona and imagination of Gaudi. Oh, and he wanted 'to sing like Sinatra, dance like Elvis and ride like Rossi'. This was no bland money-maker.

He then suggested the best thing in life is to have defects and be comfortable with them. But people are never happy with who they are. What he wanted was charisma. He liked Cantona above

Ronaldinho because he was an *enfant terrible*. 'Since I was little I was always captivated by arrogance and since my dad was like that too, a bit cocky, I followed his example.'

The broken ankle certainly imbued him with a degree of charisma. 'It's very difficult because the bone is very delicate,' he said, rubbing a thigh. 'It's best I keep all my weight off, but when I ride it hurts a lot, especially when I have to change direction.' Lorenzo's theatrical ways predictably struck a chord with the paddock dramatist Dr Costa. 'It will be a race of suffering, pain and tears,' Costa said ahead of Lorenzo's return to action.

He had fallen in love with bikes when he saw one in a shop window aged two. At the age of three, his father, Chicho, decided he was a future star and removed his brakes so that he would learn to skid. Seven years later he teamed up with Dani Amatriain, one of Spain's top team managers, and continued to rise through the ranks, quitting school and forging a reputation as a spoilt brat. Chicho and Amatriain then fell out bitterly over a sports psychologist Lorenzo was using. Lorenzo was forced to choose. Did he want his father or his mentor? Lorenzo plumped for the latter, sparking a long-standing family rift.

Chicho was told to stay away from races and he, in turn, demanded repayment for all he had invested in his son. It was ugly and Lorenzo preferred not to speak about it. 'We got to a point where we didn't have confidence in each other,' he said. 'I love my father. He will never be a poor person, but at that moment I thought that he shouldn't ask for money from his son.'

The Lorenzo I saw was the one that had been schooled to curb the excesses of his temperament. He had undergone hypnotherapy to boost his confidence and had taken on a communications coach. No longer did he throw his helmet around the pitbox and refuse to speak to his mechanics. Instead, he belittled Pedrosa, sucked on a lollipop and carried a copy of the film *300*, a bloody retelling of the Spartans' victory at the

Battle of Thermopylae. 'It's important to feel that, as well as being quick on the track, your behaviour has evolved. I still carry the fury within me, but it's not like it was three years ago. I have my priority in life, but it is not to please other people. But I am happy to have another fast Spanish rider, because it means the sport gets more popular at home. I respect him [Pedrosa] very much.'

He believed he would emerge stronger from his troubles. In his first three races he had three pole positions, two broken ankles and one win. Nothing, it seemed, would be ordinary with Lorenzo. 'I remember doing a wheelie and the rear tyre sliding,' he said of his crash. 'Then I was flying. Scared. I thought, "When I hit the floor this will be bad." But you learn more from crashes than wins. You need these experiences.'

The following day, after two more crashes in practice, Lorenzo was an incredible second to Rossi in Le Mans. The Italian went to the top of the standings for the first time that season, three points clear of Lorenzo and Pedrosa. It was Rossi's ninetieth win, drawing him level with Angel Nieto, the thirteen-time champion who had once threatened to tear [Rossi] a new arsehole after he upset his rider in the 125cc class back in 1996.

That was ancient history. Now Nieto wore leathers emblazoned with the lettering 'BRAVO VALENTINO' and gave him a celebratory pillion ride. It was a symbolic act and proof that heroes come and go. Once Nieto had been feted as a megastar in Spain and before that he told me he worshipped Mike Hailwood. Like the man on the back.

'Hailwood was my hero,' Nieto said. 'He was a legend. I remember being a sixteen-year-old kid, racing in the 50cc at Clermont-Ferrand. Hailwood was riding the six-cylinder Honda with all three exhaust pipes dragging on the floor. There's a photo of it. I was only a kid and if he shook my hand I refused to wash it. For me he was always number one. Agostini was impressive, a great rider, but everybody copied Hailwood. If he bought a car, two or three of the same model would appear in the paddock. He was the first rider to put any colour on his black leathers, just a little stripe, but in the next race everybody had the same. He was fast on a two-stroke, a four-stroke, a 125, a 250; he'd be just as fast in MotoGP.

'He was level on points with Phil Read, level on wins, but he won the 250cc title in 1967 on points average. It was at Mount Fuji, Yamaha's test track. I was with Hailwood and we jumped balconies to the room next door. It was Gary Nixon's room and he was in bed with a Japanese girl. We watched the whole thing through the window. If Hailwood told me to jump then I jumped. Eventually, Nixon saw us and came screaming towards the door, but when he opened it we sprayed him with shaving foam.'

Hailwood, Nieto, Rossi and now Lorenzo. They formed a time-line of talent. Rossi came in off his pillion and went to the podium. Lorenzo staggered there on his crutches and sat down. The photographer called the three racers together, but Lorenzo refused to move. Instead, he stayed seated and asked Rossi to sit on his knee. It was an excruciating moment. For once, Rossi looked unsure of what to do, as if he was fearful of being upstaged. Then he obliged, wondering about the sauce of the apprentice. It was already a hell of a season.

LAP 12

The drunks were still drinking and the gamblers were still losing when Mike raised himself in the wee small hours. He looked at his watch. Four o'clock. Jesus. It was the day of reckoning. *The comeback* would happen later that afternoon and the world would discover whether he was a washed-up has-been desperately refusing to grow old gracefully. He was clinging to the coat-tails of his past and knew it. God, it was cold; vicious, breath-sapping cold. Later that day he would sit on his bike at the start of the Formula One race and try to wash away the pain. He busied himself with the minutiae of the present and refused to squint at the big picture, refused to think about the big slide.

It had come to Clay Regazzoni five years earlier at the 1973 South African Grand Prix. The Swiss driver hit Mike's Surtees, which had been clipped and left stranded in the middle of the track. They ripped off the tarmac and Mike saw the flick of flame around him. Thinking slowly, moving fast, he managed to quash the danger with his fire extinguisher. Then he noticed Regga's BRM. Regga was unconscious inside a ring of fire. The bitter orange scorched his face. Mike tried to haul his rival out, but his legs were trapped. He turned away from the burning tentacles and then dived in again. He shut his eyes and the incandescent rage bleached everything white. Mike was on fire too now. The yellow flames spread and speared. For a nanosecond Mike might have wondered if he was going to die. Death by someone else's Big Slide. How very ironic. But he got Regga out as the marshals worked and panicked. He got him out and then was doused himself.

Mike returned to the pits and jerked a thumb at Pauline. 'We're off,' he said. She picked up her helmet and wondered what had happened. They left in silence on his motorcycle and she knew better than to disturb Mike when he was like this. It was only the next day, back at Paddy's house, when she read the papers that she realized. 'Why didn't you tell me?' she asked.

'You know, it was nothing much. Anyone would have done it.'

During our discussion at Monza House, John Surtees said, 'It was the sort of thing I'd expect of Mike. It was the natural reaction of any right-thinking person, but others were standing back when Mike went in. The fire overalls back then were not much good and he knew they weren't going to protect him. There are people in this world who you'd want to be in a tight corner with and people you wouldn't. Mike was one of the former.'

Neither respect nor the George Medal he got for heroism was enough to keep his job at Surtees. Mike seemed to be on the rise and Surtees was happy with his performances, but money spoke. Bang and Olufsen agreed to bankroll Surtees' cash-strapped team to the tune of £100,000, but there was a condition. 'The price I had to pay for that deal was to get rid of Mike,' Surtees said with regret. 'The manager of the programme insisted I had Jochen Mass. I had to tell Mike in America. I'm still sorry now. He was one of our best assets, but the deal allowed us to get new engines. He was sad about it, just as I was. In hindsight I should not have done it, but that's hindsight.'

Ago was also finding that success was no barrier to falling.

People said he had it easy but there was pressure in expectation. It had been strange at first without Mike and his enthusiasm dimmed. But then a new generation came gunning for him. He met Enzo Ferrari and, as he had with Pietro Germi, he turned him down. 'I am number one in motorcycle racing, I am the king,' he explained. But then it all changed.

The beginning of the end came when the Count died. He was an awkward bastard but he knew his racing. Without him the control passed to his brother, Corroda, and later his son, Rocco. 'When he died nobody had the same power,' Ago would explain. 'So after a few years the factory was sold.'

On the track he was under pressure from the genius of a young Finn named Jarno Saarinen, and from that smug braggart Phil Read. To his horror, MV even signed Read to partner him. He had been under pressure before, of course. Ago reckoned that ninety per cent of riders would quit if given the option just before the start of a race, and he sometimes envied those at the back of the grid, the ones who brought their families and laughed and joked and cantered to happy mediocrity. Not him. He needed to win. He had to. Or, as happened at the start of 1973, he would find himself somersaulting out of favour.

He was troubled. Saarinen was on a four-cylinder factory Yamaha, a combination that heralded the pace of change, and Ago fell badly in France. Read was quickly elevated to blue-eyed boy status. 'Phil Read was not like Mike,' he said. 'He didn't care about anyone. Mike wanted to win with power. Phil Read did not care how he won as long as he did. He had always been fighting, with Bill Ivy, Mike, Jim Redman. He had to be the best even when he was losing.

'If I said one thing he would say the other. He liked to disagree. He also talked a lot with the Count's son. He turned him against me. Agusta was my family but he came in and broke the friendship. I might say the engine is no good and so Phil would say it was fantastic. I told the boss that if Phil liked it so much he could try it. So he did in Monza and the engine broke after three laps and he flew back to England after one hour. Phil then had a son and he called him Rocky, after Agusta. He was the favourite. Me, I also saw the two-stroke was the coming force and so I had enough. I quit and went to Yamaha.'

Suddenly, Ago was no longer peerless. He lost the title for the second year running in 1974 and was damned for his attitude to the TT. He had been the darling there once and had given Mike the race of his life, but now he was older and Parlotti's death had turned him against it. 'At the Isle of Man you have everything,' he said. 'It's 200 miles of first-gear and fifth-gear corners, uphills, downhills, the lot. When you win there it's like winning the World Championship. It's a huge pleasure but after three, four, five people die every year you begin to think, "Why?" I lost a lot of friends. I said if we crash then we must have the chance to stand up again. I asked why we had to accept this. People turned on me, but you have to think about your life and your life is more important than any race.'

Mike felt the same. He sat down one night and drew up a list of all the people he had known who had been killed racing bikes and cars. One of them was Jarno Saarinen, destined for greatness until he hit Renzo Pasolini, Ago's great Italian rival, at Monza in May 1973. Both were killed. Mike turned the page and kept writing. Five years later he rose at 4 a.m. for the last rehearsal. He felt the cold of the island and ignored the dangers veiled by morning mist.

CHAPTER FIFTEEN

THE RECKONING

It was mid-season and Valentino Rossi was sitting in a transporter at Assen reading a book. It was a *Rolling Stone* anthology of interviews with a black and white photograph of Johnny Cash on the cover. Rossi was in good spirits, as he should have been given that he had won in Italy, come second in Great Britain and now led Dani Pedrosa by eleven points.

'You like Johnny Cash?'

'Yes, very much,' he said as we sat secluded in the lush leather seats. 'I watched the film of his life, *Walk the Line*, twice in a row. It was so good. I cried.'

' "Ring Of Fire"?'

'Yes, I like that one.'

It was five days since the race at Donington Park, a day when Britain's great hope went to hell and back and a teenage tyro stole his thunder. James Toseland crashed and burned, ending up teary-eyed as he gave his customized St George leathers to a punter, while Scott Redding won the 125cc grand prix; he was 15 years and 170 days old at the time, the youngest GP winner of all time, two years shy of the age Rossi had been when he first stood atop the podium. Redding celebrated by sitting in the back of his motorhome playing with his Meccano set. He was driven to Hull but was too late for the ferry to Assen, oblivious to the irony of missing the boat while rewriting the record books. 'Ah yes,' Rossi said. 'I hate him – he is half my age.'

Casey Stoner had won the British Grand Prix but had been booed. It was an ugly response from a minority of the British crowd and Stoner had, most definitely, been spitting blood afterwards. 'I had it last year when I won as well,' he snapped. 'On my slowing-down lap I was getting loads of abuse. I mean, what do people want? Are they here to even watch bike racing or are they here to abuse people?'

I sipped my espresso and Rossi considered his response to the issue. 'It was very strange, for sure, but I think the relationship between the English and the Australians is not great, like the Italians and the French, yes? The people were unhappy because Casey always says, "This track is shit, this place is shit, the weather is shit." They weren't happy for that reason.'

It was a remark that would not go down well with Ducati's PR machine, but Rossi said he had no problem with Stoner. They were all bonded by shared fear and danger, but Rossi found the Australian straight and true. 'The relationship between me, Casey and Dani is more normal, whereas Biaggi was always saying bullshit. That made it difficult. But I beat those old guys and now I'm trying to beat these young ones.'

I had not seen Rossi so relaxed for a long time. He was open and animated and made the remarkably candid admission that he had not tried as hard as normal in 2006. 'When you win five titles you think a sixth will happen. It is natural. I did not give my all in 2006. Then, last year, I took lots of risks because we were not competitive. When you're not fast enough you try to push more and it's dangerous. I was scared, but it's clever to be scared because this job can hurt.'

Indeed it could. Physically in terms of broken bones and

mentally in terms of failed friendships. Rossi had set up a new management company, VR/46, and Davide Brivio, his team manager, was playing an influential role. So too was Graziano. 'People in Italy were saying a lot of bad things about me last year,' Rossi mused. 'That was hard. I have modified my organization and my style. Graziano is my right-hand man, but I am my manager.'

Maybe it was moving back home that had relaxed Rossi. He was always an enigma, an extrovert showman who craved privacy and put huge store by age-old friendships. 'He had this innate way of connecting with people through a television screen but he was actually very guarded with those not in his immediate circle,' Ali Forth said. Rossi, himself, remarked, 'People in Tavullia, they try to save me. They treat me as normal again. It gets bad if I go 15 kilometres from home, but I am happy. I am training harder and I get to bed earlier now, maybe 2 a.m. now.' He added that he felt rejuvenated, that he could go on until he was thirty-five. I pointed out what he had said about getting out at the top at twenty-seven, like George Best, like Mike Hailwood. 'Ah, things change,' he said wistfully.

Rossi had changed. I had seen him become a global superstar, the sort of person Brad Pitt would rhapsodize about. 'I would give anything to be like him,' Pitt told an Italian journalist. 'That guy is a real magician. He could hypnotize me. He's like a ballet dancer, it's pure art. For me watching him in action is like reading a poem.' It had been a hell of a ride and, leaving him to his Johnny Cash interview, it was obvious he was not finished yet. The face was older, the skin not the marbled olive I'd first met by the Thames in 2001, but he was still dancing inside the ring of fire. He still wanted to do a Hopper and light up the whole god-dammed valley.

I left Rossi and went to find Redding in the much more basic Blusens Aprilia hospitality unit, effectively a conservatory. I had spoken to his father, Adrian, on the phone and asked if he would pose for a picture with Scott for *The Times*. Adrian was more your stereotypical biker dad, with 'love' and 'hate' tattooed on his knuckles and a pierced eyebrow. A part-time window fitter, Redding had long been attracted to bike racing, while his father still fitted bikes for the TT races. His brother, Daryl, had helped plough every penny into fuelling his boy's dreams. Did he worry?

'Look, he was doing over 100mph at the age of nine so I'm used to it,' Redding senior said. 'It's been tough for all of us. Everything has been on hold from the age of six. I phone my boss three days before I come home from a race and he tries to find me some work. Scott contributes to the travelling costs and hotels now. He's looking after us. It's payback, I suppose. How much have I spent? I reckon it's probably £250,000 so far.'

Adrian did not come across as the pushy parent, although Graeme Brown, the photographer, did get a playful picture of him throttling his son as he sat on a paddock scooter. He had not pressurized Scott into a high-speed career but he was confident of success. 'I am ninety per cent sure that he will be the world champion next year,' he said. 'The bike's old, nothing special. If he gets on the new Aprilia next year and rides it like he's doing now, the sky's the limit. I've told numerous people at work to put some money on him.'

Scott, from Quedgeley in Gloucestershire, was unflustered by such paternal enthusiasm. 'If I get a good bike and everything works out, hopefully I *will* be the world champion in 2009,' he echoed. 'I didn't think I'd get a win so soon, but I thought a podium was a possibility.'

I could not help sparing a thought for Bradley Smith, the kid who had been earmarked to be the future. He still had the chance, but Redding had beaten him to the punch. They were different characters. Redding was a more earthy type, a rebel racer in the making, whereas Smith was cleaner cut and incongruously mature. I had seen him complain about having to give an inter-view to someone from Radio One when he wanted to be in the garage. He was already the consummate pro, whereas Redding struck you as someone having the ultimate blast. They also had contrasting views on the merits of the Spanish-based MotoGP Academy. 'I went backwards in the academy,' Redding said from behind impenetrable shades. 'It did not suit me. It's too serious in there. It's racing and nothing else. It's not like a family. The hand problem did not help. It would come on during a race and leave my hands numb. Couldn't feel what was going on so I had to guess. That was pretty scary. I pulled out of the first race. In the next one I slowed down. The one after that I just went with it.'

Adrian was unimpressed when it was suggested Redding have an operation. 'They were going to cut open both his arms to get blood into his hands,' he said. 'I didn't agree because he was so young. I made him squeeze a ball every evening instead. He still has it and, touch wood, the problem hasn't come back.'

A year in the Spanish CEV championship followed before his grand prix debut with the Blusens Aprilia Junior team. It had taken only eight races to score a win. Redding said that nothing worried him but would not talk about crashes. 'I never have and never will.' Superstition? 'Yeah.'

Intriguingly, Alex Barros, the Brazilian veteran, was his hero. Why? 'Well, he never had the best kit, but when he got the good stuff he was battling with Rossi straight away,' he said.

Redding did not live and breathe racing. 'We get home and he goes off on his mountain bike and we don't see him for the rest of the day,' his father said. He got on well with Danny Webb, another young Briton in the 125cc series, but said that Smith needed to lighten up. 'Me and Danny mess about on photo shoots, but Bradley's done the MotoGP Academy and is too seri-ous,' he said. 'You only have to get serious when the helmet's on.'

The next day Rossi crashed on the first lap. 'I think I am a dickhead,' he answered when asked what went through his head. He was still thinking quickly, though, and remounted. The damage limitation ended with an eleventh place, but Stoner was too good and, when he added a third successive win in Germany in tandem with Pedrosa crashing and breaking his left hand, he was suddenly back in the title race.

And then they came to Laguna Seca . . .

Stoner was vulcanized Aussie steel. Across the garage poor old Marco Melandri reflected on the news that his contract was not being renewed. He could scarcely complain. The Italian had found himself utterly incapable of taming the Ducati, backing up Stoner's opinion that his own talents were undervalued in the media. At least Melandri was fit to race. John Hopkins had beaten himself up in Assen and was on crutches, his disappointing season disappearing in a miasma of bad fortune. The paddock began to cackle with more sniffy remarks about whether Hopper was worth a six-figure contract. Hayden was fighting in the middle ground against Toseland and Chris Vermeulen, the World Superbike graduates, but 2006 seemed a distant fable now. Lorenzo's crashes had increased and his title tilt faded amid the cracked bones, but he was still a courageous fourth. Pedrosa failed to start because of injury. It was beginning to look like the title would come down to two men – Stoner and Rossi.

Tom Cruise was the latest Hollywood star to side with Rossi, trying to squeeze his entourage into the Yamaha garage, but the star turn was Stoner. His pace in practice and qualifying had destroyed the opposition and he looked well set for a flag-to-flag victory. What followed will remain in MotoGP lore for decades, an inflammable race between two world champions.

Rossi had said the only way to beat Stoner was to start 30 seconds ahead of him, but he was inwardly delighted to be on the front row. He knew it was his only chance. It took a couple of corners for the speed to straighten the field. Stoner was in front and his pace and aggression opened up a half-second lead by the first split. Hayden briefly held second but tried to go round the outside of Rossi and found himself third. Behind them Lorenzo's chequered season continued as he was thrust high into the Californian sky on the first lap. Battered and bruised, Lorenzo now broke three more bones in his right foot. It had been a brutal first season for him, the genius of the first few races tempered by the gravitational pull that tested his will. That he kept going proved that it was no act.

It was left to Rossi and Stoner to bludgeon each other into submission in a bare-knuckle prizefight at the front. Rossi took Stoner at the top of the Corkscrew, that dizzying drop, but the Aussie hung on to his rear wheel and slipstreamed him at the start of the fourth lap. He edged out and flew past. It was audacious, gung-ho stuff with no thought given to a safe points haul or the percentages. The title was forgotten. This was just two racers wanting to be the fastest, hardest, best. Thinking fast, moving slowly, all action speeded up to a static blur.

Rossi stuck an aggressive overtaking move on Stoner, but the younger man then leant over so far that he almost defied physics to take him on the outside. The crowd gasped and roared at the same time. This was the DNA of motorcycle racing, two obdurate daredevils risking all. For Stoner, there was a year of frustration wrapped up in each corner as he showed just what a star he was. For Rossi, this was payback and comeback merged together. He had been down and beaten twice but he was back. He was Valentino Rossi. Fuck them all.

It was blink-and-you-miss-it blood-letting. Graziano watched and felt the adrenalin pump. So did Uccio and Tom Cruise in the garage. Stoner's parents, Colin and Bronwyn, mixed pride and trepidation. Lorenzo was oblivious as Dr Costa examined his latest injury. It had been his year for three races but now he was a patched-up warrior, hanging together with Band-Aids and raggedy seams.

At the top of the Corkscrew, Rossi moved again. He went under Stoner at the entrance, but then had too much speed and not enough angle. He ran on to the hard dirt and threw up a smokescreen. He gripped the handlebars until his fingers whitened and wrestled the bike back towards the tarmac. As he did he hit the rumble strip and wobbled. He was jolted upright and across the track, almost taking out Stoner who had held his line. Shit! That was too much. Stoner bristled. The bastard had nearly taken him out. In the Eurosport commentary booth Toby Moody and Julian Ryder, his effusive partner, were lapping up the action. 'The people at Ducati are going to be having kittens,' Moody said. 'Valentino Rossi has never been afraid to dish it out,' Ryder responded.

They stayed within a couple of tenths of a second as they circled the track. Plotting. Thinking. Hoping. Stoner used the Ducati's speed and his positioning skill to move into the lead again at the start of lap fourteen. This was heady, intoxicating fare that cut through all the gripes about tyres and electronic aids. This was pure racing. Man against man. Nerve on nerve. No sooner was he through than Stoner, conscious that Rossi was all over his rear end, ran wide at Turn 1. His next task was to save himself and turn back into the track before he hit the gravel. With a wobble he managed it and did not breathe before he set back after Rossi.

If anything Rossi had an advantage because of the Yamaha's slightly more nimble handling. It meant by the time Stoner had got his bike into line he had precious little time to get on the gas out of the last corner. The upshot was he was taking an almighty risk on every lap by chancing everything. He was using every iota of guile and every ounce of strength to hold it together, but then it happened. He hounded Rossi into the final bend with inches between then, but the Ducati was shaking its course to parity. The rear wheel flipped off the ground. Rossi was too focused to know. His own rear tyre was beginning to wear away and tiny fragments of rubber flitted into the air. Rossi turned and readied himself for the exit, but Stoner found he was a few yards ahead of himself. The plan faltered and he slowed and turned a rigid arc. He ran off the track, across the white line and into the hard, compacted gravel. He was not panicking and was contemplating coming back when he moved a few inches too far and hit the darker, deeper gravel. The front wheel sank into the trap and Stoner fell. He picked his bike up and was so far clear that he still had second place wrapped up, but the race was gone. The mother of all races.

The aftermath was just as juicy. Matt was down in parc fermé as usual and collared the podium riders for a soundbite as they returned. Chris Vermeulen was straightforward as his third place was better than expected. However, as Matt began speaking to Stoner, Rossi timed his move. He sauntered over with a huge grin and said, 'Great race.' He offered his hand but Stoner ignored it and glared. 'Come on,' Rossi said, the grin widening. 'This is racing.' Stoner let his anger merge with his frustration and barked, 'This is racing, huh? We'll see.'

It was easy to understand Stoner's mood in those moments, but the moves were generally seen as borderline but not illegal. The one at the top of the Corkscrew where he had forced Stoner wide could scarcely be deemed a deliberate attempt to rattle the younger man, given Rossi hit the dirt and had his trajectory altered by touching the rim of the rumble strip.

Stoner did not calm down. On the podium he told Rossi he had lost all respect for him because he'd been racing for many years and had never suffered anything like that. Rossi, genuinely thrilled by such a titanic duel, was disappointed by that remark, and also angry.

By the time of the press conference Stoner was still fuming. 'Most of the time it was very nice, very clean. Valentino was riding a great pace at the front and he was riding very well. But I just felt that some of the passing moves were maybe a little bit too much and past the point of fair or aggressive. It was just some of the most aggressive I've had in a long, long time.'

Whatever the rights and wrongs of the debate, Stoner's remarks were self-defeating. Not only did it reinforce the view that he was a whingeing Aussie, it also gave Rossi the moral high ground. Stoner also undermined his argument, saying he was unhappy with three manoeuvres, but amending that to 'a couple' within the same sentence. He did praise Rossi for riding a great race, but that was lost amid the criticism. Rossi was fed all the comments and he dismissed them as playground stuff. 'If he's been racing for many years, I've been racing for a lifetime,' he said. 'And I don't know who he's been racing against, but I remember all my races being like that and my rivals always fought that way.'

It did not help that it was the summer break and so Rossi had a month to reflect on his new twenty-five-point lead and Stoner's upstart status. In the meantime I flew to Cannes to spend a day with Toseland for a magazine feature. I met Muir the photographer, who was used to snapping rock stars and artists, and we took a cab to Theoule, a small town built into red rocks on the Mediterranean. We checked into our hotel and called James.

He knew he had landed on his feet. He had begun his MotoGP career well, above many people's expectations, but had started to drift back into midfield as he struggled with his set-up. Nevertheless, he refused to feel sorry for himself. He used to live in a static caravan in Doncaster, but has just bought a terracotta villa with a swimming pool on the French Riviera, a fast ride away from Monte Carlo. He gave us a lift to the villa, introduced me to his brother and his wife, and stripped off for some pictures in the pool.

He had bought a place here on the advice of his manager, Roger Burnett, who had one down the dusty road, and was in the process of doing it up. He dried off and we adjourned to the kitchen, where he gave his nephew an ice cream and told me he vividly remembered the day he knew he was rich. 'It was the end of 2004 and my bonus came in,' he said. 'I walked into the kitchen and said, "Mum, did you know you've got a son who's a millionaire?" We had a glass of champagne and looked at the zeroes on the statement.'

There is an old adage in biking that problems usually stem from the nut connecting the handlebar to the saddle, but Toseland was an enigma because, while no nut, he was happy to talk of 'taking it to the limit' and then pose for action photographs a few feet from a sheer drop up a cliff. 'You don't think about the danger or death,' he said. 'You just need to push it to the brink of the edge. It's when expectation outweighs ability and you think you're the dog's danglies that the trouble starts.' Everyone crashes when you race at 200mph but the good ones know how to fall and roll and walk away. 'But if the bike hits you or you hit the barrier, well . . .'

He had taken some flak this year, from the riders who said he was too aggressive and the punters who felt he had been side-tracked by the piano-playing. His gigs had been varied. He had played with a classical violinist in Jerez, in front of 50,000 at a festival on an Italian beach and in assorted pubs with his whimsically named band Crash. At Laguna he even tried to crack America, playing a huge concert in California ahead of the USA Grand Prix. A proposed record deal with Sony had been put on hold so he could concentrate on his racing, but music was his future.

Toseland changed into a crisp white shirt and took us for dinner at his favourite restaurant, the beachside Marco Polo, mentioning with a tinge of embarrassment that his instinct was to reply to the French waiter in Italian. He had moved to this small town because it was the perfect base for travelling around Europe. 'I'm away for 260 days a year,' he said. He was now a tax exile, with a base on the Isle of Man, the spiritual home of biking, but he suited France because, although he said he did not set out to be, Toseland was different.

Life had not always been like this. Toseland shared the family caravan with his parents, brother and pet Labrador until he was three. Five years later, having moved into a house, he heard someone on the piano that his grandparents had bought for him. 'I knew my mum and brother didn't play so I wondered what was going on.' He crept downstairs and peeked around a corner at a man playing twelve-bar blues. 'I gave him the death stare. Musicians don't like anyone touching their instruments – even when they're eight.'

The pianist was called Ken and his combined love of bikes and music rubbed off on Toseland as he began a relationship with his mother, Jane. He learnt about Chuck Berry and racing with boyish wonder. When Ken and Jane argued, he would stay with the man who was his passport to the motorcycling world. 'He took me to the races and without him that was impossible,' he said. 'But the rows got worse. Finally, I realized my mum was mentally ill. Depressed. I was always Ken's key to getting my mum back, but this time I went with her. "Someone's going to end up very poorly," I said. And that, for him, was the last straw, and I guess that's why he took his own life.'

Ken gassed himself in the family garage when Toseland was fifteen. 'I later found out he was schizophrenic, but that night I rode to the top of an old slag heap, stretched my arms out and screamed. I felt shock and a lot of guilt because it was my decision that had pushed him, but most of all I felt anger at him for taking the easy way out. I started flying around on my bike doing things I shouldn't have. I was bubbling up inside. I was either going to go off the rails or get on the bike and risk everything.'

Toseland said he 'ached to cause trouble' but just did not suit the role of rebel rouser. He puts much of that down to the fact Ken had programmed him to be clear-thinking when racing, but the arguments wore him down and he would go to sleep with a pillow pulled over his head. When Ken killed himself and then Toseland's beloved grandpa died at the age of fifty-eight a few months later, he was scared his mum was crumbling and so bikes went on the backburner.

A chance meeting with a racer, a runner-up in the British championship, while tearing around a disused colliery saved him from giving up altogether. 'I think he thought, "Who's this kid?" because I was keeping up with him.' It was the turning point. Toseland borrowed £15,000 from his mother – 'she looked at me like I was on drugs when I asked her for it' – and entered the CB500 series. Progress was swift but troubled. He lost a cousin to a motorcycle crash and then in 1998 suffered a horrendous crash at Monza. That same weekend Michael Paquay, his team-mate, was killed. 'He was hit by two bikes and they tried to restart his heart,' Toseland recalled. 'He died while they were operating. He was twenty-four and looked like a future world champion. You never know.'

When he did get back he suffered the worst accident of his career when he landed flat on his back at Cadwell Park and wondered if he was paralysed. 'I was relaxed, almost out of my body and then blacked out. I spent 45 minutes on the side of the track waiting for the air ambulance and that really tested my will to live. I was never suicidal or anything, but it had been bang, bang, bang. I wondered what I'd do if I couldn't race again. There was no light at the end of the tunnel. I remember thinking, "Jesus, give me a break." '

Later Toseland showed me the cellar of his new French home. Hanging from the roof were his old leathers, like a calendar of cadavers. He laughed at the holes in the old ones and explained how new leathers were made from kangaroo skin because it was tougher and lighter. A mannequin sat on the bike with which Toseland won the World Superbike title the previous year. 'Took me three hours to get the leathers on it,' he said. 'I was going to use it as a scarecrow.'

He opened up his past and home, but his manager called him the 'Secret Squirrel' because he hid so much behind the good looks and deadpan wit. It used to be so with his music. 'Biking is rock 'n' roll in many ways. It's a super-cool, very masculine sport, but the piano does not really fit in. Motorcycles masked my love of playing and enabled me to carry on with my lessons without getting grief. It helped in the dark times. I never told anyone and used the bikes to get some street cred, but deep down I was a working-class lad who wanted to go to the London College of Music. It was a bit Billy Elliot.'

Inevitably, his cover was blown. He remembered a race at Brands Hatch in 2003 when he was up against Neil Hodgson, then the World Superbike champion-elect. A capacity crowd packed the circuit and Toseland could still see the banner. 'It said "Hodgson's no pianist – he's World Champion". That showed how strongly people believe you have to adhere to the biker stereotype.' Hodgson would later indulge in a show of ill-fated machismo after 'getting leathered' in South Africa. 'He convinced himself he could walk barefoot over hot coals. He'd seen a TV programme and said it was mind over matter. We spread the coals from a barbecue on the floor. Of course, he was in such a mess afterwards, with blistered feet like nothing you've ever seen. He had to ride in Japan like that.'

He met his bandmates in 1998 and their first gig was in front of a handful of punters at a Sheffield working men's club. 'You could see the whites of their eyes and they were like, "Come on, entertain us." I was terrified and wished I'd had my dark visor on.' As his fame grew he guested with Jools Holland in front of

25,000 people at Newmarket racecourse. 'I'd had blond high-lights that looked awful, so I shaved them off and turned up with a skinhead. I bought a trilby. I looked a prat. And then there's Jools Holland saying, "What key do you want to play in?"'

Some people mocked him for his music, but it was beyond a hobby. 'It was my number one passion until bikes came along. It's the only thing that takes my mind completely off racing. People may think they know me as a biker, but I like the slushy stuff, Coldplay and Elton John, composing my own songs.' One of those was for his mother's upcoming marriage. Toseland got the couple together after seeing them talk at his brother's wedding. 'I rang them both, asked them out for a Chinese meal and then did not turn up. After all the drama I'm fiercely protective of my mum, but he's a diamond bloke.'

Dutiful son (he paid back the £15,000 as soon as he could), multi-millionaire, good racer and, after he gives me a pillion ride and I hook an arm around his middle, I can confirm owner of a granite six-pack, Toseland was about as eligible as bachelors get. So what of the women who strut around the paddock with their VIP hit list and PVC hot pants? 'There are pretty girls left, right and centre, but by the time the helmet's off and the adrenalin has worn off they've gone home. I get some fans coming up and slipping me a phone number or sending gifts.' I mention a rider who says he has a suitcase of women's lingerie. 'Really? I've never felt the need to pinch a pair of pants from a girlfriend.'

His girlfriend joined us later at Marco Polo's. She was a student in mental health, but he was not ready to settle down. After all the gritty, grimy years, Toseland was relishing his place in the sun. He could not believe his luck in riding for a motorcycle manu-facturer that also made keyboards. This was a dream realized, but he still craved more. I pictured him at Assen when mechanical problems had frustrated him and his arm throbbed with pain.

That was what it came down to. The trappings, fripperies and seven-figure bank statements counted for nothing if the biking was not going well. Speed was still the drug and the disease that both killed and cured.

They all had stories and had all been through mills. Toseland had been forced to deal with suicide, death and depression before it came good. Stoner had, as Chaz Davies told me, 'had it tough like you would not believe'. Rossi had had to cope with his parents' separation, the tax saga and the loss of Badioli. They were all survivors. When they reconvened in the Czech Republic, Stoner apologized to Rossi. In the great scheme of things a spat over one move was not worth it. The pre-event press conference began in the frostiest of atmospheres, but then, as Hopkins spoke and contemplated his return from injury, Stoner leant over and shook Rossi's hand. He was smart enough to know it was twenty-eight days late, but the hatchet was buried. 'At times we overreact,' he said, pointing out Rossi had done the same with Toni Elias. The difference was Elias was not a title contender and did not have the wherewithal to turn a slight into an advantage. 'Sincerely, I am not angry with him,' Rossi said. 'I know when you lose that type of battle you are pissed off. After the race you are hot with a lot of adrenalin and it is possible to say something that is wrong. I have done the same in the past.'

It was magnanimous of Stoner to instigate a reconciliation, but the damage was done. Rossi had the momentum and the popular vote. Some portrayed Stoner as a callow apprentice currying favour with the wronged master. Never mind Stoner's world title, the image was born and wormed its way into the consciousness. And then Stoner fell in Brno and Rossi won. The lead was suddenly fifty points. In San Marino, twenty minutes from Rossi's home, Stoner fell again and opened up an old scaphoid injury. Was it a problem with tyre temperature? Or had he been mentally destroyed in the same way that Biaggi and Gibernau had? It did not matter. Rossi won in Indianapolis, breaking Agostini's record of sixty-eight elite wins, and the lead was up to eighty-seven points. It would take a miracle now.

LAP 13

Mike crashed at Braddan Bridge in his last practice as the dawn of a new day sent hazy shadows through the clouds. It was race day and he was on his arse. He checked himself over and the pain quickly succumbed to embarrassment. Jim Redman had always been worried about his teeth when he crashed. Mike felt his nether regions and reasoned that Jim had his priorities wrong. It was a small mishap but it was a reminder.

Some had already written off Mike, but they had done the same to Ago four years earlier. He started 1974 on a Yamaha after moving from MV. He went to Daytona for his first race, a gruelling 180-mile test of endurance in the East Coast sun. The vultures were circling. Phil Read, the new champion, had damned his departed team-mate for always wanting things his own way and being a bad loser. He said Ago would find it too tough against the new generation in Daytona. Ago arrived and met Kenny Roberts, heralded as the new star of motorcycle racing. Ago had been given a Chevrolet to run while he was in America and they had stencilled '13-time world champion' on the side.

'I'm the world champion, not you, not Phil Read,' Roberts told him.

'Why?'

Roberts scowled. 'Because the world is America, not Europe.'

But Ago had won and turned back the clock. There was a legion of pressmen waiting for him at Milan's Malpensa Airport. 'Ago Conquers America,' shouted their headlines. He had showed he could win without an MV. He had shown them. The disbelievers. Phil bloody Read.

It was March 1974. As Ago rejoiced in a new-found popularity, Mike took his McLaren to third place in the South African Grand Prix. 'He had a lot of problems early on in his driving career, especially with the unreliability of the Surtees,' Pauline recalled. 'He found the drop frustrating, from being the best to being very good. It did not come as naturally to him as the bikes, but by the time 1974 came around, he was getting it together. Everything was going well. Our son was born and life was good. But then he went to Nürburgring and that changed our lives.'

He still got nervous. Ralph Bryans had seen that when he visited a race early that season. 'He had bitten his nails and chewed his fingers to the bone,' he recalled. 'He was extremely edgy. I'd never seen him like that.'

He was fourth in the World Championship by the time they got to Germany. Paddy Driver and a few friends had gone over to watch. 'We were watching the race and saw Mike come through on the last lap. He was in third. We packed up and went back to our hotel where we started a drinking session. Some time later a mechanic from one of the other teams came in and said, "How's your mate?" I said, "What do you mean? He was third." The mechanic realized we didn't know. "No. He crashed on the last lap." Well, we went straight to the hospital. We saw Mike and he said he had heard his leg crack when he hit the Armco.'

Pauline was in England. The phone rang. The call she had dreaded and the one she had always known was coming. 'I was worried sick. I was stuck at home with the children. They were telling me they were trying to get him back to London. It was a dreadful time. His heel had shattered into so many fragments and lodged itself up around the ankle joint. He lost about an inch or so. They could not get the heel back down and had to put staples around it just to hold the pieces together. He had a huge plate down his leg as well. The outer bone had split downwards. That had to be bolted back together. The other leg was broken too.' It had been a big slide. It was 4 August 1974, the last of the glory days.

After the crash they had gone back to South Africa and wondered what lay ahead. Mike's insecurities surfaced. He asked how she could love him and wondered how it had come to this. She said her love went deeper than fame and fortune and even his physique. In a way she was glad. She, too, had lost a string of friends to the sport and each one had been a sobering experience. Bill Ivy's accident had been particularly hard. 'With each one it becomes gradually less of a shock,' she said. 'It effects you slightly less. Now, when I speak to people and they still have their mum and dad, and they've only lost one or two distant people in their lives, I think, "You just don't know." When Mike's racing world finished I was glad, but it was a blow that took him an awful long time to come to terms with.'

They were living in South Africa. They decided Pauline should get residency status, but the people at the office sneered at her common-law partnership. She told Mike how they had looked down at her. How puritanical they had been. Mike was in the bathroom and listened. 'Oh well, better get married then,' he said. Pauline checked herself and turned the comment over and over in her head. 'Did he say that? No, he can't have done. But it sounded like it.' It took her another day before she dared bring it up again.

'You know when we were in the bathroom yesterday, did you say, "Let's get married"?'

'Yeah, if you like.'

Pauline said they could have heard her reaction back in England. She had never thought it would happen. Even when she fell pregnant, Mike had resisted marrying until his career was over. The long wait ended with a five-minute service in Maidenhead Register Office where they used a passing porter as a witness.

Denny Hulme, Mike's old team manager, was retiring from McLaren and was moving back to New Zealand to buy into a marine business. Mike was kicking around for something to do and got roped in. He said Denny was a shrewd guy and that, if he said it was OK, that was good enough for him. So they sold their homes in England and South Africa and packed. Then Denny pulled out. 'I did not know what to do then,' Pauline said. 'We'd sold two houses and everything we owned was on the high seas to New Zealand. It was only weeks before we were due to leave.'

She sat down at the kitchen table one night, 'What on earth do we do now?'

Mike limped over with a cup of coffee. 'Only one thing we can do.'

So they went to New Zealand. 'It was all right there for a while,' she would recall. 'It was a nice outdoor life. We designed and built a house for ourselves and that took his mind off things. It helped him get over the fact that his racing was over. But then he came to England in 1977 and that started to put ideas in his head. Jim Scaysbrook, a friend, saw him ride in New Zealand. It was the first time he'd really been on a bike since. He said you could still pick him out from the crowd. He still had that easy way on a bike. I thought, "Oh no" when I heard that and started to get nervous. I could see that he still had that vitality about him. I was upset because I thought it was all behind us.

'I knew that once his mind was made up then that was it. When I found out he was actually a long way down the line with *the comeback*. He kept it quiet for a while because he knew I wouldn't have wanted him to do it. There were no arguments. That would have been a waste of breath. And anyway, I didn't want to be the sort of wife who would say, "You can't do that". He wouldn't have listened and I didn't want that. Mike was a man's man.'

So Pauline and her children, David and Michelle, went to stay with her parents in England, while Mike flew over to the island with Jim. He looked out of the window and drifted back to the treble and the titles and the battle with Ago in 1967. Ago had retired the previous December, but not before he had won the 500cc world title again on the Yamaha in 1975. They were two greats who had tried to hang on. To make it like 1967 again. 'You don't just eat it, you taste it,' Ago said in his biography, *Fifteen Times*, of the food they ate. 'It's not just sex, it's sex with flavour,' he said of their women.

Mike thought about Ago and how some said his wins had come easily. 'They should try this game,' he thought. Any of them could have gone at any time. The day Bill died he had forgotten to fasten his chin strap. Poor Bill. 'We were so close,' Ago would say of those days with Mike. 'So close that when we exited a bend it looked like there was only one bike. We merged as one.' But there was no Ago this time. Mike was on his own. This was his show. Life with flavour. Eat it. Taste it.

CHAPTER SIXTEEN

MOTEGI, 2008

The clock is ticking and even Valentino Rossi suffers from nerves. He stays up late, looks at his bike longingly and wonders about consummating his revival. Together they have come a long way from the time he sat on the Yamaha for that first race, among the arid fields and rednecks of Welkom four years ago, wondering if he had made the biggest mistake of his life. They won and then they lost. Twice. It still hurts.

Motegi is the venue for what he hopes will be his return. With Casey Stoner suffering from falls, broken bones and a newly brittle self-belief, Rossi is almost home. He has an eighty-seven-point lead with four races left. If he finishes on the podium then he will be the 2008 champion. This is his show. Life with flavour. This is the reckoning. Eat it. Taste it.

There is a strange atmosphere at the track north of Tokyo. The breath is not so much bated as short and sharp. People are worried and it goes beyond the title race. The gossiping grapevine throbs with talk of tyres. Dani Pedrosa's shock move from Michelin to Bridgestone has thrown the cat among the pigeons and, while the top people from the tyre companies are keeping quiet, many suspect the deal has already been done and MotoGP has decided to go to a single control tyre. They are right. 'It won't make it more equal,' scoffs one tyre technician pushing a trolley full of rubber. 'If they have a control tyre they'll still give the best one to Rossi. It will just be a different sort of uneven playing field.'

Below the control tower is a room with white chairs arranged in an arc. Across the paving stones is the canteen, where mechanics, weary of the wholesome pasta and cold buffet on offer in the team cabins, tuck into burgers and chips. A couple of Japanese fans clad in Rossi regalia are asleep on the grass bank to the rear.

Nicky Hayden walks past in blue shorts and his Repsol shirt. In the other direction goes Andrea Dovizioso. It is a symbolic crossing. Dovizioso walks into the press conference room and takes his seat in front of the arc. Hayden is oblivious, thinking only of tyres and, maybe, fleetingly of next year and Ducati when he will be faster, harder, better.

Mack is there in front of a microphone. He introduces Dovizioso and hands over to his Japanese colleague, who confirms the Italian's move to the factory team for 2009. 'Andrea moved up to MotoGP this year. His dedication impresses everyone. Andrea is fifth in the championship. HRC will provide the best possible technical support to enable him to fulfil his true potential and we look forward to a happy relationship.'

Dovizioso looks awkward. It is an excruciatingly formal appearance for a rider. He has a race in two days' time and he knows the questions that are about to come will not all be easy. 'I am happy to be here,' he says, his eyes wide and suspicious. 'One of my dreams is coming true. I believe in Honda. We can make a good season together in 2009.'

It is easy to sense the unspoken cynicism in the room. This is Honda, once the most powerful team in motorcycle racing, but the one that let Rossi get away. The one that won the title with

Hayden in 2006 despite hamstringing him with their attitude and favouritism to Pedrosa.

It is Pedrosa's position that means some people are looking at Dovizioso with a degree of sympathy. Pedrosa is a deft brute who wields most of the power at Honda. Now that he has succumbed to the mother of all hissy fits and demanded to ride on Bridgestone tyres, the old wounds have been reopened. Hayden started it, telling a Spanish journalist that his partnership with Pedrosa was a fractured one. 'I don't like the fact that there's a wall separating the garages and that we're not sharing inform-ation,' he groused. 'We're both on the same team and we should be working together.' With his exit strategy arranged, Hayden let rip, all the submerged angst of the past three years spilling over, a finger pointed at Pedrosa's manager. 'Puig has too much influence on the team. In theory, he works for Dani, not Honda, but Puig is the guy with all the power at Honda, not Dani. It's Puig who runs Honda. I know I'm not supposed to say so, but that's the truth.'

The truth hurts. First Rossi damned his old employers for their bureaucracy and lack of people skills, now Hayden has followed. In every word the anger he had felt in 2006 resurfaced. Puig did not take the attack on the chin and responded by suggesting that Hayden was worried that he no longer had Pedrosa's telemetry to fall back on. This, he claimed, was essential for Hayden because, 'He never knew how to set up a bike.'

The inevitable question-cum-bear-trap then comes. How does Dovizioso feel about riding with Pedrosa because Hayden did not have a good relationship with him? Dovizioso raises his eyebrows. 'Pedrosa, for me, was always a good rider. I battle with him in 125 and 250 and always he arrive in front of me. I prefer to have a good relationship, but if he does not want it then it's not a big problem for me.'

'What about the wall?' someone shouts.

'We don't want a wall,' Masumi Hamane, HRC's president, says.

The day drifts on. Friday is a day for hard graft and tinkering. Hayden is fastest in morning practice but few expect him to stay there. Rossi is a tenth of a second down and Stoner another seven-tenths. In the afternoon Stoner is the fastest from Rossi and Pedrosa. Dovizioso is fourth, just adrift of Pedrosa, a scenario many see repeating itself in the coming year.

I catch up with Rossi in the alleyways between the grey cabins that house the team officials in Motegi. There is no grand paddock here. It is brass-tacks racing. Rossi is clowning around with Marco Simoncelli, the rider with wild hair. His bouffant is so big that he has been forced to order a larger helmet. Although Rossi has long got rid of his 'wolfman' look, the pair are cut from the same cloth, maverick figures who mix fun with a macho belligerence. Both have fostered fan bases and long-standing rivalries, Rossi with the departed Biaggi and Gibernau, and Simoncelli with Hector Barbera. The latter feud has been developing since the huge accident in Mugello when the pair collided on the penultimate lap and Barbera was sent somersaulting through the air. It was a crash that prompted reflex thoughts of Kato and Locatelli and Phillis and Hocking. Barbera had been lucky.

It is early evening and Rossi will soon return to the hotel on the hill. The teams are sequestered far away in Mito, a hotchpotch of neon shopping centres divided by a green river. This is the race where a rider can feel alone.

He is in good spirits. Today, Rossi knows he is almost home. Back on top. He sits down in the small room, his picture stuck in the window, and talks to the Italian media. This is the familiar routine. Eventually, they leave and he is left with a few Brits, two Spaniards, a Dutchman and a German. Willy, a newcomer to the FIAT Yamaha press corps, has wandered off and so we are alone with a megastar. I can't help thinking this would not be allowed in other sports.

As always on these occasions the talk starts with tyres. 'I have some problem on the right because this track is not fantastic for me,' Rossi begins. 'We suffer a bit on the exit from the slow hairpin. Improving that is one of the main issues. But anyway I am not so far from Casey and Dani. Nicky is in good shape, especially in the wet, he has a good feeling on the bike.'

This is the stuff the trade papers want but not much use for a national. Rossi, though, is reliable and you know he will get there in the end. 'I am worried about Pedrosa for some reason,' he continues. 'First, he has a great motivation to improve on the Bridgestones, he wants to prove he can win on them, and second this track suits his weight and style. For sure we are not at the maximum yet. The Bridgestone tyres have a different quality. I need to ride on different lines because, with Michelin, it is possible to use more of the track. With Bridgestone I have to make the same line every time.'

Tyres are all-consuming but this is about the man rather than the machinery. Rossi is about to end two years of having his problems rammed down his throat. He has felt victimized, pursued and, perhaps, even fragile, but he is now the Rossi of old, the man in the Elvis suit on the cover of *Rolling Stone*. Matt Birt, *Motorcycle News'* MotoGP man, asks a question about testing the 2009 bike on Monday. Rossi raises a hand. 'Ah, it is actually the 2008 point five,' he quips. 'We have three or four things to try on Monday.' Birt suggests he may have to temper the celebrations the night before. 'We need a reason to drink,' Rossi says, refusing to get ahead of himself, remembering Estoril and Valencia and the slide into support billing. 'In 2006 and 2007 I was not consistent. This year I try to arrive on the podium every race and, where possible, win. This is not a regular weekend. Usually the pressure starts on Saturday night, this time it's Friday. But, if we make good work tomorrow then I'm not worried.'

I ask Rossi if this means more than the other titles because he has suffered in the interim. 'Yes, for sure,' he says instantly. 'This year is the most difficult. Now I have an eighty-seven-point advantage, but for sure the battle was more tight. This championship has had more fighting than 2005, for example. Every championship is special, but this one means most.' Headline delivered, Rossi leaves. The sky is darkening and the paltry Friday-night crowd is departing. The lights in the garages remain peepholes to the frenzied work going on as the night drags on.

Back at my hotel I consider Rossi's achievements. It goes way beyond the mechanics of a motorcycle, the machinations of a rift with Honda and the beating of Agostini's mark of sixty-eight elite wins in Indianapolis. I think about Rossi saying 'you want some?' to Biaggi, of Angel Nieto telling him he was going to tear him a new arsehole, of the drunken homage to Pedrosa in Brazil. I think of Rossi losing millions to the taxman and saying he was serene, of his tears at watching Johnny Cash re-runs, of Tavullia town council holding a meeting in the stands at Misano and electing him mayor for the day. I think of him saying in an interview that he liked England because 'The other evening, from my flat window, I saw in the opposite building a sixty-year-old man, completely naked and fat as a pig, pot belly, miming a tennis match. On his own. The English are raving mad which is why I feel so comfortable here.' Rossi is different, a one-off, and that's why he is so loved and feared.

Saturday morning muddles on towards the qualifying sessions that will determine the grids. It is all routine enough until Barbera crashes in practice for the 250cc race. It is a bad spill. Barbera is using up his lives. 'I believe that God exists, that when it is your time it is your time,' he had said after his terrible fall in Italy earlier that summer. Then he walked away. This time he is on a stretcher.

The MotoGP world keeps spinning. Rossi is oblivious to Barbera's plight as he puts his Yamaha on to the front of the second row. Pedrosa will be next to him, Lorenzo, Stoner and Hayden ahead. Stoner has come in for a lot of flak this year, but

313

has reconciled himself to his fate. Adriana, his tall, devoted wife, follows him around and carries his helmet. She is shy and quiet. They are an ordinary Aussie couple living on thrills and hopes. Except Stoner is the world champion, a twenty-two-year-old cannonball. 'Unfortunately, when I came on the main straight to start my last fast lap, a bug hit my visor. I was trying like crazy to get the tear-off but I just couldn't do it. I couldn't see my apex points so I lost my confidence.' The prognosis on Barbera – two broken bones in his back – proved anything could happen, but at the pole position press conference Stoner is throwing in the towel. 'Look, the championship has gone,' he says. 'Anyone with two eyes can see that.'

Hayden is happier and has the look of a man with a huge weight lifted off his shoulders. 'I'm not stringing the forty-sevens together like some of these guys but I'm pretty happy. Tomorrow's the real show, though. My last qualifying lap was tough – I went pretty good, was coming out of Turn 2 and there was a group of guys. Hell, it looked like rush-hour traffic. Going down the straightaway and out of the corner of my eye I saw that not one guy turned round, and I thought, "Oh man, this is going to get ugly." So I slowed down and tried to keep a little heat in the tyre.'

Simoncelli is also there. He has put his Metis Gilera on pole. He is asked what he feels about Barbera's crash and he is expected to say something nice, that for all the antipathy between them nobody likes to see anyone hurt. 'He is not nice to me,' he says. A bit of compassion is lost in his basic English, but Simoncelli is not about to do a U-turn. He puts his arm around Stoner for a pole position photograph. It is a comical sight. Stoner is blushing, forcing a smile and all but shoving Simoncelli's arm away. Oblivious to any discomfort, Simoncelli grins, thinking they are all going to join arms. He will realize when he graduates that they don't do this in MotoGP. Rivals are kept at arm's length or, at the very least, punching distance.

Hayden speaks to Mack on his way out. He is still a popular figure. Earl and Rose have raised their bikers well. They are polite and entertaining, Nicky's Kentucky drawl and florid use of language never failing to liven up the dullest of days. Only once has he ever been anything less than utterly cordial, when he asked me, 'What sort of crazy question is that?' I can't remember the question but I remember the response because it was so unlike him. Most people in the paddock are armed with knives to plant in others' backs. It is a viper's nest of bitchiness, ego, posturing and deep friendships. Everyone likes Nicky, though. Rose used to sew 'Mr Dirt' on the back of his leathers when he was a kid, but he is Mr Clean.

The jury remains out on Pedrosa. Many view him as the pampered plaything of Honda. He gets preferential treatment but rarely smiles and is even showing traces of Biaggi in his habit of blaming the bike and the tyres and the alignment of the stars. Stoner, too, has managed to raise the hackles of many in the media. 'Just like Mick,' people say of Stoner. Faster, harder, bitter.

Rossi is the one. It is hard to see anyone dominating like he has done and, more than that, he has recovered from a torrid couple of years. The sun sets for the last time as a loser.

Rossi would normally lose himself in the huge Yamaha transporter where he has an office, the place we had met in Holland and looked at his book of rock interviews. This time he is stripped bare and there is nowhere to hide. He goes past on a scooter with Uccio holding on behind him. Inevitably, the best-looking women in the paddock are dragged along beside them.

Back in Mito I bump into some Italian mechanics from one of the 125cc teams. The garage attendant at the Holiday Inn then regales me with the wonders of his parking mechanism. To be fair to him it is a triumph of engineering. You drive your car into a room big enough for a single vehicle. You walk out, he presses a button, lights flash and the car is then miraculously transported, via pulleys and ramps, to a space somewhere down below us. When I pick it up the following morning, it is facing me, even though I have kept the keys with me all night. 'Only two in Japan,' he says. There are little miracles happening everywhere today, I think.

There is always a flush of excitement on race day, even for the most experienced, cynical souls. Today could be ordinary or it could provide the sort of drama that saw Rossi fall in Valencia two years ago, gifting the title to a tearful Hayden. Rossi is smiling on the grid but he is ever thus.

He crouches down by the side of his bike. Stoner is sheltered from the sun by Adriana's umbrella. Pedrosa sips from his bottle. 'DANI – GAS' screams a huge banner draped on the grandstand. Hayden touches his bandana. This is where it ends.

When the lights go off it is Pedrosa who heeds the banner and gets on the gas. He cuts across Hayden but cannot get in front of Stoner. The bluntness that saw him concede the championship yesterday is gone and he is thinking only of winning. Of delaying the handover. Stoner leads at the end of the first lap. Maybe, fleetingly, he thinks of last year, when he won the title with his worst result of the season, when Ezpelata had first broached the idea of a control tyre and where the fast-drying track had added to the drama.

He is more likely concerned about what lay immediately behind him rather than the distant past. As they cross the line for the first time, Stoner leads from Pedrosa and Hayden, with Lorenzo, having less to lose, ramming his Yamaha up the inside of Rossi's to overhaul him on the brakes into Turn 3.

This is the powderkeg of MotoGP. Having avoided any mayhem, Rossi is now concentrating on charging. He bullies Lorenzo into a mistake while Pedrosa gets past Stoner. Suddenly, the placings look comfortable for Rossi's title party. But Rossi knows only one way of winning. He wants the fix of glory as much as the place in the record books, he wants to ravage the brilliant, bloody here and now. So he works his Yamaha on to the back of Stoner, whose broken scaphoid bone feels more tender by the moment.

He knows Rossi is there, from the pitboard and the noise and the shadow. He also has the sixth sense of a racer telling him it is now or never. If Stoner wants to hang on to his title then he must pass Pedrosa now. He heeds his instincts and he attempts to round Pedrosa at the hairpin. It works, but his wrist is sore and his body weaker than his mind. There is a shaft of daylight and Pedrosa's small frame squeezes past, the door pushed shut after being forced ajar. On the fifth lap you realize just what it means to Stoner as he ignores his brakes and rockets past Pedrosa as they come to the sharp right before the bridge. It is a bad move, ill-conceived, brave and despairing. Pedrosa can only back off to save himself and let Stoner past. The Australian puts up a hand and looks backwards. And then they are racing again.

For someone who makes decisions in nanoseconds, Rossi is a deep thinker. He knows Pedrosa is vulnerable after being brutalized by Stoner's bellicose move. He lines him up and passes him on the inside two corners later. It is now Stoner from Rossi, the new and the old, the reigning champion and the people's champion.

This is the battle that everyone wanted. The two best riders in the world on arguably the two best bikes. Bound by Bridgestone, granite and their titles, they traverse the circuit, Rossi shadowing Stoner's rear tyre, occasionally moving out to intimidate and bully.

Stoner, though, is suffering. The mental anguish of losing his title has succumbed to the thrill of the fight, but his wrist is hurting and draining his belief. Every corner hurts and he has a legend waiting for any sign of weakness. The lap times tumble but as Rossi weaves a line around the track, Stoner is beginning to resemble a fly in a web. He cannot escape and Rossi has laps in hand. Finally, he powers down the inside, throws out his left leg, as evidence that he is on the edge, and holds the line. This is Rossi's brilliance, his ability to make passing moves stick.

Now we are counting down. Eleven laps to go. Rossi is refusing to let up and pushes his bike close to the record lap time set by the old 990cc machines. Ten, nine, eight. Stoner briefly closes, but Rossi glances at his pitboard and responds. Seven, six, five. I catch the eye of Mack again and think back to 2006 and how Hayden was crestfallen and then revived. I think about the fantastic madness and drama of this sport. Four, three, two. The last lap. I think of Agostini and how he loves this man for his showmanship. Of Hailwood and how Rossi loves his legend. In some ways he is an amalgam of both, the Latin good looks and inveterate sex appeal of Agostini, coupled with the flamboyant, fun-loving spirit of Hailwood.

He crosses the line from the past to the present and Rossi is the champion again. There are roars. Not from everyone because even the affable do not become multiple world champions without crossing people. Far away, Biaggi will take the news with barely a flutter of recognition. Gibernau, debating a comeback, must wonder if it is worth it.

He celebrates in typically colourful style. One of the Fan Club drapes him in the new T-shirt which has a clockface pointing to the number eight, signifying his world titles, and the words 'SCUSATE IL RITARDO', 'Excuse the delay', in large letters. Rossi then stops and approaches a desk that has been set up alongside the track. One of his friends is dressed in a suit and sits behind it. He is a notary and signs Rossi's helmet to make it 'official'. Some wonder whether the suit and officialdom are subtle digs at the taxman, but Rossi denies that.

'It's not news,' Stoner says as dusk falls on the press conference. 'It's not something that's come as a shock. It's been coming for a long time. My mistakes set this in place and we knew it was out of reach. I made two mistakes and that's cost us the championship. My upper body has taken a beating. I was making parts of my body that don't normally get tired extremely tired. I made a friendly gesture to Dani because it wasn't a friendly pass. I had the front brake right into the handlebars and I couldn't stop any quicker. Dani's brakes were better than mine. I could not pull it up any quicker and when Dani realized I was there I let off the brakes because I did not want to lose the front end and take us both down. Valentino has ridden an amazing season. I've got to learn from it. I don't want it to happen again.'

For Rossi *the comeback* he had craved since he crashed in Valencia in 2006 is complete. 'I have grown up very much. At the end of 2005 I felt a little bit unbeatable. We had some problems in 2006 but when you have a lot of victories you think we will fix them. That was the first mistake. When you win all is very good and everybody is friendly and positive, but I have learnt to lose. That's the most important thing. I have learnt to lose.

'At the end of 2007 we had a very strange meeting. I had a broken hand and spoke with Furusawa about 2008. We talked about what we needed to do to improve the engine and the bike. It was also important to have the right people in the right place because last year the organization of the team, especially with some of the Japanese engineers, was wrong. This time we came back with the guys who work on the engine in Japan with the guys who work with me on the track. It was very important. MotoGP is a project, you know.'

I think that Carlo Pernat has it right. He says, 'These people are born every twenty years. Like Borg, like Maradona, like Cassius Clay. These people are not just champions, they are something more. They have an appeal. They have charisma. Cassius Clay was against power. Maradona was against power. The same with Valentino at the beginning. You remember how many times he said to Dorna, "No, we will not race here because we will be dead." These people are more than champions.'

Rossi grins. He's back. 'After Barcelona Casey started to ride like a devil and dominated three races, not just the races but qualifying and practice too. I was a little worried, but Laguna was the key point. It was the battle between Stoner and me and I was able to win. It was not just twenty-five points. This has been the hardest title. The level of concentration and effort needed has been the hardest of my career. I rode the best I have ever done. I made one mistake. I am happy. But next year, well, next year is another story.'

LAST LAP

The red and white leathers were zipped up and the bike was ready. Mike looked his age with his thinning hair and a face that betrayed years of hard living. He had the gammy, gimpy leg and, for those who remembered him as a demonic Adonis in black, he looked almost middle-aged.

He did not speak much as he contemplated what lay ahead and the lessons learnt from practice and talking to Mick Grant. It was Formula One day. Comeback day. There was no turning back now. Ted had pulled off a neat stroke by getting Mike to run at No. 12, the number of TT wins he had on the island. Phil Read would be No. 1. That could work to their advantage.

The crowds fought for the best spectator spots. The island, struggling in the aftermath of having its World Championship status stripped, was buzzing again. The bars were full, the car parks tangled webs of baking metal. It was Mike the Bike, one of the most popular figures to ever sit on a motorcycle, against Phil Read, the professional wind-up merchant and the Biaggi of his time. Lines were drawn. It was not quite a morality tale, but it was an old-fashioned Western between the matinee hero and the arch villain.

Read sprinted from the line on the Honda and the race was on. All the negotiations with Martini and the team of sponsors, the subterranean efforts of Nobby Clark in his cellar full of secrets, the deals to get the bikes and the exile from his family funnelled into this moment. He sucked in the drama and breathed deeply. The clock ticked on. He would start 50 seconds behind Read.

They were all thinking about Mike that day. Tommy and Ralph and Paddy and Pauline. Even over in Spain where the Formula One circus had decamped, the racers were wondering about their old sparring partner. Someone tried to find reports on the World Service. Jochen Mass, the man who had replaced him, and Clay Reggazoni, the man he had saved, might have spared him a moment's grace. Another of his old friends from Formula One, Dickie Atwood, had upset his wife by leaving a family holiday to visit the island. 'Bloody Mike Hailwood,' his wife had complained.

Bloody Mike Hailwood was away and running. It only took eight of 223 miles for Mike to be in the lead. Stay there, thought Ted. Just stay there and we're home. But this was the island, and anything could happen.

The tannoy crackled with excitement. Many could not make out the commentary but they knew the word 'Hailwood' was being mentioned a lot. He was still there. In the pub car parks they drank deep below the banners wishing Mike well and cheered as he flashed by. He was fast and demented, beating the passing years into submission. When he came around after the first lap he was nine seconds in the lead. It was not much. Tom Herron had lapped the 37.7 miles at only 0.8mph slower. And there was still the Honda duo of Read and John Williams to concern Ted as he sat in the press box and phoned reports to Pauline.

Mike was back in the groove, though. On the bike he raced back into the past and forgot about the leg. He didn't think about the family or the fame or the folklore. Only of winning. Of going faster, harder, better.

In Parliament Square a man with bellbottom flares and a rug of black hair chased a dog off the track. The crowd laughed but the danger was real. Moments later they heard the groan of the Honda engine, accompanied by the baritone gargle of another bike. They hoped. Sure enough, as Read entered the square he had Mike with him. The 50 seconds had been swept away. Read's gripes about his Honda look justified or maybe it was just the case that a rejuvenated Hailwood was better than him. For Read and all racers, such statements were truths never aired. They blamed machinery and injury, but rarely themselves.

Read tried to outbrake Mike. He tried everything. Mike had seen it all, though. He had only once been guilty of bad sportsmanship, when he had pretended to Derek Minter that there was oil on his tyre, but he had been young and impetuous then. He went past Read and did not mess around this time. He would not pat him on the backside as he went by, as he once had with Mike Duff, the Canadian rider, and he would not wave or give a V-sign. This was serious. The passing of Read meant he was in control, but the vagaries of the island meant that was never total.

Read was desperate. He knew that it was going to be hard enough to finish ahead of Mike, let alone put 50 seconds on him. He managed to get clear after refuelling, but Mike was soon back, like a rabid dog with a bone, a blast from the past. 'He looked like the genius who had always haunted me,' he said later. 'He was a bloody nuisance.'

They were racing each other but the race was elsewhere. It was Herron who looked the most likely man to derail the comeback. He was an affable twenty-nine-year-old from Antrim who had bumped into Mike a week earlier when he was struggling with a particular corner. He asked how to get round 'this bloody bend'. Mike said he'd been trying since 1959 and still had no idea. Tom had been stopped for speeding on the way home and fined £17 and £2 in costs. The chief of police then asked him for an autograph. Tom said it would cost £19.

Tom was riding well. Despite his modesty, he knew the TT well and was the last winner of the senior race before the island was stripped of its World Championship status. The gap was down to four seconds. Ted groaned. He had faith in his man's ability but had the natural pessimism of the journalist. Then, on the third lap, Tom hit trouble and was out. Mike set a new lap record of 110.27mph. There was no way Mike could be beaten now unless he made a mistake on the last lap. That was very possible. This was the TT, Mike was thirty-eight and all over the course bikes had been dropping out. Younger men on better bikes. But Mike was proving what so many never get the chance to do – he was out of his era and he was bridging the generation gap at 110mph. He was debunking arguments about the greatest and different ages by merging the ages, just as he and Ago had once melted together at the Sachsenring.

An island waited. Maybe Mike remembered the near misses. The time he had broken down at Monza and gifted Ago the title. Or the near hits, like 1967 when Ago's chain had broken and given him the greatest win. That had been the last time. That had been the best time. Until now.

He came over the line and, as McGuinness would say some forty years later, you could have lifted the island out of the sea on the emotion. Every appetite had been sated. Mike roared to a halt and hugged Ted. 'Fantastic!' Ted cried. 'Fantastic!' Mike was speechless. A thickening throng of well-wishers threatened to choke the two friends.

Later that afternoon Read went to Mike's hotel and went up to his room. He was still wearing his leathers when he knocked on the door. Mike, with a vodka and lemonade in his hand, ushered him in. Any ancient hostilities were momentarily washed away in the emotion of what had happened. 'I felt inspired,' Read told him. 'It was like the old days all over again.'

Jon Williams was second and told a reporter that it was a pleasure to be beaten by someone like Mike. Except there was nobody quite like him. He caught Ted's eye as he was shepherded away to interviews and made a telephone with his hand. Ted got the message and tore back to the press room where he picked up the phone, to find Pauline was anxiously listening to muffled voices. 'He's done it!' Ted said. 'He's done it.'

'I could hear the crowd in the background,' Pauline said. 'Everyone was going mad. I felt like crying. All this built-up tension, all this fear, was suddenly released. I was so happy for him. I thanked God he'd done it. I thanked God he was safe.' Eventually, she got to speak to him. 'I wasn't even trying that hard,' he said, almost dumbfounded by what he had done.

'I knew he was trying to win,' Pauline said when we met in a wine bar in the winter of 2008. 'He never did anything without trying to win. I thought he had a very good chance. A lot of people did not want him to do it because they thought he might tarnish his reputation. He showed them. I went to the airport to pick him up and hung on to him the longest time. "It's all right," he said. "It's all right." He was back and he was safe. I thought that was it. And then, of course, he decides he wants to go back the following year too!'

A KIND OF LIVING

Mike did go back to the island in 1979 and won again in the senior race. It was his fourteenth triumph. 'He'd buried some ghosts and demons,' Pauline said. 'He did still have it.' He had it, but there was still a void after racing. He tried his hand at business but nothing held the same appeal. In March 1981 Mike took David and Michelle for some fish and chips. A lorry performed an illegal U-turn and there was a collision. Michelle was killed instantly. Mike hung on for two days before he died. David survived.

The horrific irony of surviving the most punishing and reckless era of motorsport and then dying in such a fashion was heartbreaking. Now, four decades on, the interminable question is whether he was the best. There is no definitive answer, but it is not hard to see why Rossi is so enamoured of the Hailwood legend.

The old timers are a mixed bunch. Some are jaundiced by time and refuse to acknowledge the achievements of future generations. Others are in awe of modern speed. Paddy Driver is one of the latter. 'It's frightening how fast they go these days,' he said. 'Just astounding. They have wider, sticky tyres and they handle better probably and, yeah, they have better brakes, but Jeez, the speed! It's almost overkill. It's mindboggling.

'If I had to say who was the best between Mike and Ago, well it's an unfair question, but I'd say Mike. I always felt he was better round the corners. He was the only guy who could control the Honda 500cc. He said to me, "They want me to come back and they're going to find another 10 horsepower." Mike said he didn't want any more. It was too bloody frightening as it was.

'The other year I was standing next to John McGuinness at the TT. He's a new legend, I guess. I was on a bike and there was a photographer around. I said to McGuinness, "Come here, young man, I'll make you famous." I bet he said to himself, "Who the hell is that old geezer."'

Tommy Robb cried when he heard the news about Mike. His old pal had been due to come up and open a new workshop in Warrington. 'I still find it very hard,' he said. 'There are twenty-seven more years of life that man could have had and they would have been good ones. He was killed by a silly lorry driver. I remember the fun most of all. I remember going back to my caravan at Spa and putting on my wife's red dress and high heels. Everyone was sitting round a campfire drinking. I pranced into the middle. There was a hush and everyone looked at this strange bird. Mike leapt up and he'd had enough for me to think that it was not going to matter that I was a man. I was in grave danger.'

John 'Moon Eyes' Cooper said, 'Mike was the Valentino Rossi of the 1960s. He was a character. I still like the bikes. I saw Randy Mamola at a classic bike festival recently and he said he'd asked Casey Stoner to get a stick and put a white handkerchief on the end of it when he went to Donington and say he did not mean what he'd said about the place. I've heard he's a misery and is not too popular. I also heard his dad floored someone for criticizing Casey.'

Ralph Bryans is no dewy-eyed romantic. 'We rode short

circuits, road circuits, everything,' he said. 'But we had it easy in some ways. You didn't change settings and there was very little you could do with the bikes. You might change the tyre pressure and that was it. Everyone used what today you'd call intermediates and there was only one company, Dunlop, making them. You had little to worry about when you went racing. Today we'd all be lost, changing this and that. It was pure in a way. Some people were quicker and that was it. Today, well, I'm a Valentino fan.'

Rossi remains a Mike fan. 'The best riders of the story are Hailwood and Agostini. I like Barry Sheene too. I met him in Australia two months before he died. I think maybe he already knew he was close to the end, but he said, "Come and have some fun." Later, I liked Kevin Schwantz. I never saw Hailwood and Agostini race, but I like Mike the Bike the best. He was able to win in cars and on bikes, he won the TT, he rode all sizes, he was very eclectic. And away from the track he had a lot of style. The best rider of the story.'

Ago himself now lives in a plush villa in Bergamo, with electric gates and room enough for fifteen bikes, one for each world title. Like Mike, he did not want to marry when he was racing because he said it was 'incompatible' with family life. In his forties he did marry a Spanish interpreter. She arrived in a carriage with ten white horses. Ago and Maria left the church on a brand new Yamaha. Then they danced the Flamenco to 'Ave Maria'.

They are still married. Ago still has pictures of Mike on his walls. Statistically, Ago is the greatest of them all with, according to the record books, 122 grand prix victories. He says it is 123 and gets his results sheet from an oak drawer. 'See,' he says. 'They don't count my last win on the 750cc. But why? It was a GP race. Hockenheim 1977. Valentino wins on an 800cc or a 990cc or a 500cc and they all count. My record is important to me. People think I will be happy if he beats my record. Why? I prefer to keep

Agostini on top. Why should I be happy for Valentino? Everybody prefers to keep what they have.

'Valentino is the best of today. I was the best of my time. Mike was the best of his. That's all you can say. The only difference is today it is safer. In 1973 we pushed for change because we thought, "Maybe I die today. In the last race Saarinen died. Then Pasolini." Now twenty people crash in practice and nobody is hurt.'

The old racers have won and lost in equal measure. Phil Read had his troubles, lived in a caravan and was angry when Sheene got his MBE before him. Tommy Robb sits in his study, eyes his shelves of trophies and tells me his son is in *We Will Rock You* and his daughter has started a new show with David Essex. 'Their mother's a dancer.'

Maria Agostini picks up her car keys and says she will drive me to the airport. Before she does Ago points out the trophy he got for winning in Daytona in 1974. Ochre leaves dance in the air. A dog warms its back against a window. 'I am nobody now,' he says. 'But Valentino rang me and said to me that if he gets to within one win of my record, he will call me and ask me if he should retire. I like that.' He laughs and his eyes dance. He is happy, content and lives like a modern-day prince, but you know that he would give anything to be back inside the ring of fire.

Index